Forged by Fire

The Battle Tactics and Soldiers of a WWI Battalion
The 7th Somerset Light Infantry

5/09 Bols

FORGED BY FIRE

THE BATTLE TACTICS AND SOLDIERS OF A WWI BATTALION THE 7TH SOMERSET LIGHT INFANTRY

by

Brendon Moorhouse

SPELLMOUNT
Staplehurst

British Library Cataloguing in Publication Data:
A catalogue record for this book is available
from the British Library

Copyright © Brendon Moorhouse 2003
Maps © Spellmount Limited 2003

ISBN 1-86227-191-7

First published in the UK in 2003 by
Spellmount Limited
The Old Rectory
Staplehurst
Kent TN12 0AZ

Tel: 01580 893730
Fax: 01580 893731
E-mail: enquiries@spellmount.com
Website: www.spellmount.com

135798642

The right of Brendon Moorhouse to be identified
as the author of this work has been asserted by him
in accordance with the Copyright, Designs
and Patents Act 1988

Typeset in Palatino by MATS, Southend-on-Sea, Essex
Printed in Great Britain by
TJ International Ltd, Padstow, Cornwall

Contents

Dedication

This book is dedicated to my wife Denise, and daughters Olivia and Helena. It is also dedicated to all of those about whom it is written.

Acknowledgements

I am extremely grateful to Lieutenant Colonel Elliot, Brigadier Fyfe and all of the staff, present and past, at the Light Infantry Office in Taunton for their invaluable assistance in my research. Also for their permission, and that of the Trustees of the Somerset Military Museum Trust, to use extracts from battalion scrap book, records, plans and photographs.

I would also like to thank Major John Cotterill and Lieutenant Colonel David McMurtrie for their tremendous efforts and many helpful suggestions. I am in further gratitude to Lieutenant Colonel McMurtrie for permission to use extracts from his father's war diary, and for kindly permitting me to use personal photographs in the book.

I would also like to thank Paddy Griffith for making the time to discuss my approach to this book, for his sage advice and also for unknowingly inspiring this book with his own work *Battle Tactics of the Western Front*. Also, I would like to thank Paul Seaton for his constant encouragement and lively discussions that in no small part contributed to this work; and Moira MacMillan for some writing suggestions in the early stages.

I would like to thank the staff at the Imperial War Museum department of documents and department of photographs and acknowledge the permission of the Trustees of the Imperial War Museum to reproduce many of the photographs and the use of extracts from records held at the Museum. I would also like to acknowledge the help and permission of staff at the Liddle Collection, University of Leeds to use the poem of Arthur Hendon. I have used extracts from Captain Foley's book *Three Years on Active Service and Eight Months as a Prisoner of War* after every effort has been made to identify the copyright holder. I would also like to thank the Editor, David Gledhill, for his kind permission on behalf of *The Bath Chronicle* to use extracts from an article used in this book, the Clerk of the Records at the House of Lords Records Office for their permission to use extracts from Lloyd George's *War Memoirs*, and, also the staff at the Royal Engineers Library, Chatham, for their assistance.

List of Maps

Preface

When the First World War started ordinary British people from all walks of life volunteered in huge numbers, joining and swelling the small pre-war regular army into what became arguably the most powerful and effective land army in Europe by 1917. Prior to the war there was no national service and, as the small regular army was all but destroyed in the fighting in 1914 and 1915, the remaining British Army had to be effectively forged by the fire of war. This book aims to show how this came about in an average infantry battalion.

The 7th Somerset Light Infantry was an 'ordinary' infantry battalion that fought in many key battles of the war, from the periphery of Loos, through the Somme, Passchendaele, Cambrai and the March 1918 offensive. The battalion was one of approximately 1,000 that saw service on the Western Front and, while the soldiers of every battalion had a unique experience, the development of battle tactics from training to field experience in this battalion is typical of many of them. The detail available in looking at one battalion has enabled the constant refinement of tactics – offensive and defensive – to be examined, alongside the changes in technology, morale and organisation of the British Army.

The mainstay of the book is the accounts of the battalion's soldiers. These accounts were often written during the war in letters, interviews and diaries; many were written in the decade afterwards. The 'evidence' of these men, in the context of the great battles in which they were involved, is all the more compelling because of its proximity to the events. The people that wrote them would mostly never have dreamt of their use in a study of this nature. Because of the passage of time I have been unable to corroborate every account but where I have, often from very divergent sources, there has always been remarkable consistency.

Today, there are no survivors from this battalion, and it is a personal regret that I have not been able to meet any of the officers and men whom I feel I have come to know through writing this book.

Some Day, Not Now

Some day, not now, shall the results be seen
Of what is happening in the while between
The ceaseless strivings and the heavy cross
The bitter failures and the grievous loss,
Some day, not now, we'll understand the scene,
Of what is happening in the while between.

Some day, not now we'll know (as we are known)
The meaning of the wanderings here alone
The sorrow loaded and the care worn brow
Shall rest with Christ, but O, not now.
Some day, not now, when all our strivings cease
We'll rest with Jesus, in His peace, sweet peace.

Some day, not now, we'll clasp His pierced hand,
And join with the redeemed in a love song grand;
The weary shall grow strong; the eyes, now dim
Shall glow with heavenly light when they see Him.
Some day, not now, we'll reach the pastures green,
And walk the meadows by the floating stream.

Some day, not now, the partings will be o'er,
And we shall meet in heaven to part no more;
The heartbreaks shall be healed, the wounds embalmed
The sea of human life be ever calmed
Some day! But now, a while, the tears and grief,
And then the victory, joy and relief.

Arthur Hendon, 7th Somersets,
Killed in action, Ypres, 12 July 1916.

PART ONE

Opening Stages

We met, we fought, we lived, we laughed,
And won the bally war.
Lt Col Preston-Whyte DSO

CHAPTER I
Formation and Training

Introduction

On a bright sunny Sunday morning, 28 June 1914, Gavrilo Princip and his fellow conspirators assassinated Archduke Ferdinand and his wife as they drove through Sarajevo. After a number of unsuccessful attempts by members of his group, Princip was able to step out of the crowd with a revolver and, while a policeman nearby frantically tried to grab his hand, fired two shots into the car. Franz Ferdinand was struck in the jugular vein and his wife Sophie was hit in the stomach. Both died soon afterwards. The Archduke was the heir to the Austro-Hungarian throne.

The assassination led to a series of demands upon Serbia by the Austro-Hungarian empire which publicly stated that Serbia was behind the assassination. The main powers within Europe intervened in the ensuing negotiations along the lines of defence treaties that had been agreed between the various states. A little more than a month later war was declared by Britain against Germany, after Germany refused to guarantee Belgian neutrality.

King George V commanded a week of court mourning after the assassination, but nevertheless the majority of people carried on their daily lives untroubled. The events that would eventually reshape the world and touch the lives of every family in Britain were reported only in passing in the local newspapers. Employers continued to advertise and fill a variety of positions such as the 'strong respectable lad' sought by a firm of fruiterers. No doubt many applied for the positions advertised by the Wireless and Telegraphy Service who were offering 'Splendid opportunities for youths and young men willing to go to sea'.

Summer was also the time when territorial battalions would gather for their annual training camps around the country. Although they appeared to have a relaxed atmosphere, there were legal obligations for those on the territorial roll to maintain military standards. Frederick Rowe from Devon, for instance, was fined 24 shillings by Torquay Magistrates Court for failing to make himself an efficient territorial over the summer of 1914.

All around the country people continued or embarked on their chosen

3

careers, like the young Mr Shufflebotham who at 18 years of age had just left school and taken up articles with a firm of land agents in Taunton. George Price, with a wife and young family, worked as a furniture packer in a removal business in Bath.

By the end of July the situation had started to be far more obviously difficult. The grave peril that Europe faced became clear when Germany declared martial law and Russia commenced a general mobilisation of her army and navy. Britain was readying her forces too with the First Fleet publicly sailing from Portland under 'sealed orders'.

Tensions rose throughout the country and Europe. David Lloyd George later summarised the state of the country at the time in his memoirs:

> The elder statesmen did their feckless best to prevent war, while the youth of the rival countries were howling impatiently at their doors for immediate war. I saw it myself during the first four days in August, 1914. I shall never forget the warlike crowds that thronged Whitehall and poured into Downing Street, whilst the Cabinet was deliberating on the alternative of peace or war.

By 3 August the crowds had spread up to Trafalgar Square, with groups of men singing the 'Marseillaise' out of taxis as they drove past. Union flags started to appear as the day progressed, with Mr Asquith the Prime Minister being roundly cheered as he set out from Downing Street to attend Parliament in the evening.

The British government issued an ultimatum to the Germans that expired at eleven o'clock on Monday 4 August (midnight, central European time). When this became popularly known, the crowds continued to grow through the day, and by eleven o'clock on this bank holiday Monday there were vociferous crowds outside Buckingham Palace, along Whitehall, the Mall and in Trafalgar Square. Ministers were loudly cheered and patriotic songs were sung. There was no response from the Germans. War was declared.

The British Army and the Somerset Light Infantry

At 11pm on 4 August 1914, when war was declared, the British Army had a total of 157 regular (i.e. full-time professional) infantry battalions spread across the globe. Most infantry regiments had one home service battalion and one that would be abroad. There were eighty-one regular battalions in Britain and seventy-six abroad. Each regiment would also have territorial battalions as part of their strength.

On 4 August 1914 the Somerset Light Infantry (SomLI) numbered five battalions. None of them were at full strength. The 1st and 2nd Battalions were regular soldiers. The 1st Battalion was stationed at Colchester as part of the 4th Division and they would see action before the end of the month. The 2nd Battalion was in Quetta in northern India (now Pakistan) where they remained for the war. Upon mobilisation those men who were on the reserve list as former soldiers were required to report to the Taunton depot and the steady trickle of men presenting themselves were, up until 7 August, sent to the 1st Battalion at Colchester.

The 3rd Battalion was a reserve battalion which was based at the regimental depot in Taunton, administratively housed in the imposing structure of the Jellalebad barracks. The battalion was mobilised formally on 8 August and was made up of the remaining reservists who were presenting themselves. Very soon the 3rd (Reserve) Battalion was sent to its war station to garrison Bull Point and the surrounding forts at Devonport. There was quick disappointment for these men as they were soon told that they would become a draft finding battalion – that they would not take the field as a battalion in their own right. The first draft was sent to the 1st Battalion in France on 26 August.

The 4th and 5th Battalions were territorials who had already assembled for their routine summer training camp on 26 July. They had been engaged in training at Bulford camp and on Salisbury Plain since then. During the war the 4th Battalion would be split into the 1/4th and 2/4th Battalions. They fought in Mesopotamia and Palestine respectively, the 2/4th joining the Western Front, where it fought in July 1918. The 5th Battalion was similarly split into the 1/5th and 2/5th Battalions which were both sent to India, although the 1/5th fought in Palestine in 1917.

Both regular soldiers and volunteers had been employed in the South African war in 1900-1 and there would still have been a significant minority of men in the ranks who had seen action against the Boers, particularly amongst the reservists who were all formerly professional or territorial soldiers.

The organisational contribution of the territorials was significant from the moment that the telegram to mobilise was received at the Territorial Association offices in Taunton at 5.15pm on 4 August. Immediately the staff began working on a war footing. The five clerks usually employed were increased to twenty to cope with the increased administration; the principal concern was the issuing of severance allowances to the wives and dependants of the men called up. A clothing department was also set up to find and issue clothing to soldiers; the territorial associations had the responsibility of finding clothing for any battalions stationed in their area and in the next few months the staff at Taunton found some 2,000 suits for men of the North Staffordshire Regiment who were stationed at Okehampton. The territorial and regular army recruiting staff combined in encouraging and processing enlistment.

The national situation

Shortly before the declaration of war, a general mobilisation was ordered calling men to arms around the whole country. The relatively small British Army was formed from the available regulars, territorial and reservists and by the end of August the regulars and reservists were largely deployed to France as the British Expeditionary Force (BEF). The Kaiser had referred to the BEF as Britain's 'contemptibly small army'; at home this was soon translated affectionately into the 'old contemptibles'. At this stage the Territorial force was retained in Britain to forestall any German landing or invasion.

It was soon realised by many, of which Lord Kitchener is largely given the credit, that the BEF was wholly inadequate in size to deal with a large-scale continental war. On 21 August 1914 the government, appreciating the need for a larger army, issued orders for the raising of the First New Army of six divisions. These were to become popularly known as the K1 divisions – Kitchener's first army of 100,000 men. They increased the British Army by adding another six infantry divisions including the 14th (Light) Division.

Within the 14th (Light) Division was the 6th (Service) Battalion of the SomLI, which included many volunteers and reservists who had signed up for foreign service for the duration of the war. Such was the jingoism and clamour to join the ranks that thousands more men volunteered than originally expected, hoping that they might see battle and gain glory before the war ended. It was largely from these additional men that the 7th Battalion Somerset Light Infantry was formed, when the government promoted the formation of another six divisions on 11 September 1914. These were known as the Second New Army or K2 divisions. The 7th (Service) Battalion SomLI, which was formed two days later, became thereafter part of the 20th (Light) Division.

On 21 August, the day the government announced its intention to increase the size of the Army, the 1st Battalion departed for France. They sailed from Southampton in the morning and disembarked at Le Havre at midnight after waiting for a favourable tide. As was common at this time, crowds had collected along the docksides to cheer the arriving soldiers bloodthirstily shouting 'A bas Guillaume' ('down with William' – the Kaiser) and 'Coupez la gorge' ('cut their throats'). Within four days they were in action against the Germans, opening sharp fire on a German cavalry patrol. The 1st Battalion's fortunes were linked to those of the other 'old contemptibles' of the BEF who fought the early battles of the war until trench warfare began in October and November 1914. Their exploits were keenly followed at home, particularly by the other men in their regiment.

The 7th (Service) Battalion

The recruiting staff at Taunton appear to have wasted little time; even before the public announcement of the formation of Kitchener's army, they sent letters to various organisations and bodies throughout Somerset requesting volunteers. For instance, on 18 August Mr Cooke-Hurie on the Keynsham Parish Council received a letter from a Somerset officer which stated that 1,000 new recruits were required for a new battalion of the Somerset Light Infantry, the old county regiment. The intention at this time was to form the 6th Battalion. The letters emphasised that it was important that they were Somerset men, and that arrangements would be made for those from the same village to serve in the same platoon or company. Travel warrants were made available for the volunteers to travel to Taunton.

Throughout the county recruitment rallies were organised. In Bath a stirring meeting was held at the theatre, where the assembled crowd was told to loud cheers that the engineering firm of Stothert and Pitt had 150 men out of 800 already serving their country. At the end the National Anthem was sung as men stepped forward to enlist and the crowd surged across the theatre entrance to cheer the volunteers.

In Bristol the Colston Hall was opened for the purpose of recruiting, with the work being carried out by volunteers. The administration was undertaken by members of the stock exchange, local lawyers and other professions. Attestation – the formal act of volunteering – was taken in the Arch room, after which the volunteers were sent into the lesser hall for a rudimentary medical examination. When attesting, a volunteer would be asked his name, age, where he was born, whether he was a British subject and whether he had previous military experience. He would also be asked to consent to a vaccination programme. The volunteer would then take the oath of allegiance which would be certified by the magistrate or attesting officer present. A total of 4,000 volunteers (for a variety of regiments) passed through the hall in the five weeks that it was open, before recruitment was moved to offices opposite.

In the rural areas the number of men volunteering was necessarily smaller. At a large and enthusiastic open-air meeting at the Cross in Glastonbury on the evening of Wednesday 21 August, Major Arthur Shee MP explained the scheme to the assembled crowd. Enlistment would be for a maximum period of three years, but if the war only lasted one year or six months, the force would be disbanded as soon as possible after peace had been declared. He did not think that the conflict could last more than a year for the reason that every nation in Europe would be bankrupt if it did. The Glastonbury Town Band played 'Rule Britannia' and the National Anthem and four men volunteered to join.

Among the men who joined the battalion were some from outside the county. A few volunteered from neighbouring counties, as did many from Wales. Many of those volunteering from outside Somerset had been born in the county and were away working, with many coming from south Wales where they had been working as miners.

Volunteering was not always straightforward. Mr Nepean was an old soldier who had served twenty-one years before being pensioned off. He had fought through the siege of Ladysmith and the Tirah campaign and he was not going to miss this war even though he was 47 years old. Mr Nepean had a friend in Lord Roberts who had commanded much of the South African campaign. Lord Roberts knew Lord Kitchener who, in September, on Roberts' recommendation, gave Mr Nepean a commission as a lieutenant in the Somerset Light Infantry. Soon afterwards Lieutenant Nepean would be in the 7th Battalion.

Typically the men who volunteered were first sent to Taunton, where they were introduced to the regiment and then sent on to barracks for training. In Yeovil for example, fifty-four men volunteered to serve after a rally on 26 August. The next day they were sent on to Taunton where they stayed at the Jellalebad barracks until 1 September when they were moved on to North Camp, Aldershot. It was here that the men were formed into platoons for training. While the men remained at the barracks they were taught rudimentary drill. Eventually, at the end of September, local police officers became involved at this stage because of a shortage of soldiers proficient in drill at the depot. The officers and NCOs were required to train the newly formed battalions. There were overwhelming numbers of men staying at the barracks at this time with up to 1,300 being billeted in Taunton in early September. The barracks only had accommodation for 350 men, and the rest had to sleep in local schools and public halls that had been requisitioned.

The 7th Battalion was formed on 13 September from volunteers who had been gathered in Aldershot. The battalion numbered 1,200, and was made up of the surplus NCOs and men after the formation of the 6th Battalion.

Major Troyte-Bullock of the 2nd Battalion was on leave from India at this time. Any hopes that he may have had of a restful time with his wife at North Coker House, Yeovil were soon dashed. He was promoted to Lieutenant Colonel and given command of the new battalion.

The early days of the battalion were chaotic. The men came in their civilian clothes and there were no uniforms for them. There were also no weapons. Training consisted of drill and fatigues. The gathered men came from all walks of life. Colliers, clerks, a sign writer and postmen had been assembled and were formed into platoons to be trained, although even this was hampered as there was a severe shortage of officers and NCOs.

The grouping of these men did not happen without certain problems. One of the main issues was soldiers getting drunk in the towns they were near to or camped in. In Aldershot restrictions were placed on pub opening hours after men from all of the battalions training nearby had caused problems. On 20 September, for instance, Private Roberts of the 7th Somersets was punished after being drunk and creating a disturbance and also for using obscene and threatening language to an NCO. Men were also punished for being found drunk in the town streets or creating disturbances at camp. Other problems were the throwing of rubbish out of barrack windows and men spitting on the barrack floors which particularly upset the battalion Medical Officer.

On 21 September the battalion left Aldershot, marching to Woking to join with three other battalions to form the 61st Brigade. The other battalions were the 7th Battalion the King's Own Yorkshire Light Infantry (7th KOYLI), the 7th Battalion Duke of Cornwall's Light Infantry (7th DCLI) and the 12th Battalion King's Liverpool Regiment (12th King's). The 7th SomLI would remain brigaded with these battalions for most of the war.

Despite a lack of equipment, training continued unabated. The men's efforts were concentrated on drill, gymnastics and route marches. On 26 September the 61st Brigade was inspected by Lord Kitchener, and three days later King George V, the Queen and Queen Alexandra also made an inspection of the brigade. By now the men were looking decidedly dishevelled from their training and lack of adequate clothing, and when the battalion paraded for inspection by the King they had to be placed at the front or rear according to the state of their trousers.

Training without equipment continued until October when the men of the battalion were issued with blue serge uniforms because of an acute shortage of khaki. At around the same time the battalion was issued with ten drill purpose rifles – Short Mark 1 Lee Metfords of 'pre-historic origin'. These had been loaned to the 7th Battalion by the 6th Battalion and were all the battalion would have until December when a further 100 Lee Metfords were issued. Rifle training was carried out so far as was possible with the men firing on the range, then passing the rifles on to the next group who waited their turn. In November the battalion was given eight sets of bayonet fighting equipment, and bayonet instruction was added to the training.

Throughout this time the whole 20th (Light) Division suffered from the same chronic shortage of equipment. The four artillery brigades attached to the Division had only four 15pdr guns per brigade with which to train. These were old guns and came without gun sights. Wooden sights and guns were improvised so that at least gun drill could be carried out. It wasn't until February 1915 that they would be given one modern 18pdr gun per brigade.

Notwithstanding the difficulties encountered, by Christmas the 7th Battalion had achieved an identity. Most of the men of A, B and C

Companies spent their first Christmas together in the army at their barracks at Woking. D Company, many of the officers and some NCOs were able to take eight days' leave over Christmas. The rest took their leave later.

Christmas meant that the men could enjoy a break from the training regime for a while. Christmas trees were found and dinner was held in the men's rooms. Thanks to Colonel Troyte-Bullock the men were able to dine on turkeys, geese, roast beef, plum puddings and mince pies. A plentiful supply of tobacco and cigarettes was also provided. The Colonel and company officers toured the dining rooms, and the Colonel proceeded to wish his men a pleasant time and expressed the hope that they would all meet again next Christmas, and that the coming year would be one of glory for the 7th Somersets.

A competition was held for the best decorated room which was won by C Company. They had decorated their room with various ornaments and with the words 'Success to our Brave Allies' emblazoned on one of the walls. By common consent the £3 prize was unanimously given to the men of the 1st Battalion who were actively engaged at the front.

On New Year's Day the whole brigade was paraded and addressed by the Brigade Commander. He wished all his men a happy and prosperous New Year as well as telling them that he felt sure that when the time came the 61st Brigade would prove itself second to none in the expeditionary force. In the afternoon the men played football, which had become a popular pastime.

In the days after the Christmas and New Year leave in particular, men often overstayed their passes. When they returned to the battalion they would usually be fined; the fine being levied in day's pay was usually the equivalent or slightly more than the length of absence.

Times of change

The early life of the battalion was full of changes. Personnel were sorted, brought into the battalion or left. Typical of the changes were those in January 1915, when Mr Fitzgerald who had joined the 7th Battalion, was selected for a commission. He left to undertake one month's military training at Keble College in Oxford before joining his new regiment, the Glosters. Similarly, in the week of 21 January the Regimental Sergeant Major Cole was transferred to the regimental depot in Taunton. He was replaced by Arthur Smith, who had been a company sergeant major. He was a popular appointment who inspired confidence in the men, as he had seen military service in the Northwest Frontier campaign in 1895–7, the First World War coming only a year after his retirement from the regular army. A new face in the battalion was Edward Hatt, who had volunteered for the Queen's Westminster Rifles, and then transferred into the Somerset

Light Infantry upon gaining his commission as a 2nd lieutenant. A young man, he had recently left the Dean Close Memorial School in Cheltenham and had intended to follow a career in commerce. His father was a councillor in Bath (soon to become the Mayor), and his elder brother had taken a commission in the 6th Somersets. By July 1915 2nd Lieutenant Hatt was given command of D Company.

The training process also revealed that some of the volunteers were unsuited to being in the army. Groups of men were often discharged from the battalion as being medically unfit, or after training, had been deemed as 'unlikely to become efficient soldiers'. A few were found to have been too young to volunteer and were discharged.

Another change for the battalion was the acquisition of a small bugle band in January 1915. The band would lead the men out on their route marches, no doubt easing the tedium of constant marching in and around Woking. The marches would often start early in the morning with 1,000 men drawn up in columns four wide, headed by the bugle band, often going fourteen miles in their serge blue uniforms and caps. Few breaks were taken, although on the longer marches a stop would be made for a sanitary trench to be dug. Fitness levels were generally high and the men would return, weather permitting, marching nearly as smartly as they had left. There were frequent complaints that soldiers marched too far apart and thereby blocked the whole road; the four-man column should have been narrow enough to keep to the left-hand side of the road and allow other traffic to pass. Gradually, as efficiency improved, night marches were introduced. These required an advance and rear guard to look out for traffic and avoid accidents. During this time other items were constantly being provided to the battalion such as the money for twenty-six pairs of field glasses that was sent to Colonel Troyte-Bullock by the Mayor of Bath in March.

On 23 January the whole 20th Division was assembled for an inspection by Lord Kitchener. The weather was appalling and the men gathered in their greatcoats in snow which turned to sleet and then rain as they marched to the parade. Their coats soaked up the rain, getting heavier and heavier. Eventually they arrived at the bleak inspection field, a snow-covered heathland, where the whole division took more than an hour to arrive and assemble. The soldiers were left standing in the bitter cold and a number collapsed and were carried off in ambulances. At 3.15pm Lord Kitchener arrived, quickly made his inspection and left. The soldiers were relieved to be able to march back to their billets.

On 22 February 1915 the battalion marched from Woking with the rest of the brigade to Witley Camp, Godalming, where training continued until near the end of March. Some of the men had been issued with khaki service dress and webbing before the move, and the remainder were clothed in service dress at Witley camp. The service dress at this time in

11

the war was with the peaked cap, helmets only being issued much later. The battalion underwent an inoculation programme against enteric fever.

Training then changed from drill and marches to include tactical schemes. As it became more realistic there was a greater effect on the population exposed to the exercising soldiers. Throughout the country battalions moved off the roads and on to farmland causing a lot of trouble for farmers. One company of the 7th Battalion were responsible for driving a flock of pregnant ewes into a private garden, upsetting both the sheep and the householder who suffered extensive damage to his garden. Soldiers from the battalion also managed to trample over a mushroom bed, which led to a high claim for compensation. Officers were asked to weigh training needs against the damage the exercises were likely to cause. The battalion also practised entrenching by digging holes on any public ground near their camp, and the officers were instructed in the use of the Vickers machine gun and in map reading.

The tactical schemes included practising manoeuvres against other battalions in the brigade. These were observed by brigade and divisional staff who would comment. Efforts were made to get the men accustomed to using cover to manoeuvre. On one manoeuvre the 7th Somersets were pitted against the 7th KOYLI and were severely criticised for un-necessarily exposing themselves to the enemy. A notice was issued to the battalion stating: 'Soldiers marched in a column along the railway line 1500 yards from the enemy. The GOC [General Officer Commanding] realises that the scheme excluded artillery, but machine guns or even rifles could have done considerable damage to so large a mark'. Other short-comings included failure to use small hills for cover, excessive bunching up of soldiers, and signallers often unnecessarily exposing themselves to enemy fire or even signalling so that the enemy could see the message.

During this time the general levels of equipment improved throughout the 20th Division. A large number of good draught horses, guns and equipment became available for the artillery, although the Divisional ammunition column had to be completed with mules. On 21 March the Division began moving to Salisbury Plain to continue training. The men proceeded in full marching order (less rifles) along the dusty roads in fine weather and arrived at their camp at Larkhill on Salisbury Plain where they would remain until 24 July 1915. Until then they continued to train hard, with field firing exercises and night manoeuvres being incorporated into the training schedules. The training of the Division, as with new Divisions at the time, concentrated on open warfare techniques. In June all of the men were fully equipped and armed with Lee Enfield rifles.

The 7th SomLI was now organised in five companies – A to D Companies (rifle companies) and a headquarters company. The rifle companies were arranged in four platoons of about fifty men each, a total of sixteen platoons in the battalion. All of the infantrymen were armed with rifles, the officers with revolvers. The headquarters company comprised the Colonel and second in command as well as orderly room, signalling, medical and transport staff. Cooks and scouts were also attached to headquarters. The battalion had four Vickers machine guns and their crew.

On 24 June 1915 the Division was drawn up on Salisbury Plain for inspection by the King. It had been nearly eleven months since the outbreak of war and this group of more than 12,000 of Kitchener's volunteers stood trained and eager. The 7th Battalion had been transformed from the postmen, porters, confectioners, lawyers and land agents who had last paraded before the King in their tatty civilian clothes into a body of soldiers. This occurrence, which was repeated throughout the land, was unique in British history.

During these early days a number of men from the battalion received the news that they had become fathers. In January, for example, Sergeant Sears and Sergeant Ley both had baby sons, while Private Beardmore's wife delivered a daughter. Sergeant Langley also received the sad news that his eldest son, Percival, had died at the family home in Bedminster, Bristol.

The training programme also took its toll on the men. The battalion suffered two measles epidemics and the long hours of training, often with the soldiers out of doors in all weather, meant that some became seriously ill. One of these, 22-year-old Private Leonard Patch, contracted pneumonia and returned home to Norton-sub-Hamdon where he died on 24 February. He is buried there in the churchyard of St Mary's Church. Private Sidney Biddiscombe died from an illness at the Military Isolation Hospital at Aldershot on 6 March and Private Frederick Grimstead from Axbridge in Somerset died of scarlet fever and pneumonia at the same hospital on 20 March 1915. By 16 April 1915 the battalion had lost five men.[1]

NOTES

1   The others who died were 19-year-old Graham Godden (died 6 December 1914); he is buried in the Brookwood Cemetery, Surrey), and Thomas Taylor (died 16 April 1915). Also shown in official records – in error – is Charles Taylor who is purported to have been killed in action on 16 August 1914 – before the battalion was formed.

CHAPTER II
Pack Up Your Troubles

Towards the sound of battle

On the afternoon of 24 July 1915 the main body of the battalion set off for France. The 878 men boarded two trains at Amesbury that carried them to a troopship in Southampton which sailed that same evening. The last view that many on board would have of England was of the lights of the Southampton docks and the views of the countryside about the Solent as their ship steamed out into the rough and darkening English Channel.

An advance party of 112 men from the battalion, together with the twenty-three carts of the transport, had set out two days before. These men had disembarked at Boulogne and travelled up the hill to a rest camp above the town where the whole battalion would eventually assemble on the night of the 24th.

The next day the battalion entrained for a camp at Wizernes where it remained for two days. Seasickness was driven away by route marches while the machine-gun officers were sent to a machine-gun school for instruction. Lewis machine guns began to be deployed into the front line units at this time and this necessitated a lot of training. Previously the battalion's main armaments were the Lee Enfield rifle and four Vickers 'medium' machine guns which were heavy water-cooled weapons that were incapable of being moved and set up quickly.

The Lewis gun was a relatively light (28lb), air-cooled machine gun that fired either 47 or 97 rounds of .303 rifle ammunition from circular drums at a rate of roughly four bullets per second. Four guns were issued to each battalion, one per company; each company had to find two Lewis gun teams of six men to be trained in the intricacies of using the gun. One was a reserve team to replace casualties.

After Wizernes the battalion marched to Notre Boom where the men camped in fields. Here the proximity to war became apparent at dawn on 30 July. At 4am they were woken by the distant sound of artillery firing. The gunfire almost certainly came from the German offensive that captured some British trenches at Hooge in the Ypres area after the first use of flame throwers. This was approximately fifteen miles from where

15

the 7th Battalion was encamped. The quiet of the following morning was again disturbed by the sound of fighting.

The battalion would spend some days here, the men being given a little time to acclimatise to life in France. Training schemes were centred on raising the fighting ability of the battalion, practising rapid redeployment as well as integrating the Lewis guns into the battalion. Physical exercise, distance judging, rapid loading and gas mask drill were also practised daily.

The organisation and training in the BEF was changing to adapt to the requirements of trench warfare. Specialist bombing sections were introduced and selection and training of officers and men for these had to be done. Most of the training was given by officers and NCOs of the two regular divisions with battlefield experience in the III Corps into which the 20th Division had been introduced.

On 5 August the battalion marched to Rossignol where training continued for the next four days. Working parties were also required to build a thirty-yard shooting range, part of an ongoing programme to build an infrastructure to support a rapidly growing British Army.

Visiting the front line

After just under one year of organising, preparing and training, on 10 August 1915 the battalion was attached to the 27th Division for training in the front line. The 27th Division was a regular army unit that was occupying the quiet stretch of front line at Armentières and would be expected to demonstrate trench warfare techniques to the inexperienced men of the 7th Battalion.

For the purpose of this introduction to trench warfare the battalion was split in half and set out for the front line that was occupied by men of the regular 27th Division. A Company was attached to the 4th Rifle Brigade and B Company to the 4th KRRC. Both companies set out from their billets behind the line at 4pm and slowly made their way into the front-line trenches along the zigzag communication trenches. The men arrived and were settled into their new surroundings by 7.30pm; the instructing battalions immediately set to work to integrate the novices into the ways and dangers of life in the trenches. Disconcertingly the Germans in the trenches opposite were well aware of the new battalion, calling out 'Hello, you Somerset cuckoos' in welcome.

C and D Companies were sent into support and reserve trenches; C Company was attached to the 2nd King's Shropshire Light Infantry (2nd KSLI) and D Company to the 3rd King's Royal Rifle Corps (3rd KRRC). They were accommodated in a farm and an iron factory behind the front line. Perhaps surprisingly to the men involved, who might have had other ideas of what being at the front entailed, by the evening the men of

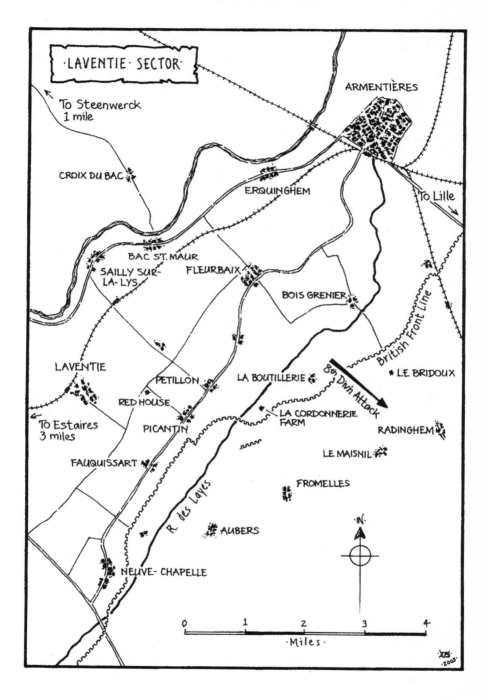

these two companies were hard at work digging a communication trench.

After just twenty-four hours in the front line, A and B Companies were relieved by C and D Companies, going to the support and reserve positions. Here the men were put to work while the officers and NCOs were given instruction on trench warfare by men of the 2nd KSLI.

One of the men given instruction was Corporal Cox, who had worked in a clerical job and also taught shorthand before the war. Corporal Cox wrote:

> I had not been up in the trenches long before the corporal I was with said 'I am going out to visit the listening patrol. Coming?' So off we went. The patrol goes out in front of our trenches, between us and the Germans, listening. Each side shoots up flares which last about a minute and light up everything around them. Then the best thing is to either drop down or stand still otherwise you get a bullet. I dropped down when we went up and I can tell you, and did not meet with anything. We paid three visits to the patrol in the two days I was up there. There is more firing by night than by day. Soon after it gets light everyone is on duty and then about five o'clock you see the chaps getting their breakfast, making the tea etc. and soon after that all except the sentries turn in and sleep.
>
> On the second morning I went down to get some water with two other chaps. We had to go to a mined house and get it from a pump. Coming back a sniper evidently spotted us because he sent three shots very quickly over our heads. We got in a trench and then wondered where the sniper was, as some of the ground we had to pass was open at the back. However no more shots came when we moved and so we got back all right.
>
> That same morning a corporal was visiting his sentries and spoke to one on duty two trenches on my left. He just turned around to say 'post correct corporal' and just when he turned a bullet caught him in the neck and came out his left ear. His number would have been up if he had not turned just when he did. When they got him outside and were taking him off the stretcher he smiled and said 'Where did they get me?'– a little expressive!

On 13 August the companies exchanged places again. On this tour the men were expected to carry out normal front-line duties. One of those going into the line for the second time was 19-year-old Private Charles Stephens. He spent part of the night on sentry duty until he was shot and killed by a German sniper the next morning. He was the first fatal casualty of the battalion in combat, and he was buried in a cemetery at a nearby farm that evening.

Later that evening a party of Germans carrying out works around their trenches was surprised by battalion machine gunners and two were reportedly shot.

After swapping front and reserve positions once more on 15 August, on Tuesday 17 August the battalion was marched by platoon out of the line until it reached Erquinghem Bridge where it met the transport. Movement by platoon was commonplace when the battalion was in range of enemy guns to reduce the risk of heavy casualties. The whole battalion then set off on a nine-mile march to billets behind the lines, ending its first spell in the trenches.

The men were billeted in farm buildings near Le Rossignol for the next week, during which time training continued in earnest. The battalion's scouts were instructed in the arts of sniping and information gathering in the trenches. British snipers were trained to work in pairs with one man observing and the other using a telescopic-sighted rifle. Both observer and rifleman would alternate in their roles through their spell on duty; they had the dual role of keeping the enemy confined within their own trenches and of observing enemy activities. This intelligence would be logged, passed to the battalion and then brigade intelligence officers who would in turn pass relevant information to divisional, corps or army level. Things of particular interest were identifications of enemy units (from cap badges. etc.), locations of strongpoints, posts or observation points and enemy activities such as reliefs.

On 28 August the battalion was marched to Estaires where the men spent the next week providing working parties for nearby trenches in increasing numbers and deteriorating weather conditions, the rain adding to the difficulty of the already hard physical labour.

Holding the front line

The battalion returned to front-line duties on 5 September 1915 moving into support positions behind the 7th DCLI. For the first time the 61st Brigade was holding the front line by itself.

On 9 September the battalion had men of the 23rd Division attached to them for trench warfare instruction. The men, from the 13th Durham Light Infantry, were given two days' instruction. At this time the 7th Battalion SomLI had only spent seven days at the front, although given that it now occupied support positions and spent its time supplying working parties, this was perhaps not too important. Some of the Durham officers were taken out on a night patrol of no man's land.

On the night of Monday 12 September 1915 the battalion took over trenches in the front line that had previously been occupied by the 12th King's. It was the first time the battalion would solely occupy front-line positions and it was an area where the enemy trenches were extremely close, at the narrowest being some sixty-eight yards from the enemy line. From the outset Captain Hatt noticed the difference: 'We arrived at night in the trenches and from the moment we got there things seemed to become more active.'

At a little after 5 o'clock on the following morning the Germans exploded two mines right next to each other underneath the Somersets. Sergeant Major Bulson reported:

> He undermined us and about 40 yards of our trench line was blown sky high. I was fortunately in the next fire bay but one from the eruption and so I escaped injury beyond a few bruises. It was awe inspiring – first the heaving of the bottom of the trench, then the wobbling of the fire step and the parados, then this mountain of earth guns and bodies thrown high into the air to come down again falling all around us.

The mines had been exploded under B Company creating a single crater about forty yards in diameter. In the process about twenty men of the company were buried. In the words of Captain Hatt: 'Then there ensued a terrific bombardment for some time, which seemed like hours but was really only about a quarter of an hour, until our artillery started and it gave them a devil of a tying up.' The German shelling was concentrated around the crater that had been formed by the blasts, and at the same time an attempt was made by the Germans to rush and capture the crater. Sergeant Major Bulson:

> We 'stood to' and opened rapid fire to keep the enemy back and I remember a snick and went to put in a fresh clip of cartridges, found that I had only four inches of my bayonet left. An enfilade bullet had knocked the rest off. One thing, we kept the enemy off, for only a few of them were able to occupy the crater made by the mine.

While the fighting was going on around the crater, efforts were also being made to find and free the buried soldiers and tend to the injured. Lance Corporal Ward took charge of the stretcher bearers who were to hand and, regardless of the fierce battle going on around him, he was able to tend to wounded men and also bring some of them to safety. He subsequently received the Distinguished Conduct Medal.

The initial explosion and the short battle that followed claimed five dead[1] and seventeen injured from the battalion. The toll would surely have been much higher had it not been for the prompt response of the artillery, which was noted by all.

Sergeant Major Bulson said: 'I would pay tribute to the artillery supporting us that morning for within a few moments of the explosion they were putting down a barrage on the SOS line effectively stopping any attempt by the enemy taking our trenches.' German casualties were apparently heavy. In Captain Hatt's words: 'I hear that they were carrying dead and wounded for the whole day out of the Boches lines. We lost only a few compared with what they must have lost.' The rest of the day was tense with intermittent shelling.

The dead men included Sergeant John Berry who was born in Reading but was working as a postman in Clifton in Bristol at the outbreak of the war. He was a veteran of the Chitral campaign in 1895 and of the Boer War in which he served with the Bedfords. Sergeant Berry was killed by a shell while he was writing a letter home to his wife. The unfinished letter was sent to his widow with an accompanying letter from Captain Nepean: 'I am sure that it will be a great comfort to you to know that his last thoughts were of you. Sergeant Berry was a most efficient NCO, and is very deeply regretted by all ranks.'

For his part in organising the resistance to this German raid 2nd Lieutenant Mitchell was later awarded the Military Cross.

Enemy shelling and trench mortar fire continued for the next three days. On the afternoon of 14 September the shelling killed two more men and injured another six.[2] The following day two men were killed and another seven injured by trench mortar fire that started at dawn and carried on through the day. One of those killed was 23-year-old Private Robert Wetherall. He suffered a fractured right leg and wounds to his head and left arm and died later that day. Another man, 21-year-old Private William Bragg, was sitting beside a dugout when a shell burst beside him and hit him in the leg. Others nearby rushed to help but were unable to stop the bleeding; he eventually bled to death.

At 9pm on the evening of Friday 16 September D Company set about relieving B Company in the front line positions. While the relief was taking place, Captain Nepean, who had tried so hard to get into this war using his connection with Lord Roberts, was killed, along with his orderly Private Albert Bennett, by one of the trench mortar bombs. The bomb rolled off the parapet and exploded close to both men. Captain Nepean suffered terrible injuries to his back and died as he was being carried to the dressing station.

On Saturday calm returned. There were no enemy bombardments although enemy snipers were active. During the next three days, three more men from the battalion were to die.[3]

Captain Hatt's C Company moved from the front-line positions into a support role within the battalion on the Saturday and he found time to write to his parents in Bath the next day:

> We were relieved last night and are now back in support billets behind the firing line after a week in the trenches. [Despite the

endurance of his men over the previous week he offered an insight into life in the trenches at that time.] One rather funny thing showing the pets one meets in the trenches. I went down one and saw a sentry watching through a parapet and close beside him and sitting on its haunches and cleaning itself was a little mouse. It was quite tame and they were making a great fuss of it. It was awfully funny. There were a number of kittens also in the trenches some of which had strolled over from the Huns.

On Monday 19 September the exhausted 7th Somersets were relieved from their first and violent experience of holding the front line. They marched to Rue de Quesnay where the men billeted in and around a farm. Although out of the front line, they were still within enemy artillery range and soon became involved in an artillery duel. Captain Hatt wrote of Tuesday 22 September:

Just another letter to let you know I am still jolly well and jolly fit after a good sleep, and furthermore a good wash. It is rather trying you know, washing out of a canteen and using the same water for a week and one welcomes a bath such as we had yesterday in the old boiler we unearthed, it was great. Yesterday we lost all the furniture we had looted as a shell came through the window and burst in the mess room and all the tables and chairs have gone, and all covered in debris. But extraordinary as it may seem we had succeeded in getting sixteen eggs which were standing in the corner of the room, and not one was broken. We were very pleased. But it was a beastly nuisance as it rather disturbed our afternoon's rest. Apart from that we slept most of the day.

The battalion was fortunate not to suffer any casualties. Quite apart from the constant dangers they faced, the soldiers were also often under personal pressures. One of the battalion's men, Sergeant Coombes, had recently been involved in trying to get his wife and children rehoused as their home in Bayford was unfit for human habitation. His letter, written to Wincanton District Council from the front, had resulted in a visit by the sanitation inspector who had told Mrs Coombes that the two-bedroom cottage, apart from having defects present, was too small for her family. She was told to find alternative accommodation or face eviction. This was more easily said than done as with seven children Mrs Coombes had great difficulty in persuading prospective landlords to let her take a new tenancy.

Loos

Although the sector of the front line into which the 20th Division had been introduced was relatively quiet, away from the main battleground of Ypres to the north and areas of smaller battles like Neuve Chapelle to the south, it was soon to change.

The area occupied by the 20th Division was soon to be on the northern edge of the Loos offensive, and fall between the main offensive to the south and a diversionary attack to their north. The main battle would start on 25 September. Accordingly the men were constantly required to form carrying parties while out of the line against the backdrop of a heavy barrage that intensified on 22 September. It was the German response to this artillery fire that had resulted in the shell blowing up the Somerset's officers' mess room. The suspense of the men grew as they became aware that a 'big show' was expected, and rumours circulated that the battalion would be part of it.

The battalion returned to the front line on 24 September, occupying trenches to the east of la Cordonnerie Farm. The weather had broken as the men returned to the front. Captain Hatt wrote:

> What a day it was, pouring with rain, and when we got to the trenches they were nothing more than huge streams of mud and water half way up our shins. Well we swam up there and relieved the [7th KOYLI] people and settled down to a dirty night.

The battalion was under orders to help create a diversion while the main attack took place, but to be on notice to attack if required. The diversion included setting down a smoke screen along the front line in conjunction with other units to mask the exact point of the attack. Also, the battalion was to fire on the enemy trenches to support attacks by elements of the 8th Division to the north and the Indian Meerut Division to the south. There was a little optimism that the Germans might fall back on this front if the offensive to the south was successful. Captain Hatt wrote:

> The morning of the 25th was very dark and misty, still raining. We all stood to at 3.30 and then at a given signal, bombs, artillery bombardment, rapid rifle fire, machine guns, smoke bombs, gas bombs and everything were let loose, and to my dying day I shall never forget the scene that went on for two hours.

The main British barrage of 18pdr field guns commenced at 4.20am and continued until 5.15am when it slackened. The heavier guns had been sent south to help with the main battle. In Captain Hatt's words:

The whole of the front was a dense volume of smoke. The air was thick with the crack of bullets and screeching and numbing according to size went the shells in their hundreds from our guns into their parapets and supports – a veritable inferno. And the Huns started but they never got a look in. His artillery pounded shells over very quickly, but they were badly aimed and did little damage.

Our men did wonderfully well and when I went up and down my company lines and saw rows of figures in their smoke helmets [an early gas mask], pounding away with their rifles, looking like divers, I thought as never before what a wonderful lot they are. It was a very trying part to play in so big a show, but I think we were very success-ful and the Huns I think were in a deuce of a funk.

At 6am the 25th Brigade of the 8th Division attacked to the north of the 7th Battalion positions between la Boutillerie and le Bridoux. They stormed and captured the enemy front-line trenches, but were driven out later that day in a counter-attack. At 6.30am the main Loos attack began to the south. Although the first day of the offensive had been a partial success, overall the offensive was in retrospect a disappointment. Despite German machine guns firing at Somerset positions all along the line, Private Bert Smart was the only man killed on 25 September.

The battalion remained in the front line throughout the first day of the offensive. Their positions were fairly active, while the German counter-attack was delivered against the 8th Division to the north with the Somersets occasionally firing rifles and machine guns at very long range in a vain attempt to help the beleaguered men of the 8th Division. They watched the odd artillery barrage from a distance. As day passed to night a heavy rain started to fall, keeping the trenches in a very bad state. The Somersets had not been called on to attack.

The following day, while the battalion stood in the front line in a state of readiness, the men received post and parcels from home. Private Herbert Miller received a package containing cigarettes which he handed out to his friends. Just as he had finished he was struck by a bullet from a rifle that had been accidentally discharged. He was severely wounded and was evacuated to a nearby field hospital where he died the next day. The same day orders were given to return to billets and the men struggled back through the cold mud and rain to billets at Rue du Quesnay. Captain Hatt said:

I think I have never been so tired as we were then. It was almost impossible to struggle along with all our packs on but we got back somehow and I slept till 11 o'clock in the morning. I am awfully fit but my feet are very sore today after being wet through for so long and not being able to take my boots off but that will be all right by tonight.

A quiet sector – Laventie

After the battalion's involvement on the periphery of the Loos offensive, it was to spend some months engaged in mundane trench warfare. October brought a return to a position near the front line at Laventie – a relatively quiet sector, where headquarters were established in a war-battered red-brick farmhouse, 'Red House'.

The British front at this part of the line was a continuous front-line trench which was entered through communication trenches that started behind the lines. The front-line trenches did not have many proper underground dugouts. Wooden shelters provided the only limited protection available. In the rearmost areas, about a mile behind the front line, were a series of posts. These were in farm buildings or specifically constructed positions where no pre-existing cover was available. Often these posts would be used by the soldiers manning them as cover and accommodation, even though they were occasionally targeted by the enemy.

The soldiers spent a great deal of time on trench repair duties – repairing parapets, parados and wire as well as draining and improving the posts. Fatigue parties would also be drawn from the battalion for other types of work.

Groups of men were attached to the 181st Royal Engineer Company who were tunnelling. The infantry fatigue parties were required to carry away the mining spoil, and also to bring up wooden supports and joists. The tunnels were built primarily to undermine and blow up enemy trench positions, but very quickly the miners also learned the necessity of digging tunnels for other purposes; as listening posts to hear enemy mining activity and also to counter-mine enemy shafts.

On Saturday 2 October, while the men were working, the Germans successfully penetrated the British tunnel and introduced poison gas into the shaft. Some of the miners were gassed and a Royal Engineer officer, Lieutenant Hobbs, together with a small group of men from the Somersets, went into the mine to rescue the poisoned men. Lance Corporal Allsop was able to carry out one unconscious man from inside the mine.

In his efforts to rescue his men, Lieutenant Hobbs was gassed and collapsed in the mine. Single-handedly Private Kell, one of the Somersets, was able to drag him to the surface, himself being gassed in the process. Another two Somerset men were also gassed. Private Baker survived and was evacuated to hospital, while Private Frederick Newman was overcome and died underground in the tunnel. In all two men died, three were admitted to hospital and six reported sick with gas poisoning. The bodies of the dead men were recovered the next day.

Archie Hurley, a soldier engaged elsewhere on fatigues that Saturday, had a narrow escape. He wrote to one of his brothers around this time:

> Just a few lines to let you know that I had your letter and cigarettes quite safe. They came in very handy I can tell you. The trenches are wet and muddy, we are covered in mud, and it is very cold at nights. I have had a letter from Fred [his brother – a driver in the artillery] who says he is going to see me the first chance he gets. I had a very narrow shave . . . Four of us were coming up the trenches with food when a couple of snipers saw us. They shot down two of my pals and left us, but I soon got under cover. I was carrying a tin of biscuits at the time. The shots came ping ping but luck came my way. We had some fun about a week ago. We were all lined up and ready to charge when we had the order to rapid fire. Our company drove about 10,000 bullets over for them.

After a couple of days at the front the battalion received two new officers fresh from training. Second Lieutenant Andrews later recalled his arrival: '[I was] 18 years old or so when I got my commission . . . came out to the trenches just after the battalion's involvement in the battle of Loos'. He had passed through training school at Crowborough where he had been attached to a regular training unit for one month:

> We felt like veterans when we reached our Depot. When the real training began however, we felt and looked like very raw recruits again. Do you remember how new we all looked in our Sam Brownes and what efforts were made to darken them? How proud we were of our swords, and what great deeds we would do with them. How anxious we were to get to the 'Front,' that mysterious place we were all destined to hear so much about during the next few weeks. Months of training passed by, monotonous drilling, musketry, marches and so on until we began to feel that the war would end before we got a look in.
>
> Then came the day when I found myself included with the next draft. I remember I went with [Lieutenant] Martin. After a confusing medley of RTOs, railheads, concentration camps, French railways and other curious things we found ourselves reporting to battalion HQ near Laventie. We were to go up the line to join the battalion.
>
> It all seemed very unreal – the night was dark, and very quiet except for the occasional 'ping' of a bullet or glare of a Verey light. We saw men asleep in the trenches, with one here and there looking over the parapet on sentry. We saw men filling sandbags or putting up wire entanglements. This was hardly what we expected – it seemed somewhat disappointing, we had visions of being thrust into the fury at a critical moment and helping beat back an overwhelming attack.

We were to learn that the normal use for bayonets was to toast bread and grill fish, that swords were only worn by 'Brass Hats', the cavalry and orderly officers at home; that the type of Mills bomb though timed for five seconds, did not always wait as long and that it was safer to throw it away on the word 'three' than 'four'. If you were a dead shot with a revolver you might be useful as a rat destroyer. We were amazed when the first relief took place. We had been taught to lead the relieving party to the trench, wait until the outgoing men had turned right in file, and then follow into the trenches they had occupied as they marched out. I often wondered afterwards what idiot had taught us such nonsense.

One of the occasional shots heard that night by Lieutenant Andrews was a short burst of machine-gun fire that caught and wounded Acting Company Sergeant Major Langley. He was carried out of the forward positions and was sent on to the casualty clearing station at Merville, where he died three days later.

After six days the battalion was relieved. Six days were spent behind the front line in Laventie supplying working parties, and then the battalion returned to its former trenches on 12 October. The next day dawned with the men huddled in their trenches and dugouts under their waterproofs against lightly falling rain.

Orders were passed along that the battalion was to take part in a fire demonstration against the enemy that afternoon, in conjunction with men of the 60th Brigade on the Somerset's right flank. The 60th Brigade would also be feigning an attack with mock up soldiers being thrown over the trenches and then being pulled back by ropes as if shot. The plan was to get the Germans to man their trenches and then bombard them so as to cause heavy casualties.

At one o'clock fire was opened on the German trenches with rifles and machine guns. At the same time clouds of smoke, that were initially mistaken for gas by the Somersets, were released by the 60th Brigade soldiers. The Germans were quick to respond with machine-gun fire that raked the British lines slightly injuring Lieutenant Pidgeon and damaging a machine gun. The demonstration ended a little over one hour later, and normality returned to the trenches.

The remainder of this spell in the front was uneventful, with the exception that the ever present danger posed by enemy snipers was underlined. On the morning of Friday 15 October a battalion sniper, Private Oliver Hill, was shot through the head. He lived for ten minutes before losing consciousness and dying. Oliver Hill had sung in a church choir and worked with his brother at the Dunkerton pit near Bath before the war. Captain Hatt in whose company Oliver Hill had served wrote: 'The whole company and my brother officers join in expressing our deep

27

sorrow and sympathy with you in your loss. Your son was always cheerful and was a great favourite with all the men and ourselves.' Two days later another battalion sniper, Private Ernest Cromme, was also killed.

The battalion was relieved on 18 October 1915 and returned to Laventie where once again many men were required for working parties. The battalion also practised attacking and bombing, and live hand grenades were introduced to the training. Lance Corporal Rideout was injured during practice at the bomb school.

While the battalion was out of the line on Tuesday 19 October, CSM Samuel Harris was shot dead in his billets by a man, Corporal Paddock, who ran amok. The incident was to some extent covered up in the public report in that it was reported that he had been accidentally shot but that the 'full particulars of the way he met his death are not yet known'. CSM Harris was a married man from Illminster who had been a regular soldier with the Somersets before the war. He had become a postman on retiring from the Army shortly before the outbreak of war.

Despite the constant small numbers of casualties the conditions in the Laventie area were later looked upon with a certain nostalgia by those present. Lieutenant Andrews recalled:

> Laventie was of course one of the 'cushy' parts of the line. The trenches were well made and afforded plenty of protection. They were also comfortable. One of my billets comprised a wooden shelter backing onto the parapet; it had a door and windows; there was a bed inside and Kirschner [the original 'pinup'] pictures were on the walls. I won't swear to it, but I believe there was even a pot of flowers there. On occasions there was the inevitable 'strafe' with its accompanying toll of casualties, and we often longed to hit back at the fellow who was causing us such discomfort. Unfortunately we seemed to be somewhat short of ammunition, so much so that our replies to a good old Bosche bombardment usually consisted of a few miserable whizz-bangs. At least, that was our view of these pip squeaks, but possibly the Bosche being at the wrong end of the shell thought differently.

There were constant reminders to all the men in the form of letters and parcels from home. One patriot, a tobacconist from Bridgwater, sent tobacco and cigarettes to the battalion. The recipient, Sergeant Howell a former gas worker who came from Bridgwater, wrote a grateful reply:

> Many thanks for the box of cigarettes and tobacco, which arrived quite safely yesterday. I've been around the battalion and divided them with Bridgwater boys, and they wish me to convey their thanks

to you. We have been out of the trenches now six weeks and go in again tomorrow (Sunday). We have six days in and six days out, and we are glad to get back for a rest, as those in the trenches don't get much rest while there.

The battalion threaded its way back into the front line on 24 October. Between the end of October and Christmas it continued to rotate into and out of the front line at broadly six-day intervals. It suffered a further ten fatalities during this time.[4] Most of the identifiable casualties were from gunshot wounds and significantly another two battalion officers, Lieutenants Melhuish and Armstrong, and another battalion sniper, Private Griffiths, were shot dead. Officers' and snipers' roles required a high degree of risk through exposure to the enemy. Private Griffiths was only 17 when he died. He had lied about his age in order to get into the Army, saying that he was 20 – the then minimum age. He was well liked in the battalion, and the fact that he was an excellent shot meant that he had been trained and worked as a sniper himself.

The only other significant change during this time was a deterioration in the weather. The battalion's men were spending their first winter in the trenches, and endured a very wet November and increasingly harder frosts as the year came to an end.

Despite the hard work being carried out during fatigues, that this was a quiet sector and that deficiencies remained is amply illustrated in the recollection of Major Preston-Whyte of an incident that occurred around this time:

> C.O. on leave Maj ____ commanding the battalion. 11pm Major arrives in my company line. We meet and he asks me what the wire is like on my front. I have often wondered myself as I have considerable difficulty in finding any. However I say it is not so bad. The Major's never been in no man's land and suggests we go and inspect wire on my front. I go with him and hope we may fall over a few strands somewhere. After looking about for some time and my continually saying 'It should be about here sir', imagine my horror when he suddenly flashes on his electric torch, waved it about and called out in a loud voice, 'I say, where is this ____ wire?' I did not wait to reply, but left him to it. Strange to say nothing happened, and on his return he asked me why I had cleared out in such a ____ hurry. 'Far be it from me'.

Christmas was at Fleurbaix – out of the line. The newly appointed Lieutenant Henry Foley, who had joined the battalion with his brother Geoff on 20 December after being selected for officer training from the 6th Battalion SomLI, said:

On coming out of the line we were billeted at Fleurbaix which was still partially inhabited, and only slightly damaged by shellfire. Here we spent Christmas, receiving on the eve of that festival of peace the seasons greetings from our friends over the way in the shape of about thirty shells, which fell in and around the village. Nobody was hurt but C Company, who were nearest the point of danger had to leave their billets, the officers providing light comedy in the scene by mustering their men clad in pyjamas.

On Boxing Day the battalion returned to the front line, where they were subject to sporadic shelling. On 28 December Lance Corporal Frank Chapman was killed by shellfire that caught him in the back. He was the last man from the battalion to be killed in 1915. Since formation the battalion had lost forty men through enemy action – the effect of 'attrition' while on active service for three months.

The 7th Somersets, like all British battalions, was now beginning to function in a far more sophisticated manner than it had been just three months previously. Specialist roles in machine guns and bombing had been created for officers and men alike; the battalion intelligence officer's, signals officer's and transport officer's roles now required great skill to be performed effectively. Most still had a lot to learn.

The battalion remained in the Laventie area until 10 January 1916 when the 20th Division was relieved by the 8th Division and went into divisional rest. The spell at the quiet sector was at an end.

NOTES

1   Five were killed outright and one wounded man later died. Those who died were Private John Orchard, 19-year-old Private Ernest Pearce, 24-year-old Private Thomas Rudge, Private Michael Bones, Private George Richards and Sergeant John Berry.

2   The dead men were Privates Edward Bristow and George Beck. Another man, 24-year-old Private Walter Fry, died of wounds.

3   On 17 September Private Thomas Jones died from wounds, Private Frederick Raison was killed on 18 September and Private McCarthy died of wounds on 19 September.

4   Private Frederick Drane died on 1 November 1915 after being shot in the head on 24 October; 2nd Lieutenant Melhuish was shot on patrol on 27 October; 21-year-old Private Frederick Tapps was killed on 17 November; Private Joseph Phillips and 2nd Lieutenant Armstrong were killed on 28 November in separate incidents; 17-year-old Private Emrys Griffiths was killed on 29 November; Private Herbert Fuller was killed on 3 December; Privates Joseph Webb and Peter Smith died of wounds near the front and Private David Williams died of wounds at home in the last two weeks of the year.

CHAPTER III
An Overview in 1916

The war until 1916

The year 1916 arrived with most of Kitchener's New Armies blooded by their first exposures to life in the trenches. The Regular battalions that had taken the field in 1914 and the territorial units that had joined them had exhausted themselves in the early battles that stopped the German advance into France, and then in the bloody and costly fighting at the First Battle of Ypres, Neuve Chapelle, Aubers Ridge, Givenchy and Loos that followed in 1915.

The decision to raise a large British army had proved fortuitous. The character of war had changed beyond anything hitherto seen in Europe. Massed armies of conscripts and volunteers faced each other in miles of front-line trenches, support trenches and reserve positions. Machine guns, rifles, hand grenades, bayonets and dense tangles of barbed wire protected the immediate front lines. Deadly artillery barrages awaited anyone who dared to enter no man's land. Meanwhile, farther behind the lines, industrialists, chemists, soldiers and even amateurs worked to develop and perfect ways of breaking the deadlock that had emerged in autumn 1914 and which the offensives of 1915 had proved incapable of achieving.

Britain's Army had been transformed from a small regular army, with reservists, into a large European army. The BEF that landed in France in August 1914 numbered five infantry and one cavalry division. There were a few British infantry divisions retained at home to forestall any German landing in the United Kingdom. Towards the end of 1915 the British and Commonwealth armies had twenty-six infantry and five cavalry divisions in France and Flanders. At this time there were also thirteen British and Commonwealth divisions in Gallipoli, the Middle East and Africa facing the Turkish and German forces there. The number of divisions in Europe was set to grow with the return of some of these units, and with planned increases in the army in the field, to the extent that by July 1916 onwards the army used fifty-three infantry divisions in the Battle of the Somme, and had in excess of seventy divisions available.

Armaments

An armaments shortage was very quickly identified at the commencement of hostilities and this continued, albeit to a lesser extent than at the early stages.

The opening weeks of the war showed that the British Army had not anticipated the type and quantity of artillery and shells that would be needed for the conflict in Europe. Experience in South Africa had demonstrated the effectiveness of shrapnel shells in seeking out the elusive Boer enemy hiding and sniping from a distance. Trench warfare, where the enemy was protected by trenchworks and dugouts, demanded high explosive shells in great numbers to literally smash the emplacements to pieces.

British shell production was pitifully small at the start of the war and high explosive shells only became available after October 1914. The shortage of artillery ammunition cannot be exaggerated. Within weeks the General Headquarters of the BEF in France was requesting both a numerical increase in artillery shells, and an increase in the percentage of high explosive munitions. By mid-September 1914 Sir John French, the commander of the BEF, pointed out the shortages saying: 'In view of the large expenditure of ammunition now taking place and to be expected this is a serious matter. No effort should be spared to send out further supplies at once'.

The provision of nearly all armaments at this time was undertaken by government contract with private companies. This may explain the impotent replies from the War Office to the effect that: 'we cannot supply at this rate until manufacturers reach their maximum output'; and from the Master General of Ordnance: 'I cannot say what our future supplies will be, as it entirely depends on the promises of the firms to which we have given large orders being kept up to date'. At the height of the crisis ammunition was being fired at twice the rate of replacement and the BEF went down to under ten days' reserves.

A strong feeling soon emerged that the companies undertaking munitions work were profiteering, at the same time that they were failing to properly support the army in its campaign. A crisis in skilled manpower quickly developed as hundreds of thousands of metal workers volunteered to fight in Kitchener's armies. Long hours and poor conditions of work along with high profits and a manpower shortage led to growing industrial action by munition workers. In January 1915 the Board of Trade were notified of ten new disputes; by March this had risen to seventy-four.

Despite the existence of censorship, letters from soldiers serving at the front were printed in local papers, such as this one from an anonymous soldier in the North Somerset Yeomanry:

Here we are only just out of the trenches and under orders to go in again tomorrow [29 May 1915] for ten days. With the wind blowing in our faces at 20 miles an hour, its ten to one against any man coming home alive. We only have 10 percent of our fellows who came out with us left. Our artillery is nothing to theirs, and we are being killed in thousands because its true that we cannot get any high explosive shells. Shrapnel is allright on infantry advancing, but you can't blow trenches to ____ with it. I'd like to put all the strikers and slackers in the trenches and let 'em get all sorts of enemy shells from a ton downwards on them, as they have and are doing to us, and hear only very occasionally a battery let fly shrapnel in reply ... I saw a transport man and he said the whole column had gone down to the base for lyddite [high explosive] shells three times and come back without one. Meanwhile we get blown to ____ out of it the next for want of them.

On 26 May 1915 the Ministry of Munitions was formed with David Lloyd George as Minister of State. The Munitions of War Act 1915 became law on 2 July; factories were taken over by the government to restrict profiteering, control practices and to introduce new procedures for dealing with industrial disputes by means of arbitration while the employees continued to work. Serious consideration was also given to curbing absenteeism caused by alcohol consumption, to the extent that prohibition was considered. The compromise reached was the introduction of licensing laws, elements of which survive to this day.

The views of an employee engaged in an Admiralty project of a 'highly confidential and secret nature' were expressed when he was prosecuted by his employers in Bath City Police Court in August 1915 for absenting himself from work. Mr Rice said that for the past thirteen months he had been engaged on overtime. He had been working over a big coke fire in a warm corner, and a blower was close to him. He said that some time ago his health and nerves had broken down and he started to lose time. People who came to that part of the shop would walk away and put fingers in their ears. The accusation being made that he spent too much time in the public house, he denied this saying that he had the occasional glass, but did not sit there idling away his time. Mr Rice then vainly tried to assert a different line of defence stating that he had 'sacked himself at a minutes notice' like the company had a habit of doing with its employees. This was refuted by the works manager, Mr Lawrence, who pointed out that since 12 July 1915 neither a worker nor his employer had any right to discharge a man that was needed. An employer being liable for a penalty if it did so. Evidence was put before the court that Mr Rice absented himself from work on average two to three days per week. He was duly convicted and ordered to pay £3 compensation and costs.

Efforts to solve the manpower shortage included trying to obtain the return of metal workers from military units, although this only achieved the return of 5,000 out of an estimated quarter of a million who had volunteered. Many skilled men were required in active service especially in units such as the Royal Engineers who were advertising for blacksmiths as late as 27 November 1915:

> Urgently required for service in the Royal Engineers for the duration of the War. Men desiring to enlist as Blacksmiths in the Royal Engineers are put through a test at their trade which is less difficult than the tests for shoeing smiths. They might for example be required to cut a length of ½ inch sound bar iron, bend into a ring of 5 inch diameter and weld complete.

Women were increasingly employed in munitions and other work to replace the dwindling labour force, the first women becoming involved in early 1915 on an ad hoc basis. In March 1915 the Board of Trade called upon women to volunteer, and by 4 June 1915 nearly 70,000 had enrolled as available to work. Of these 1,816 were given work in munitions factories on the same basis as the men, often working twelve-hour shifts.

Perhaps the greatest contribution to ensuring an adequate supply of shells was made through the formation of seventy-three national factories by the Ministry of Munitions by December 1915. The output rose steadily from approximately 70,000 per week in May 1915, to 120,000 in September 1915 and 240,000 in January 1916. These increases have to be looked at in conjunction with the huge increase in the size of the army, the ever larger part of the front line it occupied and the bigger battles being fought.

Artillery shells became a public focus of attention as they were a direct shortcoming visible to and affecting the fighting capabilities of the front-line soldier; but there were severe shortages of all equipment. Rifles for instance were being produced at a rate of some 45,000 per month in March 1915, which although an impressive figure, was totally inadequate to arm and train quickly an army of at first hundreds of thousands and then millions of soldiers. The plant and machinery required to turn out a new rifle took about nine months to make and rifle production remained inadequate until late 1915 when more machinery became available.

The number of machine guns available at the beginning of 1915 was also derisory in view of the demands of trench warfare. By 1 June 1915 there were only 1,330 machine guns of all descriptions available. In November 1915 the War Office raised the requirements to sixteen Lewis guns per battalion. Production orders far in excess of this had already been placed by the Ministry of Munitions, and funding was provided to expand production capacity. Broadly speaking the annual production of machine guns through the war was:

Year	Total produced
1914	300
1915	6,100
1916	33,500
1917	79,750
1918	120,850

These are total figures and include weapons for aeroplanes, tanks and the Royal Navy.

New and improved weapons

The 28lb Lewis machine gun made its appearance towards the end of 1915. This revolutionary air-cooled weapon was initially deployed with teams of six men manning it although later it would be operated by a two-man team. Although the gun could be carried by one man, the others provided support and carried ammunition. The Lewis gun provided a considerable increase in mobile firepower of infantry units and was increasingly relied upon as infantry assault tactics developed throughout the war.

At the same time constant refinements were made to existing weapons. For example, hand grenades went from unpredictable 'home-made' bombs at the beginning of the war (often made in Army workshops), to a standard and relatively much safer (to the user) Mills No. 5 bomb.

With the development of standard grenades the rifle grenade was made possible. In 1915 this was a Mills bomb welded to a stick and fired with a live round from the rifle – thus ruining the rifle. By 1917 a cup discharger and ballistite cartridge were widely used. Increasingly teams of men were trained to provide close support to the riflemen of their battalion. Because of the trajectory of the bomb, these weapons could be extremely useful at close range in the trenches and were particularly effective at suppressing enemy strongpoints.

Another significant contribution to the infantry arsenal was the Stokes mortar which was issued to infantry brigades at the beginning of 1916. It was essentially a 'light' trench mortar that, when first deployed, fired an 11lb bomb up to 400 yards, although the range increased considerably as the weapon was refined. It was deployed in or near the front line and was thus able to support an attack more directly than heavy artillery or mortars which usually operated to a set time-tabled fireplan or with pre-arranged barrages.

Also, by the end of 1915 significant progress had been made in the development of the tank. The Admiralty Landship Committee had started to develop prototype tanks after early experiments by the Royal Naval Air Service that involved adding armour to armed patrol cars. The first prototype of the vehicle that would become the familiar British tank Mks I–V ran on 16 January 1916, although many refinements were required before even the flawed Mark I was deployed in battle in September 1916.

Poison gas was first used in quantity by the Germans on 22 April 1915 and was then rapidly employed by other nations. Many types of gas were used. Some were intended to incapacitate through temporarily blinding, by irritating the nose, pharynx and eyes or by inducing headaches and nausea. Often these irritants were added to high explosive shells. Other gases were intended to kill through a variety of means. Some, like phosgene, attacked and damaged the lung lining causing the victim to die from oedema – the lungs filling with body fluids until the victim drowns. Another fatal toxin, 'mustard gas', was introduced on 12 July 1917 and would burn the skin on contact. Mustard gas was persistent, and unlike others, would seep into clothing and remain on the battlefield in shell holes in effective strength for days.

The delivery of gas was a problem for all sides. Discharge from cylinders was initially used but it required a favourable wind, both in direction and speed, which meant that gas could not be easily co-ordinated with large scale attacks. After Loos, where there was a failure in the effectiveness of cylinder released gas, most cylinder releases were used to support raids. Cylinders were unpopular with the infantry who had to carry them into the trench and then often live with the inherent risks of leaks or ruptures from enemy fire, until the gas was released or removed.

Projectors were then employed: a cylinder containing the gas was fired from a mortar-like tube using an explosive charge with a range of 1,000–1,500 yards. The British used enlarged 4 inch bore Stokes mortars. Projectors had the advantage of being capable of delivering a large concentration of gas in a short period of time from behind the front line, and were less affected by the wind.

The other main method used gas-filled shells, which had the advantages of greater range and surprise in delivery. But these advantages were balanced by the relatively small amount of gas that could be delivered and initially the Germans used irritants in their shells. German gas shells would often be marked according to their content with coloured crosses – yellow, blue or green – which were used by the gunners and the recipients of the shells alike to identify the contents.

Towards the end of the war the British devised the release of large concentrations of gas from cylinders in 'beam' attacks. These were facilitated by loading up a railway carriage with a large number of cylinders which would be discharged simultaneously from immediately behind the front line when the weather conditions were suitable. It meant that the British front-line soldiers would have to be withdrawn temporarily, but the suddenness and concentrations of gas delivered was reputed to be very effective in causing large numbers of enemy (and civilian) casualties.

A feature of the Great War was the extent of innovation in weaponry. New weapons, and refinements to existing weapons, required new tactics for their effectiveness to be fully exploited. By the end of 1915, many of the weapons were only in their relative infancy in the sense of their limited deployment and novelty to the troops they were issued to. Two years later, successful developments would start to be fully integrated into tactical thinking, altering the nature of warfare.

CHAPTER IV
Flanders Fields

Divisional rest

The battalion left the front near Laventie on 11 January 1916. In two days the men marched to the village of Steenbecque eighteen miles from the front line; easily out of enemy artillery range. They remained there until 22 January refitting. It was the first chance for a complete rest from front-line duties and Bugler Harper from A Company wrote to a friend asking for a football:

> We are now out of the trenches for six weeks rest after six months in the trenches, and I expect during that time we shall have a good deal of spare time and, as you know, a game of football eases the monotony of the situation. It seems rather funny back here out of the sound of the guns after the time we had while we were in.

On 23 January the 20th Division was administratively transferred to the newly formed XIVth Corps of the Second Army which held the northern sector of the British front. The XIVth Corps included the Guards, the 6th and the 20th Divisions and was commanded by Lord Cavan. After this the battalion moved to a village just west of Cassel where it remained until 3 February.[1]

News filtered down to the men that they would soon be deployed in the Ypres area, which had been heavily fought over. From the town of Ypres and its Yser canal running north–south the British held a salient (or projection) from a base-line about eight miles long which jutted east into German-held ground for an average of two miles at this time. The salient ended in the area of the Messines Ridge to the south of Ypres. The whole salient was overlooked by the Germans who held the higher ground. Five officers and eight NCOs were sent to the area to reconnoitre the land to the north. Lieutenant Andrews: 'We were told quite frankly that it would be no picnic up there.'

Over the next ten days the battalion moved closer to the salient, and on 12 February 1916 marched to the divisional rest camp west of Poperinghe. The next day they moved to a hut camp about two and a half miles to the east, between Poperinghe and Ypres. This stretch of road and the surrounding area was lined with tents, huts, hospitals and supply dumps that supported the soldiers in the Ypres salient.

The battalion stayed at this camp for eight days preparing for active duty. Equipment was cleaned and the men underwent typhoid inoculations which laid most of them low and made them feverish. The weather had become poor with a cold rain falling and a strong gale blowing.

A Machine Gun Corps (MGC) had been formed by royal warrant on 22 October 1915, but official resistance meant that it was only in early 1916 that changes started to be implemented. The grouping of the sixteen Vickers machine guns within each brigade into a machine-gun company was effected to permit a greater development of specialist roles for the heavier guns. The MGC set up its own training schools for gunners where techniques were developed and taught; for example, the use of grouped machine guns in an indirect fire role similar to an artillery barrage. Also, the establishment of the MGC ensured that the Vickers machine guns were deployed on a brigade front whenever a sector of the line was held, rather than being left to individual battalions to site. The objective was to ensure use of the best fields of fire and a better integrated defence.

In practical terms, for the 7th SomLI the formation of the MGC meant the removal of the Vickers guns to brigade control at this time, and this meant a loss of personnel to brigade. It also meant that greater reliance now had to be placed upon the Lewis light machine gun within the battalion. Another change was the issue of steel helmets, which replaced the old peaked cap.

On 22 February the battalion prepared to go into the trenches again. Sergeant Howell wrote to a friend in Bridgwater:

> Our battalion are just moving into the trenches after a month's rest, and I think we are going into the hottest corner of the line. The trenches we are going into have changed hands so many times and its now called the 'international trench'. I hope the Somerset lads will be able to hold their own and let other battalions see what we can do. We have a little snow this morning, and its not much good for the trenches.

The next day the battalion went a short distance by train to the village of Vlamertinge where the men got out at a level crossing and marched to the front, passing briefly through the cobbled streets of Ypres and into the wintry cold and muddy salient. The Somersets were in fact headed to the north of the salient near to an area called 'international corner', so called because it had formed the boundary between the British and Belgian or French Armies. 'International trench' was to the south-east of Ypres and was not visited by the battalion. By the time they arrived in Ypres, the cloth-making town that had previously had a population of 17,000, it had suffered terribly from the ravages of the war. The area had already seen two major battles that had resulted in the destruction of many buildings.

Ypres canal

The 7th Battalion moved into the front line on Wednesday 23 February 1916. The positions were a series of shell-hole posts linked by shallow trenches from south of a position called Lancashire Farm running in a rough line to a position called Grouse Butt. Conditions were appalling. The 'trenches' lacked proper drainage and the men would often have to sit on the fire steps with their legs immersed up to their knees in icy cold water. There were no dugouts in the forward positions at all, and only the company headquarters were allowed any form of shelter.

The support and reserve positions were along the canal bank. The canal itself was virtually empty, with puddles of stagnant water in the bottom. The tow paths that ran along either side had an embankment and it was in this that the dugouts had been built. Lieutenant Henry Foley wrote:

> Both banks of the canal were honey-combed with dug-outs and shelters of all descriptions, none of which to my knowledge were anything like shell proof; but of course after the memories of the front trenches they seemed perfect havens of peace.

Because of the conditions the men would be rotated between the forward and support/reserve positions with much greater frequency notwithstanding the increased danger they were exposed to during reliefs. Lieutenant Andrews:

> The trenches there offered far less cover than we had been accustomed to, and movement from one place to another was usually accomplished by doubling oneself in half from the waist. This uncomfortable proceeding was rendered all the more necessary from the fact that there were some deadly snipers in the trenches opposite us. It was on our arrival at Ypres that the wearing of steel helmets became compulsory, and until we got used to them and grew to appreciate the protection they afforded, many were the sighs for the old time comfort of a 'balaclava'. Here we knew what it was to get shelled from the back as well as the front, and the blame fell inevitably on our own Artillery until we learned that it was the Bosche, who were potting at us from the sides of the salient.

Even the few dugouts were rustic. Major Preston-Whyte described the scene on one occasion:

Raining hard. Company headquarters consists of three iron sheets overhead and a running stream 18 inches deep under foot, and an old pig trough to sit on. Self and two subalterns in occupation. One of us always has to remain and look after pig trough, while the other two go round the line, or else it would float away and someone else would get hold of it.

Lieutenant Foley is left at company headquarters while I and my other sub go round the line. He takes this opportunity to dig out our rations and get something to eat. Rations consists of one loaf bread, one tin butter, etc. I do my round and return. 'Well Foley', I say, 'What about some grub?' 'Right,' he replies, with his mouth full, and starts looking round. 'Where is the bread?' I ask. 'Now where did I put it,' he says. I look about and see the bread on top of the iron in the rain. I point this fact out to him with a few choice remarks. 'Oh, I am sorry,' he says, reaching up for it and knocking the butter off the pig trough into the stream. 'Thanks,' I remark, 'I hope at any rate you have not opened the bully yet'.

During the first four days at the front, the battalion was subjected to constant bombardment for the first two. Before it was relieved three men had been killed and ten injured.[2] The next few days were spent with the battalion providing night-time working parties. Under the guidance of the Royal Engineers, the men worked at draining the front-line positions, a constant and insoluble problem in Flanders because of the low-lying land. Two more men were killed doing this work.[3]

The 7th Somersets relieved the 7th DCLI on 3 March at night to prevent the watching Germans noticing what was happening. The relief was complete at 4am by which time it had started to snow again. The men found the trenches in an appalling state. Efforts were made the next day to improve the wiring in front of the trenches but the working parties found the ground too sodden to dig. It had snowed continuously throughout the day and the water in the posts was very cold. Lieutenant Andrews recalled:

One night I went out on my first night patrol with a Corporal and two men. I don't think I was feeling particularly brave at the time, but I must say that I was considerably impressed by the efficiency of the arrangements made by my company commander to prevent my being shot in the back by our own sentries. However on arrival at the sally-port the sight of a stretcher bearer squad drawn up there in readiness properly put the breeze up me, until I was duly assured that they were only there 'in case'. The patrol was carried out quite successfully, the only incident being that the Corporal was temporarily put out of action through falling into a disused trench

42

that was full of muddy water. He was by no means happy when we hauled him out as the night was cold and quite inappropriate for moonlight bathing.

The battalion spent another four days in the front-line positions during which time another two men were killed. Four days of providing working parties for the Royal Engineers then followed while the battalion was in support. One man was killed on a working party on 9 March.[4]

When the Somersets returned to the front line on Sunday 12 March the weather had cleared a little which allowed more accurate artillery fire as the artillery observers could see the fall of the shells better. Monday was another clear day, although there was some mist at night. Early the next morning Lieutenant Geoffrey Foley went out to visit the posts hoping that the mist would cover his movements. An enemy sniper clearly saw him and let fly with a volley of shots. The first seven bullets missed, the eighth struck Foley in the leg causing severe injury. Unfortunately for him the dawn light meant that no one was able to carry him back into safety until nightfall and he spent an agonising day lying between the posts in no man's land. Lieutenant Henry Foley recalled the incident involving his brother:

> In the evening of March 13 I went over to B Company headquarters to get some tea, and heard that Geoff had been hit by a bullet in the thigh early that morning. The C.O. with ready sympathy knew that I would like to see Geoff before he went down. When I got there the stretcher party was just coming down. The C.O. was there himself, with Captain Whall; it was not wise to keep Geoff about in such an exposed place, so we just wished him luck and off he went, cheery and smiling as ever.

Foley was evacuated from the battlefield, and the next day was transported to the Duchess of Westminster Red Cross Hospital at Le Touquet where he began a long convalescence.

The men were relieved in the early hours of Tuesday 14 March, had entrained at the crossroads east of Vlamertinge by 2.30am, and by 4am were back in the huts they had occupied before going into the salient.

Life in the salient

The battalion was able to spend a week out of the line at the camp at Poperinghe. 'Pop' was the forward base for the Ypres salient and as such was always teeming with transport, horses, mules and lorries of all descriptions. Although the Germans occasionally shelled Poperinghe, no significant damage had been caused and the hotels and estaminets provided relief and distraction for the soldiers coming out of the trenches, as well as a last stop for the many thousands heading into them. In the main the weather was very good, although it started to rain again towards the end of the week.

After a week of rest the battalion was sent back into the salient and the front line at Ypres canal at a quarter to one in the morning. The weather had deteriorated markedly with persistent rain and, later on in the week, a heavy snow storm covered the desolate landscape.

Captain Jones, the battalion's signal officer later recounted:

> Whenever the battalion occupied a trench sector everything gravitated to the signallers dugout. Signallers, battalion or company, fixed their office or exchange in close proximity to headquarters. Communications were maintained by morse on a field telephone, for visual methods were impractical in those days of static trench warfare.
>
> Two men were on duty at one time – all messages buzzed by morse as there was a danger of conversations being overheard. The enemy used amplifiers to secure information from casual talks from one telephone exchange to another. Code names were introduced to serve as camouflage for all units great or small.
>
> Each station used to ring up, or rather buzz up by morse calls every other station with which it was in communication every quarter of an hour so that it was possible to see if your wire was intact. If he concluded that it was 'dished' a couple of linemen would be sent out to follow the wire until the break was discovered. It was not an easy task to carry about the wire reel apparatus and the telephone instrument. The latter was used for tapping in to ensure that both ends of the wire were in communication with each other. The line man would join the broken strands and ring around to make sure everyone was OK. He would send a message 'That the Sets?' He would hear a voice 'No you're on the Kings' and he would then test the line until he found the correct station.
>
> Up to a dozen strands might follow a line. When the line man found the break he would have to search for the other end. Sometimes up to 50 yards radius. Sometimes people removed the wires if they were an obstruction in the trench. Sometimes multiple breaks meant completely replacing the wire.
>
> No matter how heavy the shelling might be, whenever a break in one of the battalions or companies lines was reported the lineman would leave the security and snugness of their dugout and proceed to repair the damage. It required just as much courage and tenacity to work the electric lamp. Frequently from an exposed position in the front line – almost where a glimmer of light at night was almost certain to draw enemy machine gun or minenwerfer fire.

Wednesday 22 March through to Sunday 26 was largely uneventful. In the early hours of the morning on 27 March, 31-year-old Corporal Henry Dainton was shot and killed by a sniper. A little later, at about 5am in the early dawn, sentries from B Company noticed figures in no man's land approaching the British wire. Lieutenant H Foley said:

> They were forthwith challenged, but answer came there none, so the man fired, whereupon one of the two figures was seen to crumple up, and was heard to emit groans and presumably curses. His companion, seeing his plight would not leave him and, when the light had sufficiently increased, we were able to persuade him (the uninjured one), partly by means of bad German, but chiefly by covering him with a rifle, to exchange his present mode of life for the joys of captivity.

The man who surrendered was taken away to brigade for interrogation. The other man was unable to be brought in because of the approaching light and lay injured near the wire for a large part of the day, dying later. Lieutenant Foley continued:

> Meanwhile the report of these doings, along with our captive reached the powers that be in the rear; and the fun began. The fuss that was made over that wretched corpse was immense. Orders and instructions screamed in all day and the telephone fairly hummed with questions and minute stage directions. It was absolutely essential, we were told, that the body should be brought in that night, as valuable information was expected from it. It was at the same time considered practically certain that the enemy would make a strong attempt to regain the body themselves. Ropes and chains were promised us, covering parties were ordered and brigade even contemplated a hurricane bombardment of the Hun front line. All this we regarded with huge inward delight, but complete outward calm. As soon as dark fell, one of our men slipped over the parapet, threw the Boche across his shoulder, and was back with his burden inside three minutes.

On the same afternoon the enemy began a trench mortar barrage. One bomb landed near a trench in which one of the battalion's scouts, Charles Andrews was sleeping. Private Andrews was lying on the firestep when the nosecap of the bomb struck his leg. He was carried out of the line, cheerfully telling one of his comrades to 'Write and tell my mother its nothing serious'. He died before he reached the forward casualty clearing station, aged 19.

The next morning the Germans bombarded the Somersets with trench mortars again. Eighty bombs were counted by the men of B Company who were on the receiving end, although no severe harm was caused. British howitzers retaliated and the Germans ceased their activity. That night as sleet fell, Private Gilbert Cooke and Private Sidney Smith were killed, both shot in the head.

After another very cold spell in the trenches, the battalion was relieved on Friday 31 March and went out of the trenches for another four days. The weather improved again while the men were out of the front line. On 2 April Private Charles Best died of shell wounds.

The psychological toll of the war was now beginning to manifest itself in cases of shell shock, the term used for psychological and often physical breakdown caused by war experience. Corporal Lee and Privates Baker, Dobbie and Griffiths all left active duty because of it after little more than seven months' exposure.

NOTES

1   During this time, on 31 January, Private James Plymton died at home.
2   The dead men were Private Benjamin Langford a 37-year-old married man, killed on Thursday 24 February; Private Bertie Wright (killed 25 February); Lance Corporal Arthur Morrish (killed 26 February).
3   Lance Corporal Frederick Cross and Private Herbert Watts (both killed on Monday 28 February).
4   Private William Bullock (killed 6 March). The 27-year-old's body was never found. Private George Shepherd (killed 7 March), Private Ernest Bussel (killed 9 March).

CHAPTER V

Let Honour Rest

Ypres canal

The battalion returned to the front line near the Ypres canal at the end of March and remained until 8 April for a period of shelling and gloomy weather. During this time six men were killed or died of wounds.[1]

The only aggressive action during this time occurred on 7 April when a raiding party comprising Captain Hatt, 2nd Lieutenant Sparkes, Sergeant Dillon and fourteen soldiers gathered in a forward trench. The bombing patrol had the objective of destroying the enemy post that had been detected at a nearby road. The men slithered out of the trench into the dark of no man's land in the cold rain. They made their way in the direction of the road and the post. They reached a spot near to where the post had been seen but were unable to find the enemy and returned to the British positions.

While in support on 10 April, Major Preston-Whyte was supervising the progress of a new trench when he was shot in the shoulder. He was removed from the front line and sent to England to recover. He would be away from the battalion until August.[2]

The next day the bad weather returned with a steady rain falling for most of the day. At 1pm the enemy started a violent barrage on the canal bank positions, which then switched to the front-line trenches occupied by the 7th DCLI. From the Somersets' positions it was clear that the Germans had bracketed a forward sector of the British lines. The enemy barrage fell on the front line. It also fell on either flank which was intended to prevent supporting troops on the flanks from helping to fend off an attack. The battalion was ordered to stand to at 5.30pm and was concentrated in the canal bank area.

The bombardment severed the telephone lines and it was impossible for soldiers out of the front line to see what was happening ahead because of the darkness. The 7th DCLI were in it by themselves. The Somersets in reserve saw the 7th DCLI send up an SOS flare at about 7.15pm and a short while later a runner brought a message requesting ammunition. On seeing the flare the 7th Somersets crossed the canal bank to the eastern side.

Colonel Troyte-Bullock, commanding officer of the 7th Battalion, ordered small arms ammunition to be taken forward, and the task fell to 2nd Lieutenant Tawney and his platoon from D Company. The men gathered up all the ammunition boxes they could carry and the platoon was split in half. Sergeant Bristowe led one half, the other being led by 2nd Lieutenant Tawney. The men set off through the heavy enemy barrage. Tawney was knocked off his feet twice by explosions which injured four men from the platoon, although the platoon made it through and were able to deliver the much needed ammunition to the Cornwalls. Tawney and his men remained in the front line and helped to repel a German attack delivered at that part of the line.

The 7th DCLI were also attacked at one of their posts a little farther up the line, and there the men were at risk of being overrun. A request for more support was made and Lieutenant Andrews and his platoon from D Company moved forward. They too had to pass through the barrage and were fortunate to do so without any casualties, coming to the post that had been attacked by about fifty enemy. The Germans had already been driven off. Another German attempt to attack a nearby post was caught by British artillery shrapnel causing many casualties. Only about sixty of the enemy made it to the British barbed wire, and the combined efforts of the 7th DCLI and Lieutenant Andrews' platoon were able to repulse the attack. Lieutenant Andrews' platoon emerged unscathed.

Behind the front line the situation was still unclear, because of the cut telephone lines, and Lieutenant Cartwright was sent forward to find out what was happening. He was blown by a loud explosion into 'a very unsavoury pond', and scrambling out unhurt, and again moved on towards the front line. Later he was able to return with a detailed report on what had taken place. The 7th DCLI had suffered between fifty and sixty casualties, the Germans many more. The Somersets had four wounded in the action by the time the German attacks stopped at about 10pm. The whole 61st Brigade were relieved that night and started a move by stages to Calais for a complete rest.

Calais

The men were fortunate to be able to spend Easter away from the front line. The weather became milder as spring set in, and the soldiers spent many days refitting, checking equipment and generally relaxing. Football games were common, and there were also lectures, bathing and concerts. Lieutenant Henry Foley later recalled; 'We spent ten days here. It was an exquisitely happy time, drilling and manoeuvring by day, and need I say? making merry by night'.

From 26 April 1916 the battalion gradually started to make its way back towards the front line, stopping at ZutKerque, Mercheghem and Wormhout. By this time the weather had occasionally become very hot.

The battalion remained at Wormhout until 7 May when it moved to a camp some fourteen miles away.

Here the battalion was given training in a variety of subjects from gas helmets to bayonet fighting. On 6 May the men were given a demonstration of the effects of lachrymatory gas by being marched through a courtyard where a bomb had been exploded. The gas was intended to incapacitate a person by causing temporary blindness through eye irritation, although it could be fatal in high concentrations. They were also marched through a room where a weak mixture of chlorine gas had been released in order to experience the effects. The same day senior officers from the battalion were given a demonstration of the capabilities of the Stokes mortar. They came away impressed by the accuracy and rapidity of fire of these weapons that had recently become available. The battalion also competed with other battalions for prizes in boxing, bayonet practice, wiring and draught horses. There was some success in boxing but little else.

After just over a month out of the line, the battalion returned to the front line on 19 May arriving after a short train journey at Ypres and detraining at the asylum.

Potijze Wood

The Somersets relieved the 2nd Battalion the Coldstream Guards at 12.30am, which was completed without casualties, occupying positions about two miles due east of Ypres. Almost immediately the enemy began firing on the front line with machine guns and artillery. The gunfire quickly caused a breach in the parapet and cut the defensive wire. The breached parapet crossed a road that ran through the battalion front line, and the enemy kept it under fire throughout the night to prevent it being repaired. The attacks killed two men with shrapnel, Sergeant Ernest Wagner, who was hit in the chest, and Private Walter Sanders.

The next day the German fire stopped the parapet from being repaired and attention was also paid to the wire in no man's land. Nothing appeared to happen until 12.45am, when Private Dare was in a listening post. The Germans crept up on the post and threw a bomb at the occupants. Private Dare was flattened by the blast, but was able to recover quickly enough to get hold of a box of bombs and started hurling them back. This successfully kept the enemy away at this point and caused some casualties among the attackers.

The enemy also raided two other places, one of which was held by B Company. Sergeant Bulson recounted what followed:

> They had evidently crept up to our wire via a ditch running at right angles to the trench line. A few moments before-hand a hail of

machine gun fire had swept our parapet, no doubt to keep all the sentries' heads down and so prevent the raiding party being spotted. I was further along the trench to the right of B Company Sergeant Major's dugout. Joe Sears was the CSM to the best of my recollection and was in the line for the first time on duty. I was with him on that occasion as B Company Lewis gun sergeant. Word came down the line that we were being raided and bombs were wanted. Joe and I dashed along the trench picking up a box of Mills No 5s on the way and found No 8 platoon in the thick of it. One officer [2nd Lieutenant Willcox] was badly wounded in the head and there were several other casualties. A Lewis gun team including privates Toby Veale and Hill, both Bristolians, fired umpteen rounds of ammunition until their gun got a jam and the excitement was intense for a while.

Bombs, Lewis guns and the bayonet were used to drive the attackers away, although the surprised defenders had suffered several casualties as the raiders managed to lob a number of grenades into their trenches. At company headquarters dugout efforts were made to summon artillery support. Sergeant Bulson continued:

Lieutenant Knight and some others tried to send up an SOS rocket but got tied up with the darned thing and eventually it fizzed off and shot back along the ground towards the support line like a snake. Major Preston-Whyte was fuming and Lieutenant Knight was jumping about with burnt hands.

As the Germans fell back from this part of their raid, they were pursued by Sergeant Tanner and two bombing sections along the ditch that ran between the two front lines.

The centre party of the Germans failed as Lewis guns and rifle fire from the two SomLI platoons and those of two platoons from a working party were able to drive off the attackers. It was fortunate that the other platoons were present, as the length of line held at this point meant that positions were normally thinly held.

The battalion suffered one killed, Private Albert Williams, and twenty-four injured including 2nd Lieutenants Willcox and Addis who lost one of his feet and had the other seriously damaged. Private Dare was awarded the Distinguished Conduct Medal for his quick-thinking action. As the sun came up the next morning, three dead Germans could be seen hanging from the wire in front of the Somerset trenches.

Private Walter Gomm, one of those injured in the raid, was taken to the Canadian General Hospital in France from where he was able to write to his relatives:

I am sorry to say that I was wounded in the forehead and chest; but only a slight wound in the head. The Germans made a bombing attack on one part of the line we were holding. I was lucky as I had about twelve bombs close by me. I am hoping to come to England later on.

The following two days were relatively quiet, with a little enemy rifle and machine-gun fire as well as a few artillery exchanges.

The battalion was relieved on 24 May when the men marched back to Ypres and then travelled by train to Poperinghe. They remained there until 8 June and were joined by a draft of fifty men and NCOs. On 1 June the Germans attacked the Canadian positions at Mount Sorrel, Observatory Ridge and Sanctuary Wood and drove them from these positions. The Somersets were kept in readiness because of the enemy attacks until 8 June when they returned to the front line. When behind the lines the Lewis guns were positioned in an anti-aircraft role.

Railway and Y Wood

The battalion relieved the 6th Ox & BucksLI on 8 June taking up positions that stretched between Y and Railway Woods. These were south-east of Ypres and the Somersets' trenches were just to the north of the new defensive line held by the Canadians after the German attacks. The Canadians had unsuccessfully tried to recapture the lost ground on 3 June.

The next day the trench mortar fire killed Privates Howard Champion and 35-year-old Frederick Mear. Fred Mear was a married man who was a keen local football player for his village team. He had also been a bell ringer at the village church for the past twenty years. Retaliatory trench mortar fire by the 61st Brigade's own Stokes mortars stopped the German fire. The battalion also spent this day improving and patrolling their new trenches.

The 10th was a very quiet day, although Private Atkinson managed to shoot himself in the foot while cleaning his rifle, raising the inevitable suspicion that he had done so deliberately. Soldiers from the battalion could make out German activity aimed at consolidating their new positions west of Hooge which was harassed by British artillery fire. That night the trenches were occupied by men from the Gas Brigade who started to place cylinders into the Somersets' trenches and this continued for the next two nights. The cylinders were dug into the front-line trench and then covered with sandbags to protect the occupants from leaks or from the possibility of shelling rupturing them. During these days the battalion lost four men.[3]

On 12 June the battalion was briefed on operations that it would take part in to assist in a second attempt by the Canadians to recapture the lost ground the following morning. C and D Companies, that were in support and reserve, were each to provide a raiding party that would attack the Germans in order to create a diversion for the main attack. Lieutenant John Peard, the holder of the Military Cross which he gained with the 1st Somersets in July 1915, was put in charge of the C Company raiding party. Because of the boggy conditions the raid by D Company was cancelled. Lieutenant Peard outlined the preparations for the raid:

> In order that the enemy should have no warning of our intentions it was decided that there should be no preliminary reconnaissance of the ground. The only opportunity I had of acquaintancing myself with the lie of the land was by inspecting it from our front line trenches through a periscope on the afternoon before zero night. A distance of about 100 yards lay between the point chosen to leave the trench and attack the German position from.

The plan was that the raid was to be preceded by a short bombardment of enemy trenches and wire, trench mortars being concentrated on the wire. Gas was to be discharged immediately after the bombardment, and after it had passed over the enemy trenches, the raiding party would cross to the German trenches and do as much damage as possible and bring back a prisoner 'if any Germans were found to have survived the bombardment and the gas'. The whole operation was to take no more than fifteen minutes. The raiding party was Lieutenant Peard and twenty other ranks. Two were detailed as wire cutters. Two were tape bearers – to lay tape between trenches to guide the party back. Lieutenant Peard was to lead with the wire cutters, with the main party a few yards behind. He was given a horn to signal the return to trenches. Gas helmets were to be worn. Lieutenant Peard continued:

> Bombardment was followed by gas followed by gas followed by German SOS rockets followed by a very heavy bombardment of our trenches by enemy artillery. At zero hour I got out of the trenches accompanied by wire cutters and followed by the tape bearers and party and made a bee line for the German trench. The night was dark as a bag and it was raining hard, and soon I realised that, muffled in a gas helmet, there was little chance of me finding my way across no man's land. I therefore took my gas helmet off before I had gone far. Even then I found it very difficult to find my way, and the wet state of the ground and numerous shell holes made progress slow. However the wire cutters and I reached the enemy wire all right, though at a point to the right of where we were arriving. Unfortunately the wire was practically intact – apparently the trench mortars had not done their job very successfully – and so we had to

start cutting our way through it. The tape bearers and main party should have followed. But the tape bearers had got the tape tangled on the British wire and the party had stayed with them – resulting in loss of contact between the main party and the wire cutters.

While we were cutting the German wire a machine gun opened fire almost in front of us and I was hit in the thigh with the first burst of fire and fell into a saphead, which ran out from the enemy trenches. The saphead happened to be full of barbed wire and it took me a few minutes to disentangle myself and climb out of it. There was now a tremendous strafe going on as the Germans had realised that we were attempting to raid them, and I therefore took cover temporarily in an adjoining shell hole – which happened to be half full of water – and took stock of the situation.

There was no sign of the wire cutters or the remainder of the party. There was no hope of the raiding party doing any good. I therefore blew my horn as a signal for the party to make its way back to the trenches. I did not appreciate the humour of the situation at the time, but I have often thought since what a ridiculous figure I must have cut sitting in a shell hole up to my waist in water and blowing a horn. A revised version of Little Boy Blue!

I couldn't help thinking that the prospects of getting back to our own lines were not very rosy at the time. I had to crawl back across no man's land which appeared to resemble an inferno. I was reluctant to leave the shell hole but realised it would soon be getting light and my progress would be slow with my wounded leg. So I got out my shell hole and started crawling as quickly as I could towards our trenches.

The firing was still pretty heavy, with the occasional bursts of still greater intensity which forced me to stop and take cover several times in convenient shell holes. I had succeeded in getting about two thirds of the way back when another burst of machine gun fire drove me back to ground again. This time I was most unlucky in my choice of a shelter. The nearest shell hole into which I crawled, proved to be an old and very big one, more than half full of water and with slippery sides. I slithered into it and found myself slipping further and further in until I was completely under the water, head and all. When I tried to crawl out again I found that I could get no grip on the slippery sides and kept on sliding back again. By this time I had become rather exhausted owing to the loss of blood and my strenuous efforts in crawling, and fright, and for a few moments I really thought that I was going to drown in the shell hole. However a last despairing effort was successful and I crawled out and lay exhausted outside for some minutes.

I decided to avoid shell holes in future, no matter how fierce the firing might be. After what seemed like ages I reached our own wire and there I found two of the raiding party who had come out to look for me. They helped me through our wire and over the parapet into the trench and while they were doing this I was hit in the chest by a machine gun bullet. Fortunately it was a glancing shot which didn't do much damage and only made a superficial wound.

It was only just in time as it was beginning to get light. More than half the party had become casualties, without apparently having accomplished anything. I heard afterwards that the counter attack was completely successful.

One of the soldiers who had gone out looking for Lieutenant Peard was Private Jenkins and he was subsequently awarded the DCM for carrying the injured officer back into the trench. Sergeant Dillon was injured along with eight other men from the raiding party. Two of the raiding party had been killed. The bodies of both had to be left in no man's land. A Company had also suffered in the raid as the Germans' SOS had resulted in a bombardment of A Companys' trenches. Four men from the company were killed[4] and eleven men injured, including Captain Brown and Bugle Sergeant Gale.

The attack by the Canadians that had led to the diversionary raid of Lieutenant Peard and his party was partially successful. It had resulted in the recapture of nearly half of the ground that the Germans had wrested from them.

The battalion was relieved later that morning by the 7th DCLI, with the majority going to Ypres. Some of the soldiers were billeted at the old fortification ramparts on the east side of the town, and while there they were called upon to provide working parties to remove the gas cylinders from the trenches they had recently occupied. Even when empty the cylinders were extremely heavy (they weighed 180lbs when full), and had to be carried slung on a pole by two men. The work was especially hard as the men had to wear gas masks and negotiate the zig-zag path of the communication trenches with their ungainly load.

The battalion remained at Ypres until 17 June. During this time three men died from shrapnel wounds. Private Herbert Castell and Sergeant Herbert Law both died on 14 June. Private John Scott on 16 June.

While the battalion was in Ypres, and when not engaged on duties, some men were able to wander about and explore the town. On 16 June, while he was doing just this, a stray shell exploded near Captain Parker, the battalion's medical officer, and 2nd Lieutenant Edwin Wright, the Lewis gun officer. Lieutenant Wright died almost instantaneously. The doctor was badly wounded and died shortly afterwards.

The relative period of rest allowed one man, Sergeant Allen, to write home to his father at Parkstone Terrace in Bridgwater:

Glad to tell you that I got through the last bit alright. I only had a bit of shrapnel in my finger, but it was proper hell. I was in the front line about 35 yards from a German sap. We were under a rain of thousands of shells for three days and nights, and it rained all the time. We were up to our waists in mud and water. It's all mild clay like that outside Barham's yard [a brick and tile works]. I am enclosing a bit of poetry composed by one of a platoon outside a dugout.

Let Honour Rest on the Men from the West

As the sun was setting o'er Ypres town
A band of warriors was standing around
Bespattered with mud and covered with grime
For they'd just returned from the firing line.

They were tired and weary with battle's dread din
And their thoughts wandered back to their own kith and kin;
As the deadly shells whistled and screamed overhead
Their thoughts wandered back to where their comrades lay dead.

Those heroes belonged to the 7th Somersets
They'd been fighting like hell and squaring old debts.
Giving Fritz socks mids't the gas's dread stench
While Canadians charged and regained their lost trench.

For five days they stuck it without thought or pain
With shrapnel and bullets falling round them like rain,
All covered with mud and wet through to the skin
In that hell upon earth mids't the guns deafening din.

So tired and weary, those men from the West
Are going back to 'Pop' for a well deserved rest;
With a glass of French beer and a cooler of ale,
They'll forget those five nights that they suffered in hell.

And when all is over and we're at peace once again
And the Canadians return to their homes o'er the main,
There's a regiment they'll praise all through life till they die,
Thats the old 'Western Bulldogs', the 7th SomLI.

(Anon.)

The battalion moved to 'Pop' on 17 June where it stayed for ten days.

Potijze and Ypres

On 27 June the battalion went back into the front line, travelling by train to Ypres and then marching under shellfire along a road into the front-line trenches. They took over their new positions with Privates Harry Lomas, Joseph Meiris and James Rossiter along with Lance Corporal Lee Narcott occupying a dugout together. The dugout received a direct hit killing all four. Another man killed by shelling was Private Bradbear, who died as he was putting on his boots in a dugout. He was due to take his turn on duty in the trench. George Bradbear was 36 years old and left a widow and three children.

The next day the enemy were extraordinarily quiet which enabled the soldiers to carry out repairs to their new positions although there was some shelling that evening.[5]

That night the brigade to the right of the Somersets raided the Germans. Private Woodall was in a communication trench the next day when he identified a party of three Germans behind the battalion's lines on the right flank. On challenging the men, he found them to be unarmed and took all three prisoner. It was believed that they had become cut off after the trench raid of the previous night. That day Private Samuel Jones was killed.

The battalion went out of the line early on the morning of 1 July 1916. While the Somersets were leaving the front line, to the south thousands of soldiers waited in their assembly trenches for the Battle of the Somme to begin.

NOTES

1   On 4 April 18-year-old Lance Corporal Stanley Purnell was killed. On 6 April Privates Charles Harris, Sidney Slade and Charles Troake were killed; Lance Corporal Frank Jones died of stomach wounds on 8 April; Lance Corporal Leonard Nurse was killed on 10 April.
2   On 16 April Private Percy Matthews died of wounds he received on the 10th.
3   On Whit Sunday, 11 June, Privates Mark Bridges (by shell) and John Pendry (by rifle grenade) were killed. Another man, Private Clifford Brooks died at home. On 12 June Private Isaiah Trask was also killed.
4   The dead men were Privates Joseph Winzer, Frederick Stubbins, Reginald Green and Leonard Holder. Another killed was 35-year-old Private William Holland who had worked as a signwriter with his father before enlisting in November 1915. He had joined the battalion in the draft that had arrived six weeks before his death.
5   On 28 June Lance Corporal Percy Mees died of wounds received in Lt Peard's raid on the 12 June.

PART TWO

The Somme

It did not do to let oneself think too
much in a place like that
Lieutenant Henry Foley, 7th SomLI

CHAPTER VI

From Ypres to Guillemont

1 July

The first day of the Somme offensive was 1 July 1916. Across an eighteen-mile front fourteen divisions attacked the Germans after an unprecedented week-long barrage. By the end of this day the British had suffered nearly 60,000 casualties; 19,000 of them were dead.

The Germans occupied three main defensive lines, each between 3,000 and 5,000 yards apart. Each line comprised a thinly held outpost line, then the main defensive battle positions and then a reserve line which held counter-attacking troops. Between the first two lines were a series of interlocking communication trenches that made formidable defensive lines in their own right. The front was protected by dense layers of barbed wire fences, and on the whole of its length the Germans had fortified villages and constructed strongpoints.

Two areas of the attacks would hold significance for the 7th SomLI. The first was near Beaumont Hamel, the second to the south near the meeting of the British and French sectors. There the initial attacks were successful and the fighting would eventually reach the village of Guillemont.

Beaumont Hamel

As day dawned on 1 July, approximately 5,000 men from six battalions of the 4th and 48th Divisions waited to assault the German trenches north of the village of Beaumont Hamel. They could see and feel the barrage smashing down on the enemy front line a short distance away, and at 7.20am this was punctuated by the explosion of a 20-ton mine under the Hawthorn Redoubt just south of the village.

At 7.29am the first waves of men clambered out of their trenches and began forming up in no man's land. The barrage continued on the German front line for another minute, and then switched farther back, bombarding positions to the rear. At this, the first three battalions began to advance side by side, and the next three assembled behind in readiness to follow.

Each battalion formed up on a frontage of one company, and advanced in four lines of men, each two paces apart. In the centre of the attack, the

1st Rifle Brigade (1st RB) were the foremost battalion; behind them came the 1st Somersets. The sight was magnificent to those able to watch as the eight lines of infantry started to advance at a slow trot towards the enemy line, while hundreds of shells tore up the ground behind the German trenches. Then things started to go wrong.

Unsuppressed German artillery began to fire into no man's land and on the British assembly trenches, cutting swathes in the attacking ranks. To the front the Germans were still silent, but on the right of the attack, machine guns were set up and they started to sweep the attackers with their relentless fire. The two battalions on the right faltered. The 1st RB suffered heavily and the 1st SomLI changed the direction of their attack to the left where progress was being made despite the men encountering uncut barbed wire.

Within minutes, no man's land was littered with dead and injured soldiers, although on the left of the attack the German front line was reached and the soldiers began a desperate fight over the Quadrilateral strongpoint for the rest of the day. Amidst a fierce hand grenade, rifle and bayonet battle, shells from British and German artillery tore up the battlefield and further mangled the living and the dead. The dwindling number of attackers fought on in trenches littered with bodies, the wounded calling out in vain for help and water. By evening the attackers were all mixed up, and only small parties of men remained. All of the 1st SomLI officers had been killed or injured. Sergeant Major Chappell took command of a group of about fifty men who were eventually relieved at 11pm. (He would receive a commission as a result of his leadership and later joined the 7th Somersets.) A few remaining men straggled through enemy shellfire back across no man's land to their start line.

The attacks had captured virtually no ground in this part of the line. By the end of the first day, the attackers had suffered appallingly. More than 3,000 became casualties; the 1st RB had suffered 474 casualties, and the 1st Somersets 464. Dead and injured littered the battlefield.

The fight towards Guillemont

The day was not a complete failure, for at the southernmost part of the battle, a combined British and French assault achieved most of its objectives. The British offensive would lead eventually to the outskirts of the village of Guillemont, but only after many weeks of heavy fighting.

The 9th (Scottish) Division and the 30th Division launched their attacks at 7.30am as part of the overall offensive. Their success was attributed to many battalions entering no man's land before the barrage lifted and then rushing the German positions. Also, the Germans had less artillery support and poorer defences in this sector. By mid-day they had advanced nearly a mile and the shattered village of Montauban had been captured.

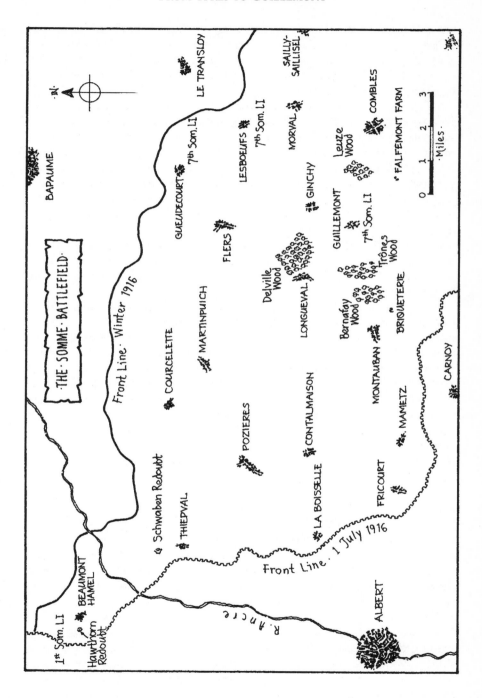

THE · SOMME · BATTLEFIELD·

On the night of 2 July nearby Bernafay Wood, at that time in its full summer growth, was seized with only a few casualties. The wood was shelled heavily by the Germans in the following days so that only shattered tree stumps remained. Farther to the south the French had similarly met with success.

The attacks in the south continued. About 500 yards to the east of Bernafay Wood lay Trônes Wood. It was the last piece of high ground on a slight rise before the main German second-line positions and had to be captured before any proper advance on those positions could be made.

Trônes Wood was different to Bernafay Wood. It was protected by a network of trenches and barbed wire entanglements, and it was itself a dense tangle of trees and undergrowth that had been untended for two years. Machine guns had been placed within it, and a concrete emplacement built by the Germans.

On 8 July 1916 the British and French attacked Trônes Wood. Over the next five drizzly days attacks, counter-attacks, artillery barrages and gas were used. The 30th Division sustained 2,300 casualties in the wood before being relieved.

A night-time attack on 13 July also failed. The attacking soldiers quickly lost direction in the dark, wet and misty entanglements of the wood and deadly short-range firefights resulted in many British casualties. The next morning the 8th Middlesex Battalion moved into the wood. They spread out from side to side and advanced in a line, firing into the undergrowth as they moved. German resistance, that had hitherto been unshakeable, crumbled. Those who were not killed in the wood fled and many were shot down as they ran for cover. The fighting had completely destroyed Trônes Wood. Tree stumps, tangles of barbed wire, the concrete emplacement and hundreds of decaying bodies was all that was left. The way was now clear to attack the German second-line defences.

The fight for Guillemont

Before the war, Guillemont had been a small farming village, with a railway station and a quarry. Horses, carts and farm machinery could be seen in the high street, a wide road dotted with single-storey shuttered buildings. Villagers would pass the time talking to one another while children played in the street. Approaching Guillemont from the west one could walk through Bernafay Wood, across four hundred yards of field on a slight rise and on through Trônes Wood. The single-track railway line from Montauban to Guillemont curved gently through the woods before passing through the station to the north of Guillemont. Emerging from Trônes Wood, the village lay to the east across about seven hundred yards of open countryside which at first sloped gently down and then rose again. A small road ran from the wood to the village with a small copse to the right. On reaching the village the quarry was on the left and, if one walked along Mount Street and through the village, one came across a slight rise in the ground towards Leuze Wood which was about one thousand yards ahead. A small village cemetery lay on the right-hand side of the road a little way out of the village. About one thousand yards to the north of the cemetery lay the village of Ginchy, and about the same distance to the south lay Falfemont Farm.

Before the Somme offensive, the village lay about two miles behind the front-line positions. Trenches along the west side of the quarry formed the first line of the second German main defensive positions. Thick belts of wire protected this trench network. The village had been turned into a fortress and tunnels and bunkers had been built within it. To the north, the village of Ginchy, and to the south Falfemont Farm were also strongly fortified. They provided mutual support in the defensive line.

Shortly after the capture of Trônes Wood on 14 July, the attacks to the north captured Longueval village and the ferocious battle for Delville Wood began. The wood overlooked the approaches to Guillemont from the north and was a significant factor in the failure of early attempts to capture it.

Lying about half way between Delville Wood and Guillemont station was a sugar refinery and farm called Waterlot Farm. This was an area defended by the Germans in strength, and plans were immediately drawn up to capture it. The attacks succeeded on 17 July after a few days' fighting, during which the farm changed hands a number of times. The area was practically destroyed.

The first assault on Guillemont was on Sunday 23 July. It was carried out by soldiers of the 3rd and 30th Division who attacked from the trenches north-west of Guillemont at Waterlot Farm and from Trônes Wood, to the accompaniment of a heavy artillery barrage. Soldiers fought their way into Guillemont but were unable to consolidate any positions. Some managed to escape the village, while many others were cut off and killed or captured.

The next attack was one week later using fresh soldiers from the 30th Division. They attacked at 4.45 on a misty morning from Trônes Wood after assembling overnight under a barrage of gas and high explosive shells. On this occasion soldiers of the 2nd Royal Scots managed to fight their way into Guillemont. Although reinforced, they were driven out by counter-attacks and were all but wiped out in the process.

Attacks by the 55th (West Lancashire) Division on 9 August also failed. Despite careful preparation, including digging trenches closer to the village, a heavy artillery barrage, and mist to cover the advance, most of the attackers were cut down by machine-gun fire as they tried to cross the wire. Again some were able to get into the village. Again counter-attacks drove them out.

The Somersets march south

On 1 July and for several days afterwards, the Somersets were billeted in Ypres at the prison, which would occasionally be shelled with 5.9s. While here working parties were provided to build a new trench in the salient.

In the evening of 11 July the battalion entrained for the front line, eventually reaching their positions at 1.55am. The soldiers occupied a series of craters and parapet trenchworks. Almost immediately the Germans fired rifle grenades at the positions, injuring four soldiers in one of the craters and killing a 21-year-old poet from Bath, Lance Corporal Arthur Hendon.[1]

The following six days were quiet. Eight men were injured, six by artillery fire and another two from machine-gun fire on a wiring party. Battalion snipers scored some success by shooting a German officer who was observing mortar fire.

On the night of 17 July the battalion marched away from the front and away from the Ypres salient. On the 20th they were moved by motor bus to Dranoutre and the following day they marched near to Bailleul, where they eventually billeted. Lieutenant Andrews later recalled this time:

> As to Ypres itself, it always seemed a most unsafe place to have billets in. My most vivid remembrances of it are of the quarters we had in the prison which the Bosches used to shell regularly with great gusto, and the haste with which we always crossed the Grand Place, which was a very unpleasant place to loiter in. Our tours of duty out of the line were often sadly interrupted. Alarms were frequent, and when we were not on fatigues and working parties we were constantly 'standing to'.

With the start of the move south, all men on courses were recalled to their divisions. Captain Jones was on a course at the 2nd Army School of Signalling when the division left. He eventually tracked the battalion to the Bailleul area where he ran into Lance Corporal Shell, the battalion headquarters mess orderly. Captain Jones was directed to a village where the Somersets had spent the night.

On reaching the village he found the battalion drawn up, and Captain Jones was given command of the signallers. It was a glorious morning as the battalion marched out, with Captain Jones in his new role ahead, the bugle band afterwards and the battalion following by company. Captain Jones described the march: 'As we jogged along through the smiling countryside, a merry, chaffing, laughing column, it was difficult to realise that this was the first stage of our journey to the Somme battle area.' The Somersets marched west along the main road carrying rifles and backpacks, sharing it with passing traffic and the billowing clouds of dust that it raised. 'At last in the middle of the afternoon smoking, singing and white with dust we marched into billets at Hondeghem, a pleasant old world village of thatched cottages and flower gardens.'

In the afternoon of the next day the battalion marched along quiet country roads to the station at Bavinchove, where it entrained for an undisclosed destination. The officers travelled in cramped conditions in 3rd class compartments, the men in the notoriously uncomfortable cattle trucks 'Hommes 40, Chevaux 8'. The train moved very slowly through the countryside, crawling through Hazebrouck and farther south into the twilight. As night fell it passed through Lillers and Bethune. The soldiers, few of whom were able to sleep, could make out the glows of blast furnaces through the gloom as they passed through the industrial areas near the towns. Through the night the locomotive hauled the carriages, arriving at a station lit up with flares. In the eerie flickering light the battalion detrained. They had arrived in Doullens.

The battalion fell in and started to march out of Doullens through the back streets, only able to glimpse the main thoroughfares, as dawn broke. As the soldiers marched out of the town along a broad road that rose and fell, snatches of song rose from the ranks. Captain Jones:

> The rolling uplands were dotted with patches of woodland. As far as the eye could see there was either a sea of golden corn or endless rows of sheaves. It was a splendid scene, which contrasted strikingly with the ugliness and sadness of life in the salient.

Although the men had had hardly any sleep and carried nearly sixty pounds of equipment, most of the day was spent marching to a hutment camp at Bois de Warnimont, where they stopped. A testament to the organisation and military postal service was the arrival of mail for the Somersets shortly after they arrived. It was not long before almost everybody was asleep.

Wednesday 26 July came, and after breakfast and a church parade, the battalion marched down the road to Burles-Artois, a village with few houses within seven miles of the front line. Captain Jones continued:

> The men were unhappy. Beer could only be obtained at exorbitant prices, as available supplies had been exhausted. The wells and pumps had been dismantled by the villagers who sold water in buckets to the troops . . . We were close enough to the line to hear the sound of the heavy gunfire.

Early next morning the march resumed, and the battalion passed through the villages of Bertrancourt and Beaussart. The marching formation changed after this and the battalion proceeded by platoon intervals as the

German guns had the range to shell this area. Mailly Maillet was eventually reached, an abandoned village, which the population had left after securing their valuables by locking rooms inside their homes. Attempts had been made to protect the church by cladding it with straw and sandbagging the door. The village had leafy apple orchards full of ripening apples and elm-lined roads which led out to meadow-land where sheep still grazed. The abandoned houses that had suffered relatively little damage afforded relatively comfortable billets. Orders came that the Somersets were to go into the trenches the following day to relieve the 13th Royal Welch Fusiliers (RWF) at and near 'White City'. Captain Jones' brother was serving with that battalion and he was able to undertake a reconnoitre of the trenches where the two men met up.

On Friday 28 July the Somersets relieved the 13th RWF in daylight, a stark contrast to the night reliefs in the Ypres salient where every movement was overlooked by German positions. In the afternoon a flurry of German trench mortar bombs and shells landed on the battalion's positions, injuring one soldier.

The 7th Somersets at Beaumont Hamel

The trenches that were occupied were those facing Beaumont Hamel in the area where the 1st RB and 1st SomLI had attacked four weeks to the day on 1 July. Sergeant Ellis described arriving:

> After marching and riding for several days we found ourselves in the trenches, where the 1st Battalion had put up a good fight. Yes it must have been a terrible battle and it gave us our first insight into what the 'great push' really was.

The ground was still covered with bodies from the attack, and the former and now unoccupied British front-line trenches were in a terrible state.

The battalion stayed there for a week of good weather and set to work reclaiming the front. At night soldiers donned gas masks and worked in no man's land, burying the dead and filling up and digging out the old trenches. The stench of decomposition of shattered bodies that had lain on open ground or buried for four weeks in weather from rain to hot summer days was appalling. Thousands of flies buzzed about the front, their maggot larvae feeding on the bodies lying in the open. The men working at night were subjected to trench mortar bombardments by the Germans, the bombs leaving their customary red spark trail until they crashed into the ground churning up the battlefield even more. Lieutenant Henry Foley described the work:

> Out in front of our wire we could see several sad reminders of the

fierce struggle that took place on that first day of July. In our parapet a cross marked the spot where Whitgreaves, whom I had known well as a Sergeant, had been buried. The remains of the old trench told silently but unmistakably the tragedy of that first early dawn of July. In every bay and traverse we found the remains of the poor fellows who had been caught there by the German counter bombardment as they waited their turn to advance; when that time came hardly a man can have moved forward. Our work now was to clear this ghastly shambles and make it once more into the semblance of a trench. In many places earth, tumbled sand bags and bodies were so hopelessly intermingled that any thought of a decent burial were impossible, and we could but hack a way through the deadly nauseating debris. The atmosphere of the place, after the days that had elapsed since the attack, was unutterably vile. It did not do to let oneself think too much in a place like that. These torn fragments of flesh and bone had once been splendid men. And now 'missing' would, after many months, be their epitaph.

Despite the work undertaken, the living conditions in the deep dry trenches was good. Captain Jones: 'Far to the South we heard the roar of the guns in the continuous fighting between the Ancre and the Somme. At night the sky was lit by the ruddy glow of shellbursts and by the multi-coloured rockets that were fired from the lines'. In the day it was possible, from the observation post, to see the huge crater formed by the Hawthorne Ridge mine and across the lines into the battered villages of Beaumont Hamel and Serre. The battalion headquarters was slightly concealed by trees that had only suffered minor damage from artillery fire, and at dusk officers were able to hunt and catch hares and partridges in the long grass nearby.

The time here was generally quiet. Only three men were lost. On 30 July Private George Perry was killed collecting battlefield salvage, and on 3 August a shell fell into a trench, killing Lance Corporal Jim Morris and Private William Burt. Burt was only 20 when he died and had worked in the boot repair business before the war. He had only been with the battalion for about two months. Fred Barrington, one of his friends, wrote to William Burt's parents: 'It is a tremendous shock to me, as we were the best of chums since we enlisted'.

Rest, reserve and preparations

After being relieved, the battalion returned to Mailly Maillet to its comfortable old billets, where on the following day all officers were gathered in the mess for new orders. Colonel Troyte-Bullock told the assembled officers that on 7 August the battalion was to move into divisional reserve. In the intervening period soldiers were to overhaul all fighting equipment, especially their smoke helmets. Badges were to be covered, and officers were to censor letters with exceptional care. It was clear that battle was not far away, and rumours circulated that the 20th Division would be used in a new attack north of the Ancre river.

Perhaps as a portent of what was to come the 7th Battalion received a gift of an ambulance from the people of Bath through the Mayor of Bath's war fund. The wheeled ambulance could carry two prostrate casualties or four sitting and had cost £20. Colonel Troyte-Bullock wrote a letter of appreciation saying of the ambulance: 'I am sure will prove most useful and a great comfort to our wounded'.

The good weather held throughout these days of rest. No fatigue parties were required, and the soldiers had four pleasant days and undisturbed nights living in houses with washing facilities. They spent many hours sitting in sunny gardens surrounded by flowers, shrubs and trees.

On 7 August 1916 the battalion was formed up after breakfast to move away from Mailly Maillet. Singing in the morning sunshine, they marched to the north, through the battle-scarred village of Colincamps near to which mass graves had been filled with the dead of the Somme, and onwards eventually to Couin, a scattered village built on a hillside overlooked by large woods. The march ended in a valley camp of tents and bivouacs in a field alongside woodland.

The next few days in divisional reserve were spent in ardent preparation. The days were very hot, the tented nights cold by comparison. The area was calm, although ceaseless gunfire could be heard in the distance and at night the flicker of gunflashes could be seen. The training was carried out with the vigour of soldiers who knew they were soon to go into battle, and it went on day and night. The soldiers practised night marching and operations, and for two days the battalion was marched to the village of Coigneux, about a mile down the road, where they practised attacking an imaginary 'brown line' and capturing a trench by bombing along it in conjunction with Stokes mortar fire. Specialists received further training, taking into account lessons learnt from the battle so far. The signallers practised their visual signalling skills using flags and lamps, because of the constant interruptions to telephone communications in the forward battle area. At night, while the rest of the battalion manoeuvred, they practised electric lamp reading skills. Officers and NCOs were given various demonstrations including the use of amplifiers and listening apparatus. The mood of the time was of calm efficiency.

On the morning of Monday 14 August the battalion made final preparations, and then marched to the front. It passed through Colincamps, this time heading east as they came out of the village, past the ruins of a bombed sugar factory and then through Euston Dump, a large supply base, and into the trenches. The front-line positions were both very close to the German trenches and far from battalion headquarters, and a system of visual communication was implemented – flappers in daylight and lamps at night.

The soldiers had not had long to settle in to their new surroundings when orders were given for a night-time action. The 20th Division, together with the Guards Division to the right, was to make a smoke and small arms barrage to assist with operations that were taking place to the south. The night appeared misty as the soldiers clambered on to the trench firesteps. Lewis guns and rifles opened fire and smoke grenades were thrown into no man's land. Artillery fire was opened along the German front line, the shells flashing through the mist and smoke of the bombs and small arms fire. The return German mortar fire caused four injuries.

The 2nd Battalion Irish Guards relieved the Somersets on the evening of the 16th, and by the next day the men had marched to the village of Authie. An advance party had acquired billets for the column. The headquarters mess was established in the village presbytery where the curé, an elderly gentleman, was most welcoming to the officers. The rectory was a rambling old house with a lovely garden on which many hours had been spent. Although the village was pretty and the officers happily settled, some soldiers experienced difficulties with villagers. Captain Jones recalled:

> Some of its inhabitants showed no interest or welcome towards the soldiers. We had a number of brisk passages with them. One lady complained that the signallers were disturbing her pigeons by moving about in the courtyard of their billet. I told her that the Germans would not merely disturb her pigeons but would eat them. Other villagers would not allow the men to draw water from the wells. This was a strange experience for men who were going forward to take their place in the battle that was being waged to expel the foreign invader from France.

The following day the march continued, with the battalion making its way to the outskirts of Doullens. The bugle band led the way, with the battalion marching in companies. Between each company the stretcher bearers carried folded stretchers over their shoulders. Behind the procession of infantrymen went Lewis gun limbers loaded with belts of ammunition and big greyish boxes of small arms ammunition. The soldiers were disappointed not to be visiting the large town, as many had hoped, before the now inevitable involvement in battle. Instead the men proceeded through the suburbs of the town and found their way to the nearby village of Gezaincourt.

After two days the battalion marched to Candas, a village to the south-west of Doullens, where it entrained for the journey south. After the soldiers had boarded the train, it sat motionless in the station for some time. Soon a troop train carrying survivors of a division, fresh from battle, passed through the station; then the slow journey to Mericourt-l'Abbé began. During the later part of the journey the soldiers were able to glimpse the Somme river and its marshy banks for the first time. When the train journey ended, the Somersets marched along dusty roads and through rolling countryside until they reached the village of Morlancourt, tired and hungry. On 21 August the battalion left Morlancourt and marched east along the dust-red road and then on to a camp in a small hollow called 'Happy Valley', between Fricourt and Bray, arriving there later that morning. From the high land around the hollow the soldiers could see Mametz Wood and other battle-scarred areas from earlier fighting. That afternoon was spent in training and preparation, including a demonstration of communication techniques between aircraft and infantry.

In the evening the officers were assembled by Colonel Troyte-Bullock when he outlined the task that had been allotted to the 20th Division. He told his men of the course of the previous fighting and that German positions in this area were centred on the village of Guillemont, which had defied several attempts to capture it. The officers were told that the British positions were within a few hundred yards of the village and that Guillemont station was held by the British. The 20th Division were given the task of capturing Guillemont. One of the officers briefed was Captain Jones:

> We were all impressed by the magnitude of the task, but we all appeared to be imbued with a resolute determination to do our best. A sense of gravity descended upon us. Battle seemed different to us now that we were on the threshold of active participation in the fighting.

NOTE

1 One of Arthur Hendon's poems 'Some day, not now' appears at the beginning of the book. With the permission of the Liddle Collection at Leeds University.

CHAPTER VII
The Battle for Guillemont

The Somersets at Guillemont

Despite Colonel Troyte-Bullock's briefing to officers, the proposed attack on 24 August was postponed to the 29th. In the meantime officers and men involved themselves in preparations, while the soldiers busied themselves with bomb-carrying parties and in training in assaulting and consolidating trenches. Then, on 25 August, the battalion took over the front line facing Guillemont. Almost as soon as the relief was complete, the Germans heavily bombarded the positions for two hours, killing Privates Henry Davey and Harry Williams and injuring ten others. That evening Captain Hatt and Sergeant Ellis, both from Bath, sat talking. Lord Alec Thynne, the Member of Parliament for the city, had been wounded in battle fighting with the Glosters and there was an eagerness to redress the harm. Sergeant Ellis said: 'Roll on when this is finished and lets get back and fight for him.' The mood was the same among many of the men, who had heard accounts from the 6th Somersets of success in capturing enemy trenches, and of nearby divisions beating off repeated enemy attacks which had caused heavy losses to the enemy. (The Germans had launched a series of strong counter-attacks in the Thiepval area around this time which were largely unsuccessful.)

The following night two companies were ordered to take up positions opposite Guillemont quarry. A Company proceeded up the communication trench known as Guillemont Alley (also as 'Irish Alley'), followed by C Company. Captain Hatt who was leading his men up the trench stopped to talk to the adjutant, Lieutenant Humphries, when a shell fell near the group. A splinter hit Captain Hatt in the head killing him outright. Four others nearby were injured. The news quickly spread through the battalion.

Captain Edward Beach Hatt was the eldest son of the Mayor and Mayoress of Bath. He had volunteered as a private in the Queen's Westminster Rifles at the outbreak of the war, rather than commence a commercial career. In May 1915 Hatt was given a commission and transferred to the 7th Somersets. He had attended the Dean Close Memorial School in Cheltenham with his brother, Arthur. The death of

71

Edward completed the family tragedy as his younger brother Arthur had been killed on the second day of the Somme offensive serving with the 8th SomLI. He had been hit in no man's land and died in the British trenches some hours later after being dragged back into cover. The Mayor lost not only his sons but also his brother who died from natural causes in the same year. Of Edward Hatt one officer wrote to the Mayoress:

> As all the officers of your son's company would like to express to you their keen regret as to his death and their sympathy with you in your loss, they have asked me to write to you to say how much they thought of your son's work as a soldier and as a friend and a man. I can assure you that no company commander was more popular with his men, or ever led them better. Always solicitous for their comfort and enthusiastic to entertain them, he never spared himself in his efforts to brighten their spare hours.

Colonel Troyte-Bullock also wrote to Mr Hatt:

> It is with deep sorrow that I have to write to you to tell you that your son was killed last night about 10pm. He was a very gallant officer and always cheerful under the most depressing circumstances. He was one of my best company commanders and will be an irreparable loss to the battalion. He like his brother, has died a noble death for his King and country, which I know will be of some consolation to you. Hoping that you and Mrs Hatt will accept my most sincere sympathy. Believe me, yours sincerely, C J Troyte-Bullock.

A memorial plaque to the two young officers can still be seen today in the Guildhall in Bath.

The battalion occupied the position opposite Guillemont quarry on Sunday 27 August. The trenches were waterlogged and the battlefield was foul with the stench of unburied bodies from the preceding attacks. A number of heavy gun officers attended the divisional headquarters requesting that the Somersets withdraw from the trenches opposite the quarry as it was proposed to bombard it with heavies. Despite objections being raised as to the feasibility of withdrawing the soldiers in broad daylight, the orders were given by staff at Divisional HQ. The main task of achieving the withdrawal fell upon the 20-year-old Captain Guy Shufflebotham who commanded A Company. Only two years before he had been articled to a firm of land agents in Taunton just after finishing at King's College in the same town where he had spent four years in the Officers Training Corps. Now the lives of the best part of his company depended upon his decisions. The withdrawal began with soldiers being sent back in twos and threes all afternoon. By the evening, with one hour

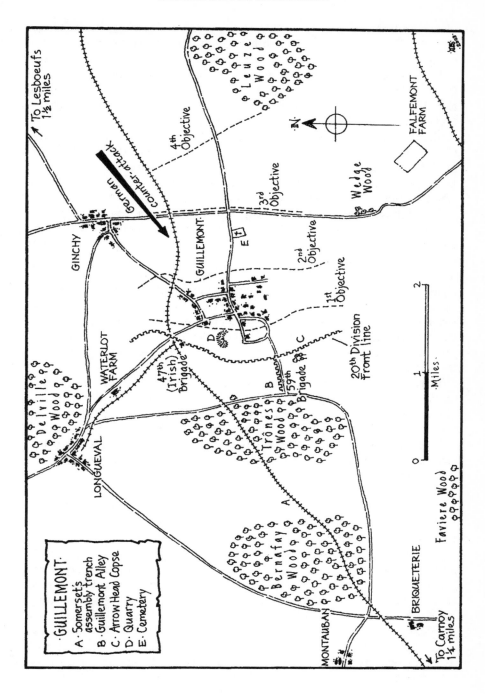

of daylight left, the whole company had been withdrawn without a single casualty. The heavy artillery bombarded the quarry for an hour and the company then returned to its former positions.

The battalion was relieved that night and afterwards moved back to the Carnoy Craters area. It had been raining persistently for four days and the trenches across the battlefield had started to become extremely muddy and waterlogged. The loose soil became sticky, making movement very difficult and the soldiers moving out of the front-line trenches found Guillemont Alley almost impassable as it wound its way through the war-mangled woods. It was easier to slither along the surface than move through the maze of trenches in the woods. It took until 6.15am for the whole battalion to reach Carnoy Craters.

The 28th was slightly drier, despite which a decision was made that the attack due the next day would have to be postponed again, because of the weather. The battle was now to begin on 3 September. Ardent preparations went on throughout the following days with nearly every man in the 20th Division being called on for carrying parties. The summer rains continued on the 29th, and the working parties had to contend with slithering about in the thickening mud created by hundreds of heavily laden soldiers marching to and from the front line to take their turn to man it, or to bring up the supplies of war. There was a thunderstorm that afternoon, and lightning struck two nearby observation balloons, bringing them down.

The battalion had been attached to the 59th Brigade of the 20th Division to strengthen the depleted brigade. Colonel Troyte-Bullock and his company commanders, Captains Shufflebotham and Mitchell, and Lieutenants 'Ack Ack Ack' Andrews and Cartwright went forward to reconnoitre the ground between Bernafay Wood and the trenches at Arrow Head Copse, as part of the planning for the coming battle. This was the ground across which the battalion would attack.

On 31 August many of the battalion were at the Briqueterie south of Bernafay Wood, when at dusk they were subjected to a bombardment of flurries of little shells that hissed as they came overhead. Gas! The bombardment continued through the night and into the next morning. The gas was 'tear gas' and caused twenty casualties amongst the troops that night and a few more the next day. The soldiers spent the night wearing gas helmets, which made walking about extremely difficult, and it stopped almost everyone from sleeping properly. The injured soldiers, including Major Preston-Whyte and Captain Blankensee, were evacuated to a hospital to recover from the ill effects. One of those injured, Private Daniel Stone, died next day from the effects of the gas, leaving three little children as orphans. The Germans had fired around 1,000 gas shells into the concentrating British forces. Also on 31 August Private Frank Pavey was killed by a shell that wounded Private Bert Daley in both his legs.

The weather had now improved considerably, and the sun began to shine. The heavy preliminary barrage on the German-held positions also began on 1 September. It was to go on throughout the 2nd, concentrating on the enemy trenches and known strongpoints. The artillery used were the batteries from the 6th and 24th Divisions. The artillery of the 20th Division had been retained in the Ypres sector.

On 2 September Colonel Troyte-Bullock assembled the battalion officers to outline the operational orders for battle the next day. The orders were then relayed to the soldiers of the battalion in a speech. Sergeant Ellis recalled being told that:

> The eyes of the whole of the Allies were on the 20th Division. We had to take Guillemont at all costs, and the work for the 'Sets' was to take the German third line, after being in reserve while the first and second lines were taken. Little groups of men could be seen conversing together over what had to be done and they all agreed officers and men 'We will do our best'.

Emergency rations and small arms ammunition was issued and the ammunition cleaned; bombs were checked and fused and gas masks were given a final overhaul.

The plan of attack

The task of the 20th Division was the capture of Guillemont village itself. To the left the 7th Division had Ginchy as its objective; to the right the 5th Division was to capture Falfemont Farm.

The plan was drawn up by Major General Douglas-Smith the Division's commander, and it was to capture the village in a series of attacks to seize four objective lines. The first three lines represented the main German defensive positions. The fourth objective was a line on which it was planned to occupy and dig in on. The attacks by the Division were to be undertaken on a frontage of two brigades. Because of the reduced number of men available due to casualties and sickness, the Division was given the assistance of the 47th Brigade which was borrowed from the 16th (Irish) Division. The 47th (Irish) Brigade were the Brigade on the left. The 12th Kings were attached to the 47th Brigade. On the right was the 59th Brigade from the 20th Division. The 6th Ox & BucksLI and 7th SomLI were attached to the 59th Brigade for the battle.

Each of the four stages was to follow broadly the same pattern. Half of the artillery would be used to put down a stationary barrage on the objective line. The other half would be employed to create a creeping barrage behind which the infantry would advance. The creeping barrage was set to advance at fifty yards per minute, and the stationary barrage would lift when the creeping barrage reached it. The stationary barrage would then fall upon the next objective line.

The first objective was the sunken road in the village and the quarries, with the Irish brigade deploying the 6th Connaught Rangers and 7th Leinsters to capture the first line; the 59th Brigade deploying the 10th King's Royal Rifle Corps (with one company of the 11th KRRC attached), and the 10th and 11th Rifle Brigade in the first lines of attack. In support of these battalions was the 6th Ox & BucksLI who were to pass through the front wave and assist in taking the first line. The plan was for these battalions to advance under cover of the barrage until they were very close to the German positions before zero hour, so that they would have far less ground to cover when attacking. Zero hour was midday.

The second objective was a line along the road on the eastern edge of the village running to Ginchy. To the left the 8th Royal Munsters had this objective. The 59th Brigade were to use the four battalions from the first objective attack supported by the three remaining companies of the 11th KRRC. This attack was due to commence at 12.50pm.

The third objective was the Ginchy to Wedge Wood road. The 7th Somerset Light Infantry were tasked to capture this; the attack to commence at 2pm starting from the second objective line on the far side of Guillemont village. The 6th Royal Irish and the 8th Munster Fusiliers were to advance to the left of the Somersets on the 47th Brigade front.

The fourth objective line was from the western edge of Leuze Wood, north-west towards Ginchy, as far as the railway line. Although no battalions were specifically tasked to attack this location, it was assumed that the foremost troops would consolidate and entrench along this line. The Royal Engineers and the 11th Durham Light Infantry, the 20th Division pioneers, were to be available to assist with this consolidation.

Careful planning had taken place to ensure that known areas of heavy resistance were dealt with adequately. Following two days of artillery fire, at 6am on 3 September a series of deliberate bombardments was made upon selected areas. At 8.15am a 'Chinese' attack was made, where all the batteries delivered a burst of rapid fire on enemy positions to feign the start of the attack. At 8.30am all of the artillery of both Divisions in support turned their attention to an area north-east of Guillemont known as 'the trap', an area that had deliberately not been previously shelled. Howitzers then opened fire with gas shells.

There were also specific plans to deal with a troublesome machine-gun position in the first sunken road in line with Arrow Head Copse. Just before noon, zero hour for the attack, liquid fire was projected from the British trenches at the emplacement. At the same time a 'push pipe' mine was exploded, unsuccessfully, with a view to destroying the same emplacement. The mine had struck a stone and had turned back causing a 120-foot long shallow trench to be created in no man's land. The emplacement was destroyed by artillery fire in the end.

Behind the front line, aid posts were set up in front of Trônes Wood and at Waterlot Farm to deal with casualties. All of the stretcher bearers came under a centralised command based at the bearer camp at Bronfay Farm, about one mile south-west of Carnoy Craters, and there were advanced bearer posts at the Briqueterie near Montauban and also in Bernafay Wood. At Montauban a loading post was established, where casualties would be transferred from stretchers on to ambulances. This was as far forward as the ambulances could go, as there were no discernible roads beyond this point. The movement of incapacitated casualties would therefore be by bearers from the battlefield to the aid posts, and then by relays back in stages until they were taken entirely away from the battlefield by ambulance. The stretcher bearers would have to carry the wounded up to five miles on foot in some cases. The walking wounded would have to struggle back to the nearest aid post to seek assistance.

Communications between the two Brigade headquarters and Divisional headquarters were by wireless stations, in addition to the use of land cables. In advance of the old front line, messages were to be sent using runners, pigeons, and arrangements had been made for aeroplanes of No 9 Squadron to observe the flow of the battle and take messages if possible.

At noon an intense barrage began on the enemy positions in accordance with the fire plan, and the first battalions went over the top.

We will do our best

Dawn on 3 September was glorious. The sun shone brightly over the assembled battalion at Carnoy Craters. Captain Jones: 'We had all been cheered by the fine weather of the last two days. Every man was keen to take his share of the battle.' The battle had commenced with the prearranged dawn bombardment at 6am. Shells of all calibres were rained down on the enemy positions, creating a tremendous din, even in the rear positions occupied by the Somersets.

The men had breakfast at 7.30am, and an hour later marched off in columns of platoons, with fifty yards between each platoon. Colonel Troyte-Bullock, the new adjutant Foley and Captain Jones watched the battalion march past. The soldiers were carrying their battle issue of cheese and biscuits, and water bottles with orders not to drink from canteens unless water was otherwise unprocurable. Also each company had twenty-five red rockets and a box of Verey lights to carry. Each officer and NCO carried flares so that up to fifty flares were carried per company. Up the road the groups of men marched in full battle order, through the brick heaps and twisted iron that was all that remained of the village of Montauban, eventually reaching the assembly trenches that had been dug to the west of Trônes Wood. The first casualties of the Somersets in the battle occurred when a 5.9 shell landed near a platoon of D Company as they marched out of Montauban, injuring four men. The remaining troops continued unperturbed to the assembly positions, although the rearmost companies were ordered to advance cross country.

Once the battalion reached its assembly positions, what seemed like an interminable wait began. A few German shells landed harmlessly nearby as the soldiers sat in apprehensive ignorance of the battle that was under way ahead of them. The assembly trenches between Trônes and Bernafay Woods were in a slight depression and the soldiers were unable to see anything of the battle. Captain Jones said it was a time spent 'Anxiously watching watches. We could hear the roar of the guns and we were agog with excitement as it was the first time the Division was to go "over the top"'. Sergeant Ellis said:

> The sun was shining and we patiently waited the time to go forward. It was here our Colonel Troyte-Bullock came down our line his face wreathed with smiles, with the following comment 'Ah you young devils, you are anxious to get at them aren't you?' Well we were. We had had enough of trench warfare. We wanted the word to go.

Captain Jones also described the wait:

> As noon approached, every man got ready, making footholes in the side of the trenches to enable them to jump out. We could not glean much information as to the progress of the battle, but some walking wounded told us the attack was making headway.

At noon Colonel Troyte-Bullock placed a whistle to his lips, and ordered his battalion into battle. Soldiers clambered out of the assembly trench using ladders in places, moving forward in four waves of companies in artillery formation. Each company had its platoons advancing in file towards the enemy. Captain Shufflebotham, commanding A Company, led the way. Behind them came Lieutenant Andrews leading D Company, then came battalion headquarters. Behind headquarters came Captain Mitchell with B Company and behind them Lieutenant Cartwright with C Company.

The soldiers passed through the tangled remains of trees that was once Trônes Wood. The recent rains had uncovered some of the casualties of the fierce battle for the wood, and here and there body parts could be seen; sometimes an arm or a leg grotesquely sticking up into the air. As soon as the battalion crossed the Montauban to Guillemont road, they marched through a barrage of 5.9 shells which fell across their front. Sergeant Ellis in A Company said:

And away we went, through a terrible hail of shells, but we didn't take the least notice of them. You could see our boys stopping to give one another a light from their fag. Of course we were losing men, every regiment is bound to, and it was here that our Colonel [Troyte-Bullock] got wounded.

Captain Jones was with headquarters in the middle:

The platoons did not hesitate for a moment but went on in single file. We were moving over difficult ground, cut up by two months of heavy fire. A maze of shell craters and battered trenches with loose strands of barbed wire clutching at our puttees. But we advanced resolutely up the rising ground towards our goal.

The goal at this stage was to advance through Guillemont and form up on the second objective line, ready to attack the third German lines. The battalion had a long way to go yet. Captain Jones recalled:

When we got to the neighbourhood of Arrow Head Copse, the shellfire became terrific. We suffered a large number of casualties hereabouts. High explosive ripped the ground in front of us, bursts of shrapnel were showering fragments on our heads. Every other moment somebody else was hit including my batman Harry Bailey.

Captain Jones heard a whimpering cry and turned to see Private Bailey hit in the mouth by a piece of shrapnel. He was able to stop and render first aid until some stretcher bearers came to help. He continued: 'It was an uncanny sensation to walk forward while men were dropping on all sides. There was no means of maintaining formation, the men followed their officers and NCOs in groups or singly as best they could.'

Sergeant Allen: 'The two brothers Porter of Durleigh were killed and Fred Hancock was wounded. It was an awful sight to see them falling around us.' Charles Porter, 39-years-old, was last seen going towards a shell hole where his brother was. The body of the father of five was never found.

Scouts were sent forward to ascertain the situation ahead and men of the battalion came across soldiers from the 6th Ox & BucksLI as they crossed the British front-line trenches. The Somersets were told that the battle was going well but that heavy casualties had been sustained. Pressing on the Somersets crossed the sunken road that had been the German front line. In the road the attackers found many dead Germans as well as some bodies of men of the King's Royal Rifles and Rifle Brigade battalions who had led the attack. Small groups of captured Germans were also found. They had been taken as the attacking soldiers overran the

79

German positions while the occupants sheltered in their bunkers. A few of the Somersets' signallers, who had been struggling forward with an electric signalling lamp, were injured here. The lamp had to be left behind.

The battalion was then able to pick its way through what was left of Guillemont village. No structures remained above ground level. The ground itself was a mass of shell holes, and the rubble of buildings that had been pounded to dust from several month's bombardments. The passage through the village was much calmer as the Germans were not firing into it yet and the Somersets formed up on the second objective line and regained their cohesion.

For the attack on the third objective line the formation was changed. A and D Companies remained in front, but formed into two lines with each company having two platoons in the first wave and two in the second. Two hundred yards behind the attacking waves was the headquarters, and they were followed by B and C Companies. These companies occupied the same frontage as the attacking companies but remained in artillery formation, with the platoons of each company spaced apart and the men of the platoons advancing in file. Colonel Troyte-Bullock, despite his injuries and attempts to persuade him otherwise, would not leave the battalion.

At the same time as the battalion consolidated on the second objective line there was an appraisal of the overall situation. Contact had been made with elements of the 5th Division to the right, and it was established that they had been held up; they were unable to advance as far as the 20th Division. This meant that the Somersets' attack on the third objective line would proceed with their right flank exposed to the enemy. On the left the Irish had made good progress, and had reported to Brigade that they believed that there were no Germans ahead of their positions. There was little opposition at this time, with only a little rifle and machine-gun fire. The 10th and 11th RB and the 6th Ox & BucksLI were consolidating their positions and the 10th KRRC moved across to consolidate the quarry that had been overrun by the Connaught Rangers. The previous problem of Guillemont – the cellars, tunnels and underground bunkers that had hidden the German defenders so that they could emerge and cut off the attackers – were dealt with this time.

At 2pm, in accordance with the plan, the barrage fell on the third German line and the creeping barrage started moving forward to cover the advance of the 7th Battalion. A and D Companies followed closely behind. A few men in the advance were injured and Captain Shufflebotham was hit in the head by shrapnel and killed. There was no significant German artillery fire at this time and it is likely that Captain Shufflebotham and other casualties were victims of British artillery fire, by advancing very close behind the British barrage.

The enemy had dugouts along the road leading from Guillemont towards the objective, as well as in the cemetery to the right-hand side of the road. These were overrun by the attackers who pressed on to the main German trenches. Captain Jones described what followed:

> There was little resistance offered by the enemy – the garrison had mostly retired to their dugouts when our barrage fell on the trench and our men were in the trench before they could emerge. A few small groups which showed fight were quickly overpowered and then their dugouts poured forth their occupants. One German officer and forty six other ranks [from the 73rd Hannoverian Fusilier Regiment] came out with uplifted arms.

They were sent to the rear under escort.

At 2.30pm the adjutant sent for information from Lieutenant Cartwright of C Company as to the progress of the battle. 'Any news from Guillemont village? If not send out again'. The reply was:

> 2nd Lieutenant Chard [of C company] reports that on our left are MGC [the Machine Gun Corps] and Royal Munster Fusiliers. They advanced past this point 20 minutes before we advanced and I can see our men well in front of Guillemont. It is being badly shelled as they have the range of it.

Sergeant Ellis, who was with the foremost soldiers of the attack: 'It was not long before our boys got their objective, and at once began to dig in for all they were worth.' While A and D Companies consolidated their front line, B and C Companies dug a support trench with the right flank swept back. The battalion was now under machine-gun fire from a ridge that ran from Leuze Wood to Falfemont Farm. Falfemont Farm had withstood the onslaught of the 5th Division.

The men of A and D Companies dug in. Sergeant Ellis recalled:

> At about this time a large party of Germans could be seen coming towards us and the men at once thought there was going to be a counterattack, but a word from Captain Whall (our then C.O.) [and] they resumed their hard work. Another word to the machine guns and they did their work in short time.

In fact both battalion snipers and gunners from the 61st Brigade MGC broke up the enemy formation. They also suppressed machine guns that were being set up along the Leuze Wood–Falfemont Farm ridge, about 800 yards from the Somersets.

Consolidation

The battalion headquarters was set up in the centre of the new support line and efforts were made to open lines of communication with Brigade. Three signallers were sent back to fetch the abandoned signal lamp. In the meantime groundsheets were laid out to signal to one of No 9 Squadron's BE 2c aircraft. A request for more shovels was unpromisingly repeated to those on the ground by the airman for confirmation as 'We want towels'. Fortunately shovels were delivered later that night.

Captain Whall wrote a message to the adjutant at 4pm urgently requesting more ammunition. At 5pm Lieutenant Gannecliffe of D Company informed headquarters that the company had no SOS rockets and also that Captain Shufflebotham had been killed.

From their position on the third objective line, the soldiers were able to look behind them to the village of Guillemont and the ridge they had crossed. Both were now under enemy fire, with Guillemont receiving 8 inch shells from heavy guns. Each shell detonated with a loud explosion that threw up a fountain of brick dust and earth in a cloud of black smoke. The Somerset positions were largely unscathed, receiving only a few high shrapnel shells that were too far away to cause any harm. The men spent the afternoon digging in, and at 7pm they lit flares so that a contact aeroplane could determine the foremost British positions.

To the right of the 7th Battalion the 5th Division had failed to make headway. The entrenchments that were dug, therefore, bent back to the right to face the potential threat. To the left of the Somersets the Irish had made equally good progress, and held their positions on the third objective line towards Ginchy. Rumours began to circulate that the 7th Division, on the left, had fought their way into Ginchy but had been repelled by a strong counter-attack. The 7th Somerset Light Infantry, the 6th Royal Irish and 8th Munster Fusiliers to their left formed a small salient protruding in front of Guillemont.

At 7.45pm orders arrived from 59th Brigade headquarters to advance up to Leuze Wood. Given the already exposed position of the foremost troops, this was treated with alarm by the remaining officers. A situation report was sent back, and the battalion awaited its fate. In the meantime there was a lull in the battle. Captain Jones remembered: 'Everything was quiet – the men were in high spirits and dug in.' While everyone waited, 2nd Lieutenant Hill of D Company decided to reconnoitre Leuze Wood to the front of the battalion. He returned a little while later, nonchalantly smoking a cigarette as though he had been on a Sunday afternoon walk. He reported that the edge of Leuze Wood was unoccupied but that the middle was strongly held. Just after Hill had returned a runner arrived from Brigade cancelling the attack.

A little after 8pm the German counter-attack fell upon the 6th Royal

Irish Battalion and 8th Munster Fusiliers to the left of the Somersets. The attack was delivered from Ginchy in a south-westerly direction towards Guillemont. The blow also fell upon the 12th King's who had moved up through the 47th Brigade and held trenches along the road between Guillemont and Ginchy.

It soon became apparent that the Irish, who were under very heavy fire and had suffered high casualties, would give way under the assault. B Company, commanded by Captain Mitchell, rushed across to their aid and were themselves soon under heavy rifle and machine-gun fire. As the company reached the cemetery, both Captain Mitchell and Lieutenant Knight were hit and injured. Sergeants Tozer and Wiltshire also became casualties. For a while Captain Mitchell struggled on bleeding from a thigh wound. The intensity of enemy machine-gun fire increased, and Captain Mitchell, who at this stage couldn't identify where the Irish positions were located, led his men into a depression where they could shelter. Mitchell remained where he was, getting weaker by the minute through blood loss, while scouts were sent forward to find the Irish. Soon they came upon a straggler who was able to direct them to the trenches. Captain Mitchell by this time had suffered considerable blood loss and was unable to continue.

Second Lieutenant Jenne, who had only recently arrived at the front, found himself in command of B Company. He moved the men forward to help; the remaining men pressing forward in the face of the enemy fire. The company arrived just as the Irish were beginning to fall back and the attacking Germans were almost into their trench. The two sides closed in bitter hand-to-hand fighting with rifle and bayonet and the attack was repulsed. The Germans retired leaving the men of B Company occupying the trenches formerly held by the Irish. Dead bodies and the injured from both defenders and attackers were left in and around the trenches.

B Company had prevented the Germans breaking into the British front line, which would have left the 7th Somersets on the right and the 12th King's on the left with wide open flanks. B Company had sustained a number of casualties at this stage but remarkably no one had been killed. However, some of the injuries were serious and a little after 9pm an urgent request was made to the aid post in Trônes Wood to provide three stretchers. As darkness fell the remnants of the company remained in the trenches formerly held by the Irish battalion.

It was at this time, after the counter-attack had been beaten off and the trenches consolidated, that Colonel Troyte-Bullock retired from the battlefield. Sergeant Ellis said: 'After being firmly established our Colonel could be seen going back, supported by his servants arm. The boys stood up and gave him a cheer.' Colonel Troyte-Bullock had been hit in the leg by a machine-gun bullet.

Also at about 9pm an urgent request was made of Brigade for more small arms ammunition to be sent to the front line. By this time the battalion headquarters was manned by Lieutenant Humphries alone, as all the others were injured, dead or on urgent duties, and there was no one available to carry the boxes. Fortunately Brigade had sufficient numbers of people to get the ammunition forward.

Later the battalion headquarters was set up in a German dugout full of pilsner water, and Captain Whall with fellow officers was able to dine on cheese and rock hard ration biscuits, and enjoy the spoils of victory.

A roll call was taken as things settled down that evening, and Brigade was informed that there had been 127 casualties in the battalion which included ten dead. The figure was in fact higher. Captain Shufflebotham had been the only officer killed, but many officers, including the Colonel, had been injured. Fifteen other soldiers had been killed, including the brothers Lance Corporal Charles Porter and Private Thomas Porter both from Enmore in Somerset.[1]

The nature of the battle meant that even though the British were successful and had overrun the German positions, the number of casualties and what had happened to individuals often took many months to resolve. Death was then often assumed because of the last place and circumstances a man was seen in. Tom Porter, the 37-year-old husband of Ada Porter, disappeared in the battle leaving Ada and her two children desperate for news. She wrote letters to the officers and men she knew in the battalion to try to find out what had happened to her husband after he was initially reported missing. Some weeks later Lieutenant Humphries wrote to her: 'I am afraid that Private T Porter is still missing, as I have received no news of him. If I do I will let you know at once, but I am afraid he was severely wounded and I can give you very little hope'. It was only in November that she received official notification that her husband was dead.

The night passed without incident for the Somersets. The pioneers of the 11th Durham Light Infantry and the Royal Engineers crept forward under cover of darkness to help those in the trenches to strengthen them and they started erecting barbed-wire fences in front of the British positions. The night was also spent running out a communication line linking Brigade to battalion headquarters. Fortunately the weather had held fine throughout the day of the attack.

In the early hours of the morning B Company were relieved by a battalion from the 47th Brigade. They returned to the rest of the battalion, finding their way quietly at night across their battlefield of only a few hours earlier. Through the night, as the positions were consolidated, the village of Guillemont came under heavy artillery fire. As a mark of the uncertainty that prevailed that night, Lieutenant Andrews, in charge of D Company, sent a message to battalion headquarters asking: 'Will you please let me know if I am to expect rations up and ammunition this morning?'

The next day the battalion, entrenched in front of Guillemont, was able to watch the 5th Division attacking to their south. They were endeavouring to capture Falfemont Farm that had defied them the previous day. One or two machine guns were seen to check the attacking waves of soldiers momentarily, whereupon the advance continued and at last German prisoners were identified being escorted to the rear. While this was taking place, plans were afoot for the Somersets to advance later that day to occupy the fourth objective line, although the soldiers were unaware of this at the time. Sergeant Ellis said:

> After digging for almost five hours we had orders to hand over the line to another regiment, a thing we didn't relish, and go back to the second lines and there dig again. We stayed there the following day thinking we should be relieved but at 8pm we were ordered forward again.

Strong patrols from the forward companies, A and D, were ordered to move out behind a creeping barrage. The weather had turned cold and it had started to rain heavily as the soldiers advanced. The men left their trenches and, following the moving wall of explosions, they reached the objective line just outside Leuze Wood. They started to entrench along the Brigade frontage in a line from the south-west corner of the wood to the Guillemont–Combles road. The Germans retaliated ineffectively by shelling the edge of the wood with 5.9s, the shells falling ahead of the British positions. The strain of battle started to become all too evident amongst the men who would have had precious little sleep for nearly three days. Shortly after taking the new position, Lieutenant Andrews collapsed with fatigue. He was carried from the forward area. This left 2nd Lieutenant Gannecliffe in charge of the forward positions and 2nd Lieutenants Hill and Scott in charge of D Company.

Second Lieutenant Hill went on a patrol along the road towards Combles that night in the pouring rain, where he came upon a burly German sergeant major who appeared drunk. He captured the man and brought him back whereupon he was sent to the battalion headquarters for questioning. Little information was gathered other than that the German reinforcements were being caused heavy casualties from artillery fire as they marched up to the line. 2nd Lieutenant Joseph Hill was awarded the Military Cross for his courageous reconnaissances.

Through the night it continued to rain heavily although ration parties were able to make it up to the soldiers. As dawn broke Sergeant Shortman of D Company was able to make out the figures of two Germans at about 600 yards down the Combles road. He shot one of them who collapsed in a heap while the other scrambled to shelter. Sergeant Shortman then went forward and removed papers from the dead man before returning to the safety of the trench. For this act and for his bravery in clearing dugouts in the initial attack, he was awarded the Distinguished Conduct Medal. A short while later, at 8am the battalion was relieved by the 7th and 8th Inniskilling Fusiliers, which although harassed by sniper fire, passed without casualty. Sergeant Ellis: 'What with the hard cold rain and heavy shells we had an unpleasant night and the morning found us in a very exhausted condition. But we were relieved and managed to get back to our billets for a good meal'.

The battalion returned to Carnoy Craters, reaching them at 10 o'clock that morning, having lost fifteen dead and 155 wounded in the battle. The exhausted men had to struggle over muddy ground, variously described as 'shocking' and 'a quagmire'. To add to the problems the Germans were sporadically shelling the rear areas.

The battalion reached the Craters very tired but in good spirits. Sergeant Ellis saying:

> Troops who had not been up and had heard of our success came to have a good look at the boys and gave us a cheering word to help us along. But we were then done up, but flushed with pride, for we had been given a job to do and carried it through beyond all expectations.

One of those soldiers at Carnoy was Lieutenant Henry Foley: '[I] found that I was one of the "also rans", the small group of officers and men who had to be left out of an attack, in case overwhelming disaster should make such a nucleus necessary. Those who had come through were muddy, unshaven and dog tired, but apparently in the best of spirits.' The next day was spent at Carnoy Craters where the exhausted soldiers were able to sleep, eat hot meals and refit.

Retrospective

By comparison to the earlier attacks of the Somme offensive, the battle for Guillemont illustrates very well the huge advances in tactics made by the British Army in the two months of fighting. In particular the role of the artillery had changed fundamentally. The principal change was the introduction of suppressive fire to support the attacking waves of infantrymen, usually in the form of the creeping barrage behind which the infantry would advance.

Suppressive artillery fire was primarily intended to keep the enemy soldiers in their dugouts, and therefore unable to fire on the attacking infantry. Ideally, the attacking soldiers would enter the enemy entrenchments before those defending emerged from their shelters. If this was achieved, the defenders would be gravely disadvantaged, often surrendering.

The earliest Somme attacks (and those of 1915 such as Loos) had shown the shortcomings of relying upon destructive fire alone. The massive bombardment preceding 1 July, which it had been hoped would destroy the German front lines, had failed. The deep dugouts were not destroyed and where the enemy were allowed time to emerge, or simply to reinforce the forward positions from areas not subject to heavy bombardment, the attackers suffered heavily. The attack at Beaumont Hamel faltered at the first line of defence with very heavy casualties as the Germans were given time to deploy their machine guns against the attacking soldiers.

Towards the end of the Somme battle, the ability of the artillery to roll a barrage forward at a given rate of yards per minute had changed the character of British infantry attacks. One has to wonder at the ability of the soldiers to adapt so quickly to the changes in tactics. Throughout the battle, and the war, a constant circulation of ideas took place in the form of leaflets and training.

An example is the 'Preliminary Notes on the Tactical Lessons on the Recent Operations' published during the Somme offensive which stated: 'Experience has shown that it is far better to risk a few casualties from an occasional short round from our own artillery than to suffer the many casualties which occur when the bombardment is not closely followed up.' These ideas and changes had clearly penetrated to the soldiers of the 7th Battalion before their first attack. Both A and D Companies were in the forefront of the battalion's attack at Guillemont. They closely followed the barrage, overran a series of dugouts along the road out of the village and captured the third defensive line. The two companies suffered no more than eight men killed and thirty-two injured in the attack. Some of these casualties may have been from the earlier barrage that they passed through while moving up to their start line in Guillemont, and four of D Company's injured came from the 5.9 shell that landed as the battalion moved to their first assembly position. Some of the casualties may have been from random shrapnel or 'shorts' from the British fired shells, amongst them the young Captain Shufflebotham who bravely led A Company in the attack – a likely candidate given that no German artillery was firing on this area when shrapnel hit him in the head killing him.

The breakdown of the battalion's casualties is as follows:

A Coy: Capt Shufflebotham and six men killed; 2nd Lieutenant Makins injured.

B Coy: Capt Mitchell, Lieutenant Knight and eleven men injured.

C Coy: three men killed; Lieutenant Cartwright, 2nd Lieutenant Chard, 2nd Lieutenant Giles, Sergeants Winzar and Williams and thirty-seven men injured.

D Coy: one man killed; Lieutenant Andrews and thirty-four men injured.

Headquarters personnel: five men killed and sixty-six men injured.

The battle shows the tremendously high casualty rate amongst headquarters personnel – slightly more than 40% of the total casualties. Stretcher bearers, signallers and messengers had to expose themselves and undoubtedly this contributed to the high casualty rate.

The battle also illustrates the difficulties in communication between newly captured areas, Brigade and higher levels of command. Had the battalion attacked Leuze Wood as initially ordered and without artillery support, it is almost certain that heavy casualties would have been sustained if the information gleaned by Lieutenant Hill on his reconnaissance was correct (and there is no reason to think it was not). The battalion would not have been able to assist in stopping the counter-attack that developed against the Irish and the gains ahead of Guillemont would have been jeopardised. Without portable radios, the difficulty for battlefield commanders in obtaining accurate information quickly was perhaps the greatest command problem for officers of all sides throughout the war.

NOTE

1   The other men killed were Privates Thomas Kirtley and Stephen Avery from Durham, whose bodies were never found; 22-year-old Private Henry Cane; Private Oliver Dukes; Lance Corporal Arthur Bisp; Private Henry Holbrook; Private Fred Hardy; Private Benjamin Evans; Private William Clifford; Private Harold Williams; 22-year-old Private William Jarman and Private John Speed.

CHAPTER VIII
Lesboeufs

The sandpits – the calm

After one day spent recovering from the battle, the battalion marched about four miles to Méaulte on 7 September, but not before a stray bursting shell killed Private Gerald Baker, a former West Somerset Yeoman who had only recently transferred to the Somersets.

The next day the march away from the front line took the battalion to Mericourt l'Abbé, a little village south-west of Albert on the banks of the Ancre river. There they were able to remain until 11 September; new clothes were issued and the men could bathe in the river. General Douglas-Smith, the Divisional Commander, addressed the 20th Division on the good work that they had done at Guillemont. Sergeant Frank Ellis remembered the occasion:

> The following Sunday we all met up for prayers and here the General thanked us for the way we thrashed the Huns and said he knew when he wanted us again he could rely on the 20th Division to repeat the dose.

While the battalion was recovering, many of those who had been injured struggled for life. Between 4 and 12 September a further ten men died of wounds.[1]

Lieutenant Henry Foley had been given command of B Company after Guillemont and spent the week at Mericourt adjusting to command:

> Here I had my first experience of taking 'company office' which filled me with considerable alarm. At a stated hour, I would take my seat, probably a biscuit box, in my office. The Sergeant-Major would then in stentorian tones marshal the delinquent before me. With an attempt at severity, which I always felt to be extremely feeble, I picked up the charge sheet and read out the 'crime'. The witness then clears his throat and rolls out a parrot like jargon – 'Sir, on the night of the so-and-so, I saw the accused do so forth etc etc'. I then sternly enquire of the victim if he has anything to say. Words fail him at the

last moment and he murmurs incoherently. I pretend to weigh his remarks judicially and strive to appear suitably severe, but feel a frantic and idiotic sympathy with the man. The Sergeant-Major coughs scathingly, as if to imply that, in his opinion, the accused stands self convicted. Eventually I breathe hard, a cold sweat gathers on my brow, and I mutter '5 days CB' or words to that effect. It was the most terrifying ordeal that I was called upon to face in my new work.

On 12 September the battalion returned to the camp at the sandpits next to the village of Méaulte where it remained for two days. Méaulte at this time was full of British soldiers either going to or coming from the front. Supply dumps and workshops were set up all about the town and nearly every house was put to some military use. Captain Jones: 'There were rumours abroad that another great battle was imminent.' On 14 September the battalion moved to Citadel Camp which was near Carnoy. Captain Jones said:

All through the night we could hear the rumble of heavy traffic along the roads leading to the front. We had heard stories of new engines of war which were to be used in the approaching battle, and we supposed that it was these which were making the noise. Very early in the morning [of 15 September 1916] the battalion marched to the Talus Boisé, a long narrow copse on the southern side of the valley which runs from Carnoy to the Briqueterie near Bernafay Wood. As we marched we could see that some important operations were to take place that day. We passed several squadrons of cavalry and as we had not seen any mounted troops for some months we began to believe that there was now the possibility of breaking through the enemy lines. An intense bombardment had started at 6am.

The storm

At 6.20 on the bright and clear morning of 15 September 1916, fifty battalions rose out of their trenches to attack what had been the third main line of German defences at the start of the Somme offensive. For the first time the British deployed tanks. The plan was to capture the German defences from Martinpuich and along to High Wood, Flers, Lesboeufs and Morval.

The attack in the area of Lesboeufs was largely carried out by the Guards Division supported by the three tanks that made it to the front line. Originally ten were supposed to support the attack. The Guards battalions advanced behind a creeping barrage through which lanes were left for the tanks to travel in, but were met by heavy machine-gun fire from the unsuppressed flank to their right. The Guards suffered very heavy casualties and by the end of the day the line had been carried forward to the third of the four objective lines that the Division had started with. This line was in front of Lesboeufs where the attack was called off for the day at 5pm.

At the Talus Boisé, where the 7th Battalion had moved the heavy fighting could be heard. Captain Jones later recalled:

> Items of news began to filter through. We heard tales of a new landship, which would crash through wire entanglements and cross wide trenches and hopes of a sensational advance were raised. As the morning wore on we heard rumours of a very successful attack on the part of the XIV Corps of which the 20th Division were in reserve. The 6th Division and the Guards Division were said to be making good progress.

At midday on 15 September the 61st Brigade was attached to the Guards Division for use on the southern flank of the Guards Division. At this time it was believed erroneously by the XIV Corps commanders that the Guards' attack had succeeded in capturing Lesboeufs but that the 6th Division to their south had been held up. The plan was to use the relatively fresh 61st Brigade to support the Guards Division and then to interpose the 20th Division into the line between the 6th and Guards Divisions.

The battalion received orders at midday to move with the 61st Brigade to the area of Waterlot Farm. Captain Jones:

> The battalion advanced along the valley south of Delville Wood and took up positions. The companies occupied some trenches while battalion headquarters squatted down in shell holes around the pile of boilers and broken machinery of Waterlot Farm that had been destroyed in the fighting for Guillemont.

Lieutenant Henry Foley recalled the scene:

> At noon however came the order to move up to Waterlot Farm; we were all glad to be doing something definite at last, although there was every likelihood of casualties occurring long before we reached our destination. Slowly we wound our way up, past heavy batteries with their sweating crews, past other troops waiting for orders, past Trônes Wood, passed the dressing stations with their groups of happy, bandaged figures, then the field artillery, spitting away like machine guns. And once past that we were out on that great sea of

shell holes and twisted shattered trees and buildings, the Somme battlefield.

The 'happy, bandaged figures' were undoubtedly soldiers with 'Blighty' injuries – wounded severely enough to be sent back to the safety of Britain ('Blighty'), but not usually so seriously as to cause severe or lasting harm. Captain Jones:

It was a warm afternoon with bright sunshine. The Germans were shelling Delville Wood and Ginchy. A few Indian cavalrymen were seen riding past on their return from the front and now we were able to recognise the engines of war which had caused such a noise during the night. We had a close view of two of the tanks that had come into action for the first time that morning. They were returning from the battle area to refit. These armoured mobile fortresses caused us no end of surprise, they looked so ungainly and heavy, but it was wonderful to see how they negotiated trenches and obstacles.

Lieutenant H Foley continued his recollection:

Evening drew in, and still no orders had reached us. I was standing looking out across the battered ground in front of us, wondering how long it would be before we took our place in that dense cumulus of smoke that marked the battle line, when out of the mist loomed an apparition, the sight of which fairly took my breath away. Slowly it rolled and swayed towards us. For a few tense moments we gasped in dumb and awe-struck amazement; and then it flashed upon us that here before our eyes was one of the new landships. On it came unruffled and undisturbed; and now we could see its gallant commander, sitting in the little doorway in its side. We streamed across and besieged the grinning crew with questions, congratulations and cheers. Having completely flattened an elaborate shelter that Captain Whall, a painstaking man, had spent the afternoon constructing they waddled off happily in their hideous craft to the rear.

By 5pm on 15 September the British attacks had thrown the Germans back for on average one mile across a six-mile front. Captain Jones said:

Our men were chafing rather at the inaction. There was not much cover in the trenches which they were improving and the soil was continually crumbling. As the evening fell the air became cold and there was a fairly bright moonlight. The night was still and there was not much shelling. Rumours began to float around that our Brigade would have to attack the next morning to complete the work begun by the Guards. At 9.45pm orders were received that the Brigade was to attack the next morning at 9.25am.

The 61st Brigade were to form the right flank of the attack with the 3rd Guards Brigade on the left. The 7th Somersets were to form the left of the 61st Brigade attacking line with the 7th DCLI on their right. Orders were quickly given to the company commanders to be ready to move at short notice and there was no opportunity for the officers to reconnoitre the area into which the battalion was going.

Just before midnight guides from the Guards Division arrived to lead the battalion forward. Rations had just been issued to the Somersets before they set out. Sergeant Ellis said: 'After staying there (Guillemont station) till midnight, we heard that the Guards Division were held up and so about 1am we moved off across the scene of our former battlefield'. Captain Jones recalled:

We followed an absolutely unknown route; the guides were frequently at a loss as to which way to proceed, as they had only come to the area the previous evening. Our progress was slow and to add to the discomforts we experienced a heavy shower of rain.

We passed through the ruins of Ginchy where a few blackened trees stretched their broken trunks heavenwards and then followed a track or road. The right hand side of the road rose a few feet and the 'Sets' passed some guardsmen sheltering in the lea of a bank. We saw a fair number of corpses laid out on the edge of the track, and the sight of them in the waning moonlight was not calculated to inspirit any troops advancing to attack.

Our long weary trudge came to an end when we reached a deep German trench occupied by a battalion of the Coldstream Guards. Major Lyon (who was the temporary commanding officer of the battalion) went and interviewed their Colonel. He appeared dissatisfied when he came back to us. The companies were ordered to advance over the trench and dig two lines of trenches to afford cover while awaiting zero hour.

Lieutenant H Foley also recalled the return of Major Lyon:

He explained how and where we were to take up position and bade us carry on. We communicated his instructions to our men, and led them out to the allotted positions some fifty yards in front of the trench.

B and C Companies were deployed in front with a covering party ahead and A and D were in support. Battalion headquarters was situated in the Coldstream Guards' trench. Captain Jones recalled:

> The men began to dig with a will, as signs were not wanting that dawn was at hand. We were digging some 600 yards from the German positions covering Lesboeufs, but were not prepared for the excavation of a new trench – having no picks or shovels. We were compelled to do our best with entrenching tools but it was difficult to dig in a field of standing oats.

Sergeant Ellis said:

> After marching for about an hour we found ourselves being led through the front line and here we started to dig in. It was just getting light and the Bosches soon found us out, for we found we had them back and front. Our men started digging for their lives, but we were in hot soup and our losses were very heavy. The Huns showed their sporting instincts by shooting at our wounded and also at our stretcher bearers.

Captain Jones continued:

> When daylight came little progress had been made and the men improved shell craters to secure shelter. Our positions lay just below the crest of a low ridge which hid the German trenches immediately to our front but we were in view of the enemy's trenches to our right on higher ground about Morval. The Germans spotted the positions and subjected them to accurate machine gun and minenwerfer fire. Heavy casualties suffered.

One of the brave stretcher bearers referred to by Sergeant Ellis was Lance Corporal Haynes, who spent this time dashing back and forth from the British trench into no man's land, dressing the wounded and carrying many back to cover while under fire. He was later mentioned in dispatches by Major-General Douglas-Smith.

B Company managed to dig a makeshift trench in the darkness, but due to an error had to shift their positions to their left and start digging again just before light. The whole battalion was scattered and disorganised. Lieutenant Foley:

> Here we were then, in the early dawn of September 16th, crowded about in any holes we could find, and with a perfect hail of bullets flying overhead and kicking up the dirt all round us, while a light trench mortar was also sending over a desultory shell or two. As soon

as it was light I went back to the old trench behind us and asked Humphries, who was now adjutant, for orders, but they had not then arrived.

At 6am a runner dropped into the shell hole next to Lieutenant Foley with orders to attack. There were two objectives. The first objective was a 'blue line' to the west of Lesboeufs and the battalion was to occupy German positions in front of the village. This attack was to start at 9.30am. The second objective was a line beyond Lesboeufs. This phase of the attack was due to commence at 10am. After clarifying certain aspects with Major Lyon, Lieutenant Foley returned to his company.

Lieutenant Foley continued:

> Finally I had to communicate my orders to my men and this was no easy job. However, I had got about half the company done, when I felt a sharp burning pain. It was not in a very dignified place; in fact I had not experienced anything like it since leaving school. I shot into the next shell hole which contained one of my Lewis gun sections. McCracken who was following close behind me, was just dropping in too when a bullet got him in the arm. The shell crater thus became a sort of impromptu dressing station. We were both at that time in some pain, and for a few moments I lost consciousness. When I came round I felt dizzy and weak. I gave Lance Corporal Morman my orders, and told him to do his best to communicate them to the other men. Then I crawled back to the trench.

The 3rd Guards Brigade, which should have been to the immediate left of the Somersets, was nowhere to be seen. Because of the confusion caused by the previous day's fighting the 3rd Brigade would not be able to move into a position to attack until the afternoon.

Captain Whall, who was standing on the parapet of the Coldstream trench, was hit in the jaw by a bullet. Injured men began to make their way back to the relative safety of the Coldstream Guards' trench. One of these told headquarters staff that Lieutenant Foley, who was in charge of B Company had been hit in the leg. Captain Jones, one of the headquarters staff, went forward into no man's land and later recalled: 'It was almost impossible to move in the oat field as the German fire was accurate and the slightest movement appeared to be noticed and a burst of machine gun fire followed.' Nevertheless, he reached the rearmost companies and found that all officers in A and D Companies had become casualties. He wriggled back through the oat field, reaching Major Lyon to report. A runner was then sent to the Guards battalion to the left of the Somersets in order to find out what they planned to do. He became a casualty and so did the second man sent. After this Major Lyon set out to accomplish the task himself. He too was hit by enemy fire and was severely injured. At this point the battalion adjutant Captain Frederick Humphries was injured.

Sergeant Ellis talked about the enemy fire:

> They kept this up all morning and at about 11.30am I was sent for and it was then that I learned that nearly all the officers were gone and that I was in charge of my company, and that we had to attack at once. [The actual time was more likely just before 9.30am.] It was now a hell on earth. The Bosche aeroplanes had found our trenches and they threw everything at us, shells large and small, machine gun and rifle fire.

By 9.25am only three officers from the battalion remained uninjured – Captain Jones in the headquarters detachment, 2nd Lieutenant Jenne who was now commanding B Company and 2nd Lieutenant Cox who had been commanding C Company until he was found entering a dugout in the Coldstream Guards' trench suffering from shell shock.

The British artillery barrage commenced, falling on the German front-line trench west of Lesboeufs, and a very heavy machine-gun barrage was put down to cover the flanks.

The battalion attacked at 9.35am. From Captain Jones' position all he could do was watch as the men advanced over the crest of the hill out of his line of sight to attack the German trench. Sergeant Ellis was with the attacking soldiers:

> The boys were not long in getting over the brow but before I had got very far I got what I had expected, as it was impossible to keep running about on top without getting something. I soon saw the results of the lads' work for the prisoners began to come in and here a German stretcher bearer helped me back to the dressing station.

To the right of the Somersets the 7th DCLI also attacked. One of the Guards officers, Vedette, who had a vantage point from the right of the attack, later described the scene:

> It is not often in this war that a man can get a comprehensive view of an attack. To the little group of officers, cooped up in their narrow trench, was vouchsafed as grandiose a spectacle as any man had witnessed in this war. Somewhere about the hour of half past nine, a light infantry brigade over on the left attacked, and from their grandstand as the men, delighted, called it the Guards could see every detail of the advance. It was a sight to gladden brave men's eyes! For though the little brown dots went creeping forward up the

distant green slopes were swept away again and again, while across the valley echoed the loud stutter of German machineguns, yet succeeding lines went on. The tiny brown figures seemed literally to be blown away, yet others struggled forward, wave upon wave, until they were lost to view. Through the glasses one could see the wake they had left – little figures crawling about, hobbling, with stretcher bearers darting and ducking to and fro. All the valley now re-echoed to the roar of artillery and the Germans left the Guards alone while they concentrated on the attacking forces. The British supports were seen coming up through a heavy barrage, then the men began to trickle back down the slope strewn with brown figures left in the trail of the advance. What had happened? No one knew. Had the attack failed? No one could say. Little by little the artillery fire slackened, some inquisitive aeroplanes came out and hovered over the scene.

What had happened was that the Somersets and Cornishmen swept over the rise and into the German trenches. To the left of the Somersets Private William Saunders, who was only 18 years old and who had been a brick and tile manufacturer before the war, moved along the flank of the battalion. He quickly came across a German officer who promptly surrendered to him. Private Saunders sent the man back in the direction of the British trenches. He then noticed an enemy machine gun set up in a nearby shell hole and moved quickly towards it capturing both men manning the gun. These too were sent back to British lines.

The attackers quickly overran about 150 yards of trench and started to consolidate their small gain. The trench had been entered by, amongst others, Lance Corporal Hill and Private Barrow and these two men led the bombing party along the trench. While this was going on, one of the battalion's Lewis gunners, Private Hill, and another man moved about sixty yards ahead of the captured German trench with a supply of ammunition drums. His position enabled him to bring enfilading fire on to the Germans who later tried to counter-attack.

Captain Jones said:

I felt quite out of it in the Headquarters trench, for the Coldstream Guards showed no interest in our fight. So at about 10.15am, leaving Corporal Allen in charge of the headquarters party, I took one of the signallers along with me and left the trench. I went forward through the corn and we succeeded in getting through the light enemy barrage which was falling at the time. There were a number of dead and wounded Germans lying in the corn, as if they had crept forward from their trench to shoot our men as they were digging. When I reached the crest I saw our men in the German trench and in the sunken road leading into Lesboeufs. The village nestled in a clump of trees and did not appear seriously damaged by shellfire. I came up to the position that our men had taken, [the enemy trench] had been captured on a front of 150 yards on the left of the road.

There were a few men of A and C Companies at the point where the road intersected the trench. They told me that as no troops were advancing on the left of the battalion, a block had been built at the end of the stretch which the battalion had taken. A bombing fight was taking place there at the moment, and I was told that B Company bombers were holding the enemy at bay. Some of our men were searching for German bombs as our own supply was almost exhausted. The only Germans I could see were a few who showed themselves near our block.

There was no sign of the Guards supposed attack on the left and, other than two stray men from the 7th DCLI who had joined the Somersets, there was no sign of the 7th DCLI on the right. Captain Jones continued:

I went with some men into the trench on the right of the road for a distance of some sixty yards, but found it unoccupied. Then I returned to the road, which became more sunken between the trench and the village. There were a number of dugouts in the bank on the left hand side, and some of our men were examining these dugouts which showed signs of only having been recently commenced. I went forward to see what they were doing, and I found CSM Anderson of A Company with some men from three companies, A, C and D. They had bombed the garrison out of the trench and the dugouts, and Anderson told me that they had taken about thirty prisoners. I asked him if he had seen any of our officers, and he said that 2nd Lieutenant Jenne was somewhere on the left with B Company digging a new trench about 80 yards west of the piece of trench we had captured.

I went along with CSM Anderson down the sunken road to a point where a second sunken road branched off to the left. The CSM had posted a small sentry group here, and the men had shot a few Germans who had emerged from the dugouts in the second road. I thought that this post was too far forward and was likely to be cut off. So we decided to withdraw all the men who were in front of the captured trench and to establish a strong post at the point where the trench crossed the road.

The withdrawal of the men forward of the captured trench was accomplished with the exception of the Lewis gun team which had not received the order and which was left sixty yards ahead.

At this time 2nd Lieutenant Jenne and the men of B Company were carrying out the orders that they had been given to construct a trench to the west of the captured line that was to be used for future actions against the village of Lesboeufs. Captain Jones recalled:

> We could see no Germans in the village, but there was plenty of cover for any that might be lurking there. The enemy fire was directed towards the crest we had crossed in the attack. We brought back a few wounded men with us, and after leaving Anderson at the roadside, I went along the captured trench towards the block where heavy bombing was proceeding. Our bombs had been exhausted, but luckily we found a German bomb store in a dugout in the sunken road and passed on the enemy stick bombs to our bombers on the left. But the enemy were constantly being reinforced from the village along a communication trench or sunken road which lay outside our area.
>
> Suddenly a machine gun opened fire upon us from the left. I turned towards the village and was just in time to see a body of about 50 Germans climb out into the open from the sunken road which ran off to the left. They had counted on finding us engrossed in our bombing contest that they could take us unawares. But we had sentries posted who were not engaged in bombing turned to face the enemy. Rapid fire was opened on the advancing Germans; several fell, their ranks were quickly broken, and the survivors ran in disorder down over the bank.

Shortly after the German counter-attack, some men from the 7th DCLI appeared from the right. Captain MacMillan was able to tell Captain Jones that the original orders had been to dig a trench just west of the captured German trench. Captain Jones: 'I had seen B Company digging a new trench, and I had wondered why they were not consolidating the captured line. Time had been so short that the orders had not been fully handed down'.

The battalion had captured about fifty Germans and two machine guns in their advance and the attacking soldiers were exhausted. Captain Jones:

> Our little group was gradually dwindling in numbers; the German stick-bombs made ghastly wounds. Some of our bombers and bayonet men had their arms torn to ribbons. Our stocks of bombs could not be replenished; we had exhausted also those of the enemy bombs we had discovered. Fresh parties of the enemy were making their way up the communication trench on our left, and their bombing section was being strongly reinforced. As there was no further need of holding on to the captured trench, CSM Anderson and I decided to fall back to a position in line with B Company and the groups attached to it. This we did by withdrawing our men in

sections. We sent a corporal along with the first party and told him to get the men to dig a number of short lengths of trench in continuation of the new battalion line. We moved all of our wounded behind our battalion line; luckily only one of them required carrying. Though we were harassed in this operation by the enemy who tried to mount a machine gun on a tripod at the junction of the two roads, but were frustrated by accurate rifle fire, we managed to get all our men stretched in a line. They were soon busy digging short bits of trench or improving shellholes.

It was impossible to move over the open to the groups on our flanks. All we could do was to shout orders or advice to one another. I could see Jenne on the left with his company, but could not get over to him, as the enemy maintained continuous machine gun and minenwerfer fire. The Germans soon reoccupied the trench which we had evacuated, but made no attempt at further advance. Each of our little groups had by this time succeeded in making a fairly good trench, and for a time we had no casualties. From our new position, which was just below the crest of the slope leading down into the village of Lesboeufs, we had a splendid view of the village and the countryside in its rear. The village with its red tiled roofs looked very demure amid the foliage which surrounded it. It did not appear to be greatly damaged, though the church tower had been sadly battered by our shellfire. Occasionally we could see some Germans moving about in the village, but they did not linger long in sight. Behind the village I was able to distinguish men, whom I took to be civilians, engaged in reaping the corn. This scene seemed incongruous when a battle was raging so near at hand.

I was utterly at a loss to know what was happening elsewhere. The German machine gun fire rained on us from both flanks. Soon after midday a company of the 12th King's came up behind us and began to dig in some 150 yards to our rear. But no one came as far forward as our line, for the machineguns were sweeping the ground. However the presence of some support gave us a new feeling of greater security.

At 1.30pm the 3rd Guards Brigade attacked on the left of the Somersets' positions, four hours and five minutes late. They had no supporting artillery and attacked against unsuppressed machine guns. The 1st Grenadier Guards and the 1st Welsh Guards made no headway and, after suffering heavy casualties, simply halted their attack and dug themselves in. Captain Jones:

About 1.30pm the Germans began to shell our new line rather heavily, mostly with low bursting shrapnel. We had several men

100

wounded for the enemy had got our range very accurately. At 2pm CSM Anderson and I were attending to a man who had been wounded in the leg, when I was struck in the neck by a piece of shrapnel. I felt a most curious sensation; it seemed like a sharp, warm sting, and then blood began to pour over my tunic from a deep cut just below the ear. A stretcher bearer was at hand, and he used my field dressing to bind my wound, but the flow of blood could not be immediately staunched. I remained in the shell hole position for another half hour, and as the shelling had decreased and no movement on the enemy's part could be observed, I decided to make my way back to the battalion headquarters detachment in the Coldstream trench. I left CSM Anderson in charge of the groups, but he himself was wounded in the thigh about an hour later. I began to walk up the road and reached the company of the King's without difficulty, but from this point over the crest towards Ginchy my journey was fraught with peril. This area was far more thoroughly searched by enemy machine gun fire than our shell hole positions had been. I had to crawl through the corn to battalion headquarters trench, where the Coldstream Guards looked more stolid than ever. The trench was now full of troops, Coldstream, Somerset and King's Headquarters.

One soldier who later received the Distinguished Conduct Medal for carrying messages between the Somersets' position under the heavy enemy fire was Private Strang. Before the war began, he had been a pupil teacher at a boys' school and the pupils were later enthralled by an account of his daring exploits. For carrying wounded through the enemy fire, Private George Delmont was Mentioned in Dispatches. He was also injured sufficiently seriously to get him back to Stockport Hospital within days.

Second Lieutenant Cox was with the headquarters staff in the Coldstreams' trench. He had become aware of the high casualty rate amongst the officers and had sent for Major Preston-Whyte to take command of the battalion. Meanwhile Captain Jones resumed his journey to the casualty clearing station at Heilly. Captain Jones said: 'Here I met Captain Humphries, the adjutant, who told me that Major Lyon had succumbed to his wounds. Within four days I was back in Blighty.'

The battalion was relieved that night and retired to trenches near Bernafay Wood. Lieutenants Jenne and Betterley were awarded the Military Cross for their parts in the battle that had claimed the lives of sixty-five men from the battalion[2] including the temporary commanding officer, Major Lyon. Lance Corporal Shell, the battalion mess orderly who had guided Captain Jones to the battalion earlier that year was amongst the dead. Nine officers and ninety-nine men were injured. Sergeant

Symington, an excellent rifle shot who had worked as a cutter before the war, who had taken command of his company when all of the officers had been killed or injured, was awarded the Military Medal. The battalion had taken fifty prisoners and captured two machine guns. There is no estimate of the number of enemy killed or injured.

For one man from the battalion the battle only ended on 17 September after thirty-six hours of fighting. Twelve hours after the Somersets had been relieved, Private Hill from B Company, who had set up his defensive Lewis gun position with his colleague in front of the German trench, returned to the newly dug British trenches. He had helped fend off enemy counter-attacks until his Lewis gun had run out of ammunition and his colleague had been killed. Through all this he was unaware that his battalion had departed and was surprised to find Shropshire men in the trenches on his return with the empty ammunition drums and his gun.

Upon moving out of the line, it would normally be the duty of the officers to write letters of condolence to the relatives of those killed. After what Colonel Troyte-Bullock later described as 'a platoon and section commander's battle', there were few officers left to do this. The parents of Reg Brooks, a Lewis gunner from Bridgwater, were written to by Sergeant Allen:

> Dear Sir, Just a line to let you know about your poor son Reg. I was with him in one of the offensive movements that our battalion made on the Germans on September 16th. We had advanced about a thousand yards and were well in touch with the enemy. Reg was with his team of machine gunners with my company and was doing wonderful work. We had the enemy retiring all along the line and Reg was simply sweeping them down when a sniper caught him, but I can tell you he felt no pain, as he died instantaneously with his hand still holding his gun. He was a fine gunner and a splendid soldier – always ready to do his part – and our company will miss him very much.

Reg Brooks was 34 years old and had worked at the Bridgwater water works before enlisting at one of the recruiting rallies at the beginning of the war. Not all the casualties were men originally with the battalion. Private William Holland from Bath, a 35-year-old signwriter who had worked with his father, had only been with the battalion for six weeks when he was killed in this attack.

Many relatives were not so fortunate as to receive accurate information quickly. Lance Corporal Arthur Jeanes' relations could only be told that he had last been seen wounded and was now missing. He had in fact died of the injuries he sustained. The wife of Sergeant William Hunt from South Street in Taunton received official notification that her husband had been injured and little else until she later found out that he had been killed. Sergeant Hunt had been with the battalion since its formation and had been promoted to sergeant in February 1915. He had only been allowed one short leave just before Christmas 1915 after fifteen months with the battalion.

The heavens opened on 18 September. Heavy rain fell all day and the next. The soldiers had moved to Talus Boisé – a long strip of woodland east of Carnoy – where they stayed until the 19th. The battalion had suffered 175 casualties in the attack and needed to be reorganised, and this was carried out as far as was possible at the time. On 20 September the men moved to the Citadel, a large military camp that was frequently used by battalions moving out of the line. Here the men were issued with a change of clothes and then, on the 22nd, moved on to billets at Méaulte where they remained until 25 September. The battalion was further reorganised during this time as a welcome draft of experienced North and West Somerset Yeomanry joined the battalion.

As with any battle, the deaths from wounds continued after the fighting had stopped. On Sunday 17 September 21-year-old Private Frederick Dawkins, who had worked in the furniture business in Taunton, died of wounds. He was another of the battalion's Lewis gunners. He had only written to his parents telling them how he had escaped harm in the attack on Guillemont:

> I suppose you have heard of the big advance which took place a few days ago. Well I am proud to say that I was in it and came out safe. Only another fellow and myself came back out of two gun teams. We also lost a gallant officer. We advanced a mile and a half.

Casualties from the front were often quickly transported away to hospitals in France and, if they were fit to move, were sent by hospital ship to the UK. Sergeant Frank Ellis, who had been injured on Saturday the 16th, was back in England by Thursday on a hospital train bound for Newport in Wales. The train passed through Bath at about half past four that afternoon, stopping at the station for a while. Frank Ellis quickly scribbled a note for a station porter to carry over Halfpenny Bridge to his wife who was working in their sweet shop in Claverton Street just across the river from the station. Mrs Ellis, who was managing the shop, heard shouting and looked out to see her husband in the waiting train, the first that she knew that he had been injured. She was able to see him briefly before the train departed for Newport.

While convalescing at the Western General Hospital in Newport, Ellis was interviewed by a journalist from the *Bath Chronicle*:

> I can scarcely think what the outcome of this fighting is going to lead

to, for having been out there early in the war, I, with a great many more, never dreamt that we should ever see the Germans in such a sorry plight as they are now. Of course they are still putting up a fight in places, but it's only in places where they got good shelter and, as soon as you get near them they throw the sponge up and want to shake hands with all.

It is very hard fighting now, but the lads all hope they will not have to go back to trench warfare. Probably some wonder why we don't advance quicker, but our guns are the things that have beat the Huns and when we have gone a certain distance we dig in and let the guns move up. The work of our guns is terrible. It is wonderful how the aeroplanes and the artillery work together. I don't think that the German shells are as good as they were. The land torpedoes (Sergeant Ellis refers to Tanks) are a help but nothing to make a fuss over. Our boys wonder the Germans don't use their beloved barbed wire now but I don't think they have any left. Our boys are pleased with the little gifts from Bath. I was wearing socks made by Bath ladies and the writing pad I had in my pocket was from Bath when I was hit. And now, Bath readers, if there is anything for these lads, don't forget that the fag ration is not so great as it was. The men find them a great comfort in action and the first thing a wounded man flies for. Lemonade powder is most useful out there now as the water is not very good and with so much shelling the men get so thirsty.

Not all casualties who were evacuated enjoyed such happy endings. On Friday 22 September 23-year-old Private Robert Knight died of wounds at the London Casualty Clearing Station in France. He was married with two young children and had been with the battalion since October 1914. On Sunday 24 September Private John Millard from Gloucestershire also died of wounds as did Lance Corporal William Fowler. Fowler was a former Great Western Railway worker. He had been a reservist called up at the beginning of the war and been involved in early fighting when he had been bayoneted in the leg by a German. He recovered and joined the 7th Battalion in November 1915.

To the east the Somme offensive continued after the 20th Division had moved out of the line. The attacks were initially sporadic and only gradually pushed the British lines forward. On Monday 25 September a major attack was delivered by the XIVth Corps with heavy artillery support. The German front was broken and the villages of Lesboeufs and Morval were captured. The Germans fell back from what had been the third defensive line at the beginning of the offensive on to another line that they had started preparing. This became known as the Transloy Line and consisted of newly dug trenches to the west of the village of Le Transloy. Plans were immediately drawn up for the capture of this line.

Retrospective

The attack on 16 September was one of the least successful operations the 61st Brigade had been involved in. It had been ordered by General Rawlinson, the commander of the Fourth Army, on the evening of 15 September. Rawlinson required an attack at 9.25am all along the line, to be 'pushed home with the utmost vigour . . . to enable the Cavalry Corps to push through to its objectives and complete the enemy's defeat'. The orders were expected to be carried through largely by soldiers who had been involved in the previous day's fighting and no time was allowed to let the artillery register the new front-line positions. They were not able to register targets using maps at this stage of the war, and it took time to register the accuracy of each gun before reliable barrages could be fired. Another problem that made the registration of the guns more difficult was that the targets were mainly on the reverse slope of the hill. Poor weather also hampered quick registration because of bad visibility.

The reason behind the hastily prepared attack was to capitalise on the serious blow the enemy had suffered the day before when tanks were deployed, and also to carry this line before the enemy could strengthen it further. The result of the orders for the 16th was that the 7th SomLI and the 7th DCLI to their right were sent into no man's land as they came into the front line, with orders to dig trenches overnight and without previously being told to bring entrenching equipment. The men were then exposed at dawn to fire from the unsuppressed enemy positions and from unchecked artillery which caused many casualties. The orders for the attack were issued while the men were under fire and when very few officers were left. Only 2nd Lieutenant Jenne, who assumed command of B Company after Lieutenant Foley was injured, appears to have had a clear idea of these orders of attack and consolidation, with the orders not even being passed fully to Captain Jones at battalion headquarters.

The attack was supported by the creeping barrage, and to this extent the 61st Brigade battalions were more fortunate than those of the 3rd Guards Brigade who attacked later in the day unsupported. Despite the creeping barrage, it is clear that the two battalions attacked on such a narrow front that, although their immediate front was substantially suppressed and captured, enfilading fire caused many casualties. This problem would have been reduced if the other Brigades that had been ordered to attack had done so at 9.25am. The whole battle front was too chaotic to allow this.

One of the more interesting aspects of the attack was the extent to which the soldiers of the battalion – the NCOs and infantrymen – were able to carry the attack without many officers being present for leadership. It must be seen as testimony to the good training within the Brigade (at least) that this was possible.

The attack cost the battalion 175 men killed or injured, a substantial proportion of its strength, given the casualties that it had sustained at Guillemont. The casualties included most of its officers and many of the specialists. The battalion had captured the German trench and held it long enough to dig a new position eighty yards behind it, and it was able to hold this position until relieved. This new trench would remain the front line until 25 September when Lesboeufs was captured in a better co-ordinated attack. Despite the delay, which permitted the Germans more time to prepare their defences, the value of a well planned attack is clearly demonstrated.

The position gained by the 7th SomLI and 7th DCLI was significant in that it amounted to an advance over the hill crest line that permitted observation of the German defences which would assist the later attack. When compared to Rawlinson's initial orders for the day, the attacks by the 61st Brigade and others along the front are bound to have been viewed with disappointment. The German line was not broken, the cavalry did not pass through to the green fields beyond.

NOTES

1   On 4 September Privates Fred Mullet, John Iles and John Singleton died of wounds; on 9 September 19-year-old Private William Lacey died from a severe chest wound at a hospital in Rouen, and Private Robert Simpson also died of wounds; on 10 September Private Thomas Dunning and Private Sidney Willcox a railway man and keen cricketer died of injuries. One man, Private Scott Charlest, died on 11 September from injuries received in the Guillemont attack. He had been previously wounded in June 1916. He left a wife and five children. Private William Coles died of wounds on 11 September and Lance Corporal Henry Coles died on 12 September.

2   The soldiers killed were Private Charles Atkinson, Lance Corporal Edward Barber, Private Reginald Barker, Private James Bird, Private Reginald Blake, Private Charles Bray, Private Reginald Brooks, Private Walter Browning, Private Frederick Bryan, Sergeant James Bucks, Private Albert Burr, Private Alfred Cannon, Private John Carrott, Private George Clarke, Private Charles Coombs, Private Albert Davis, Private Henry Davis, Lance Sergeant William Davis, Sergeant Edward Dudden, Private George Durbin, Private Arthur Edney, Private Archie Evans, Private George Garland, Private Edward Gillman, Private William Gould, Sergeant George Groombridge, Private William Groves, Private Alfred Hanson, Private Thomas Hayward, Lance Corporal Joseph Hemingway, Lance Corporal Robert Hodgson, Private Edward Holland, Private William Holland, Private Sidney Hosegood, Sergeant William Hunt, Private Arthur Hyatt, Lance Corporal Thomas Jeanes, Private George Jenkins, Private Frederick Jones, Private Paul Jones, Private Mathew Kell, Private Thomas Kell, Private John Lamb, Private Edwin Lloyd, Major Edward Lycett Lyon, Private Arthur Mitchell, Lance Corporal Cuthbert Odams, Lance Corporal William Osborne, Sergeant Arthur Parker, Private George Parsons, Private Charles Payton, Lance Corporal George Poleyhelt, Private Richard Raggatt, Private Samuel Rice, Sergeant Ernest Richards, Lance Corporal Frederick Robson, Private Anthony Scriven, Lance

Corporal Ernest Shell, Private Albert Smith, Corporal Albert Sugar, Private Lionel Sulley, Lance Corporal Stanley Walker, Private Edwin Warren, Lance Corporal George White and Sergeant Albert Woodward. On Monday 18 September Private Frank Coward died of wounds.

CHAPTER IX
To the Green Fields Beyond

Planning the final battle

The offensive operations that were carried out while the 61st Brigade were away from the front line carried the British front forward to a position of low ground facing a ridge line that became known as the Le Transloy Ridges. The British attacks had captured a significant length of the Germans' hastily constructed defensive line forcing them back to new positions along and principally behind the ridges. Beyond the ridge lay the villages of Le Transloy and Beaulencourt.

It was evident from the recent fighting that the quality of the German units facing the British attacks had deteriorated to a very poor level. Six under-strength divisions of the German 1st Army held nearly 9,000 yards of front-line trenches from Le Transloy village, north to the village of Warlencourt. The German defenders had been repeatedly battered by attacks and forced back on to new positions. Their trenches were not fully protected by barbed wire and inadequate dugouts had been made to shelter from the British guns. There was an element of disorganisation in the command structure too, as new units were fed in haphazardly to fill gaps, rather than in any planned manner.

Sir Douglas Haig had seen significant and repeated advances during September, and also saw the state of the defences and soldiers facing his men. He started to plan the final attacks to break the German resistance. On 29 September plans were issued from General Headquarters that involved a broad attack by British and Commonwealth units south of Gommecourt and along the whole line. The plan envisaged a twenty-mile penetration of the defensive positions, carrying the British to Cambrai.

A necessary preliminary operation was the capture of the Le Transloy line. This was to be achieved as quickly as possible to prevent the Germans from improving their defences any further. A system of trenches had already been dug covering Le Transloy and Beaulencourt, and although the Germans were digging hard, no substantial trench network existed behind the main line.

The Le Transloy line

On 25 September 1916 the 7th Battalion Somersets moved with the 61st Brigade from Carnoy to the Citadel. The next day they moved forward again, this time to the Quadrilateral, part of a trench system captured from the Germans in recent fighting. The Brigade was returning to front-line duty, with the 7th Battalion in reserve. The battalion remained in this area until 30 September. Sustained German artillery fire killed two men and injured twenty three.[1]

As a preliminary to the attack on the main German line, a good 'jumping off' point needed to be established. This involved an advance of the British trench system up the slope towards the ridge, without actually attacking the German trenches. This would also identify the defensive barrages of the German artillery and location of their guns. On 1 October there were plans by the Fourth Army to attack the area of Le Sars to the north of the positions occupied by the 61st Brigade, and it was thought that it would be useful to combine the advance with the general attack to the north.

The advance began at 3.15pm on Sunday 1 October under a heavy barrage, with the 7th Somersets on the right and the 7th DCLI on their left. The plan was for parties to advance and dig a new trench about 200 yards from the German positions in some ground that was not exposed to German fire.

Leading the advance was Lieutenant Steele, an officer who had only recently joined the battalion. In the confusing battlefield, he led the men too far forward and they came upon the German trench. He was last seen standing on the parapet of the enemy trench firing his revolver until he was shot down. Command of the leading line of men fell to Lance Corporal Tucker, who quickly took over and rallied some of the men who had begun to fall back on the left, leading them back to their objective line where they began to dig in on the dead ground.

The Germans counter-attacked several times leaving the Somersets to down tools, pick up rifles and drive off the attacking parties. The Germans were unable to dislodge their new neighbours who managed to construct the new trenches as planned. The overall advance resulted in twelve men being killed and twenty-nine injured.[2] That evening it began to rain as men from the 84th Field Company Royal Engineers and the 11th DLI moved up to consolidate the new trench system by linking the various trenches dug during the day. Throughout the next twenty-four hours the Germans regularly shelled the old British front line near battalion headquarters.

The battalion would remain in the new front-line trench or in support until 4 October. Enemy shellfire was incessant. It injured forty men and killed another five including 32-year-old factory worker Ernest Reed who had only been in the army for four months as a private and had joined the battalion three days before he was killed. Ernest Reed's brother had recently been killed. He left a wife and two young children.[3]

On 4 October the battalion was relieved. Due two days' rest, it moved out of the line in the rain and mud to a camp near Carnoy. Before the relief, Private Archibald Vickery, a 19-year-old from Taunton, was severely injured. He died the next morning. The battalion remained near Carnoy on Thursday 5 October, the same day that Private Dennis Webb died of wounds. The battalion had suffered twenty men killed and 100 injured in the preceding ten days, simply in occupying the front line and in the short preparatory advance on 1 October.

The attack on the Le Transloy Ridge trenches had been due to start on 5 October, but was postponed because of the bad weather of the preceding days. It was now scheduled for 7 October. The 7th Battalion, along with the rest of the 61st Brigade, had been earmarked for a role in the coming offensive earning them two extra days' rest. While the battalion was out of the line the British barrage in support of the attack started on the afternoon of 6 October. The gunners found great difficulty in plotting the fall of their shells because poor weather sharply reduced visibility.

On the morning of Friday 6 October the 61st Brigade concentrated at Carnoy, returning to the front line that evening. The 7th Somersets went into Rose and Leek trenches, to the south-east of Gueudecourt, to the sound and sight of the British barrage of the German positions. To the right of the 61st Brigade was the 60th Brigade; to their left the 37th Brigade of the 12th (Eastern) Division.

The Brown Line

The plan for the next day, 7 October, was the capture of positions in front of and along the ridge line that would give the British a view over the German defensive positions to be attacked later. The first objective was the capture of Rainbow Trench on the nearside slope; the second objective was Cloudy Trench that ran along the ridge line – the Brown Line. The 7th SomLI were in support for the attack, with two companies behind the 12th King's who were on the left and two behind the 7th KOYLI who were on the right.

At 11.30 on the morning of 7 October a German aviator flew low over the lines undoubtedly spotting the assembling soldiers. A heavy fire was opened up by the German artillery on the British support positions to the right of the Somersets. The Ox & BucksLI battalion suffered casualties as a result. Patrols that had been sent into no man's land that morning discovered that the enemy wire had hardly been damaged at all and so further bombardments of no man's land were ordered to try to make passages through the wire.

At 1.45pm a stationary barrage was put down on both Rainbow and Cloudy trenches. Two minutes later a creeping barrage was set down in front of the attacking battalions and the men left their trenches. The assaulting battalions advanced with two companies side by side in front and two side by side behind. Each company formed itself into two waves so that in all there were four waves formed by each battalion. On the right the 60th Brigade attack came under heavy fire as soon as they reached the crest of the slope to their front where they ran into poorly cut wire. Although they suffered terrible casualties, the third and fourth waves carried the faltering first two waves and Rainbow Trench was captured. To the left of the 61st Brigade, the 37th Brigade almost immediately came under a heavy defensive barrage and had great difficulty in advancing.

When the 61st Brigade advanced, the men quickly became exposed to enemy rifle and machine-gun fire from their left flank which caused many casualties. Fortunately for them the wire to their front had been cut more effectively by the artillery fire, and quicker progress was made. The 7th Battalion moved up behind the 12th Kings and the 7th KOYLIs occupying their starting trenches with orders to move forward and help consolidate Rainbow Trench in the afternoon if that trench had been taken.

From their vantage point the Somersets were able to see the two attacking battalions advance. As they neared Rainbow Trench, many Germans could be seen coming forward with their hands up. To the left-hand side where the 37th Brigade had failed to make headway, the resistance was stronger and a short hand-to-hand battle ensued. The 61st Brigade Diary recounted: 'the extraordinary spectacle, in one portion of the line was seen, of the two lines (our own and the enemy) meeting, a moment's hesitation, succeeded by our advance and a large return of the enemy under escort as prisoners'.

With Rainbow Trench in British hands, the Somersets had the task of securing the new position, while the assaulting battalions re-formed in order to attack Cloudy Trench. The second phase of the attack was to be carried out in three waves, with the third and fourth waves of the attack on Rainbow Trench forming the first and second waves in the attack on Cloudy Trench. The first two waves in the initial attack regrouped to form the third wave in the new attack.

At 2.05pm the second creeping barrage opened up in front of Rainbow Trench and moved ahead towards Cloudy Trench and the Brown Line objective. The men of the 12th King's and the 7th KOYLI advanced again, leaving a few machine gunners and men to help the Somersets consolidate Rainbow Trench. The advance went much better with the men closing with the second trench line quickly. A few Germans remained in their trenches throwing bombs at the attackers, but were quickly overrun by the two battalions. Cloudy Trench was found to consist of very shallow excavations and many Germans were killed here by the barrage and

1. Colonel Troyte-Bullock. On leave from India at the start of the war, he took command of the 7th Somersets. He became one of the very few officers to command an infantry battalion almost throughout the whole war.

2 and **3.** Off to war. Battalion soldiers board a train at Amesbury on 24 July 1915. No 2 (top) shows Captain Hatt (nearest camera). No 3 (bottom) shows Colonel Troyte-Bullock (in trench coat) overseeing the loading.

4. The battle of Guillemont. The loading post on the Montauban-Guillemont road where casualties were transferred from stretcher to ambulance – during the attack many wounded were carried here from the front line via the advanced dressing stations. (Q 4246 IWM)

5. Guillemont High Street after the fighting. In the heat of battle the 7th Somersets moved across this area to form up for their attack. (Q 4225 IWM)

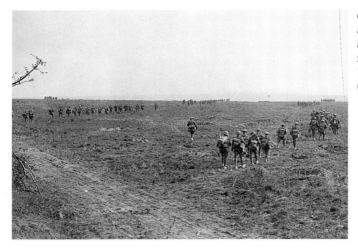

6. British soldiers in artillery formation advancing to battle near Guillemont, 15– 22 September 1916. (Q 4235 IWM)

7. Winter on the Somme. The alternate ice and muddy thaws made front-line conditions appalling. Here duck-board tracks are used by soldiers taking their turn. (E AUS 138)

8. The dreaded Steenbeek. The front-line on 16 August 1917 – defended by a series of German pill boxes including the Au Bon Gite blockhouse. (Q 17654 IWM)

9. British soldiers, probably from the 38th (Welsh) Division, making their way over Pilckem Ridge on 16 August 1917 in support of the advance on Langemarck. Note the vulnerable communication cables. (Q 2708 IWM)

10. A captured pill box and German shell fire on Pilckem Ridge. This photograph was taken on 17 August 1917, the day after the assault on Langemarck. (Q 2707 IWM)

11. A British female tank crushing barbed wire entanglements. Effective use of tanks rendered German trench systems vulnerable to attack, although their limited speed and range made breakthroughs difficult. (Q 6424 IWM)

12. Captains McMurtrie (left) and Foley as prisoners of war. Strict and often harsh discipline, poor food and the influenza epidemic made life difficult for POW's.

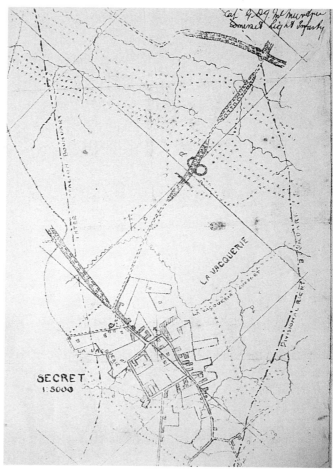

13. A secret map issued to officers before the Cambrai offensive. This one shows the Somersets' objectives and known German defences – trenches (solid lines), strongpoints (circles with arrows) and barbed wire (dotted lines).

14. La Vacquerie village. Stormed by the 7th Somersets on 20 November 1917 in the Cambrai offensive. (Q 45639 IWM)

15. 20th Division machine gunners with French infantry in hastily dug defences on 25 March 1918. The shattering German offensive meant many units disintegrated or became intermixed. (Q 1081 IWM)

16. Remnants of the 59th and 60th Brigades of the 20th Division, together with French soldiers, occupied Roye on 25 March 1918. The British soldiers are probably the remaining survivors of a battalion after the bitter fighting. (Q 10823 IWM)

17. Officers reunion in 1963. Standing left to right: J Scott, H Langdon, (Col Read), W B Giles, T G Jenne, A A Andrews, (Mrs Troyte-Bullock), H A Foley, (Col Hunt, Col Urwick, Col Graham), H Rowe, G R Colsey, S F Male; seated: L A Phelps (left), E F Blake (right). Honorary members in brackets.

attacking infantry. By 2.15pm the whole objective had been captured and the advance battalions were digging in, improving the shallow positions they had captured.

Meanwhile, it had been discovered that a gap of three to four hundred yards had opened up between the two Brigades of the 20th Division and to the left the enemy machine-gun and rifle fire persisted. C Company of the 7th Somersets was ordered to fill the gap and link up with the 12th Rifle Brigade (60th Brigade) which was done. C Company suffered forty-three casualties in the process.

Two platoons of A Company were ordered forward to take up positions on the unsupported left flank. At this time there was only one officer left in A Company and Sergeant Parker had command of the two platoons. The two platoons from A Company met a strong counter-attack but were able to drive it off. Sergeant Parker received the Military Medal for his work.

The remaining half of A and the whole of D Companies remained in and consolidated Rainbow Trench. B Company had been given the task of holding a trench to the left of Rainbow Trench running back towards the original British line to protect the left flank as the attack by the 37th Brigade had failed to make headway.

There were no more counter-attacks that day and the Germans contented themselves with shelling and machine-gunning the newly won positions. By the end of the day the battalion had suffered a total of 107 casualties, including ten dead. Joe Sears, the Company Sergeant-Major of B Company was killed, as was 26-year-old Private Stephen Hawkins from D Company who was hit in the head by a piece of shrapnel.[4] Sergeant Shortman wrote to Private Hawkins' widow:

> It was a terrible blow to me, and to all the boys in his company, as he was liked by all who knew him. We have lost a good and brave comrade who died doing his duty. We received a parcel for him yesterday, and I cannot express how I felt when I opened it. It was shared amongst his chums, as you would never have received it had it been returned. I am enclosing a few shillings which were found upon him, and I sincerely trust you will receive same. I have lost a dear chum; may he rest in peace and may God give you the strength to bear the burden which he has put upon you and his dear children so suddenly.

Seven officers were injured, including Captain Cartwright and Lieutenants Doherty, Parsons, Watts, Knight, Ross and Betterley. Most were new to the battalion, replacing casualties from the 16 September attack.

The battalion remained in Rainbow Trench for the rest of the day and also on 8 October. On the 7th Herbert Alford from Drayton, another former West Somerset Yeoman, died of injuries. The 7th Somersets were relieved on the night of the 8th by men from the 6th Division. Overall the attacks on 7 October had failed, even though in places – such as where the 61st Brigade attacked – local successes were achieved.

The battalion arrived at Montauban on 9 October where they were able to have a hot meal and then move on to Méaulte for a rest after their part in the battle. The battalion remained at Méaulte for the next five days and, while here, another four men died.[5]

On 11 October the battalion received a draft of 400 men, mostly from the Yeomanry. Two days later another draft of 140 men joined. As usual with new drafts, a lot of reorganisation took place, with the new and old members of the battalion being put through their paces in musketry, Lewis guns, bomb throwing and first aid. On 13 October Lord Cavan, the XIVth Corps commander, inspected each of the Brigades in the 20th Division who formed a ceremonial parade, and congratulated them on the part that they had played in the Somme battles. He praised the 61st Brigade for the part it had played in the capture of Guillemont and actions on 16 September when attached to the Guards Division. Lord Cavan said:

> I have asked the Army Commander and the Commander-in-Chief not to take away the 20th Division if they can help it, and they have promised to do their best. I would not lose the 20th Division for crowns and crowns.

The Somme battles were over for the division.

The beginning of winter on the Somme

On 15 October the battalion moved to Corbie and then to Allonville on the 19th. The weather had become wet and stormy. On 20 October they marched to Vaux-les-Amiens where the men stayed until 31 October. The 20th Division had been withdrawn for a rest. Throughout this time the men trained and entered into competitions in a variety of events with other battalions in the 61st Brigade and the Division. Football was popular as was running, boxing and tug of war. The battalion beat the 12th Kings at football.

The inter-battalion rivalry continued into other activities, such as one night when Vic Taverner a private in A Company, spotted a beer barrel standing at the back door of an estaminet. CSM Bulson wrote:

> Vic spotted it and without much ado gave it a push, and rolling down the slope it landed in a heap of manure, which was one of the usual back door features. Retrieving it from there, carrying and rolling, he

114

got the barrel to A Company's billet and with the aid of an entrenching tool, the head was knocked in. Canteens were soon filled and everybody was well away. The empty cask was hidden beneath some straw at the billet, and the next day when the hue and cry came nobody knew anything. The best of the joke was that the roll of the barrel could be traced towards where the 12th Kings were billeted and led to a false scent.

During this period of divisional rest, the soon-to-become-famous troupe of showmen called the 'Verey Lights' was formed. This troupe provided entertainment for the Division until its disbandment in 1919.

Training continued with the Lewis gunners, snipers and bombers undergoing specialist instruction. The men practised trench digging and also putting down a smoke barrage using phosphorous grenades.

On 1 November the battalion marched to new billets at Riencourt. The same day Private Henry Webber died from injuries in England. He had previously served in the West Somerset Yeomanry. The time spent at Riencourt was similar to that at Vaux. The men trained in a variety of skills, including bayonet fighting and a counter-attack on a trench at night. The sporting events continued with the battalion winning the divisional football competition. On 12 November the 61st Brigade held a race meeting. Various entries were contributed by the four battalions. Lieutenant Jenks recalled:

That glorious late autumn, clear blue sky, unflecked by shrapnel clouds, only an occasional plane; the dark green woods of spruce and larch, pitilessly topped for jumps for the chasers, the strings of G.S. [general service] lorries packed with excited officers and men; the gay blues and crimsons of French staff officers; marquees with welcome bottles, and wonder of wonders, a real military band. Shades of Goodwood and Ascot – what are your glories to such as these? Does Geoffrey Gilbey remember his win on his mettlesome grey, I wonder? Never shall I forget 'Saint's' good showing in the 'Scramble' with Tim Hill up, in a field of twenty nine.

But what of Malpas? Malpas made a book! And like most of the fraternity, he made it pay – till the last race. That race, no, not race, melee would be more applicable to the event for mules. Malpas laid one bet only – 10 to 1 the field – accepted, to his amazement, by a battery sergeant who took 500 to 50 francs. That NCO knew his mule – it scattered contestants, spectators and everything within reach – it passed the post like a 5.9, and Malpas' book came unstuck.

The battalion remained out of the line until 10 December occasionally moving to new camps and continuously engaged in training. Skills in night-time manoeuvres by compass, attacking trenches and defending woods at night were all developed. It had become very cold and snow covered fields and trees formed a backdrop much of the time. On 1 December Private Robert Thornton, formerly of the Army Veterinary Corps, died. On 9 December the men had whale oil (to reduce trench foot) applied to their feet in preparation for a return to the trenches. The December weather had become very cold. Winter had started early in 1916.

On 10 December the 7th Somersets returned to the front line near Guillemont, relieving the 10th KRRC on 12 December. The weather was atrocious, with the men's movements severely restricted by deep mud that sucked their boots off. Many soldiers had to be dug out as they would become stuck. To add to the misery, the Germans frequently shelled the forward areas and on 13 December three men were killed.[6] Because of the appalling conditions, the 20th Division was reorganised at this time into two groups of six battalions each, with a view to reducing the time spent by each battalion in the front line.

On occupying the front line again, the usual routines were resumed. Sergeant Major Bulson said:

> On the Somme where the mud was thickest, holding a line facing Le Transloy, we had relieved another battalion at night. There was no communication trench between the supports and front lines owing to the nature of the ground and the only means of communication by day was by field telephone to battalion headquarters, which was nearly two miles back. About one hour after the relief had taken place I set out from headquarters alone to visit Lewis gun positions in the line (at that time I was battalion Lewis gun sergeant) and found my way first of all to the company in support. From there I followed the beaten track through the vile sticky mud towards the front line and had struggled three parts of the way when I came across one of C Company's fellows lying exhausted. Poor chap, he had sprained both his ankles trying to tug his gum boots out of the mud and was properly bogged. I tried to help him but could not do so. He said 'And I've got the company's jar of rum here too', and there it was in a sandbag covered with mud, and weighing like two. I took that on and told him I would report to his company and get help sent to him, which I did. It was a relief to C Company Sergeant Major when I dropped into his trench with the jar intact (and I didn't have a drink).

While Sergeant Major Bulson was visiting the Lewis gunners a patrol had been sent out into no man's land. Colonel Troyte-Bullock would later write:

Sergeant Dawson who had always been a keen patroller went out into no man's land as soon as the relief was completed to look at the wire. He got some way into no man's land when he got hopelessly bogged and unable to move. He was found by a party of five Bosches who proceeded to pull him out. He, of course expected to be taken off to the Hun lines, but not a bit of it. They informed him that they were his prisoners and demanded to be taken across to our trenches. Sergeant Dawson had hopelessly lost his way and said so, but they said it was quite allright as they knew the way and conducted him back to our advanced battalion headquarters. On the way they picked up another of our men, also bogged, and took him along with them. Major Preston-Whyte (temporarily in command of the battalion) was somewhat surprised when the sentry shouted down there were five Huns coming down the stairs.

Sergeant Major Bulson:

After visiting the gun posts I started back towards battalion headquarters again, but did not get far before falling into the second in command, Major Preston-Whyte. He had turned an old Bosche dugout into an advanced headquarters and would not let me go any further as it was breaking day and I should have been exposed to the enemy. I went into this dugout, sat down at the signallers' table done up after wandering about all night and dropped straight off to sleep. The next thing I remembered was the Major shaking my shoulder and saying 'Sergeant Bulson, search these prisoners,' and on opening my eyes there were two Germans standing beside me. I wondered where on earth I was for a minute. On searching them I found that both were holders of the Iron Cross and actually carried their medals about with them in their pockets as well as wearing the black and white ribbon. They were evidently both brave men and picked for the patrol they were out on when collared. Incidentally while being escorted back, the party found the fellow I left in the mud and two prisoners had to carry him.

The battalion was relieved on 14 December going the next day to a hut camp at Carnoy. The Germans shelled the trenches heavily while the relief was taking place. Major Wardlaw, Lieutenant Betterley and three other soldiers were injured and Private James Salter was killed.

Before the relief Private Benjamin Gaylard from Stoke-under-Ham in Somerset had been found by his comrades sitting up in the trench quite dead. His feet were frozen and with no visible sign of injury his death was attributed to 'shell shock', although exposure is more likely. Benjamin Gaylard had only recently married. After the very short spell in the trenches, the battalion medical officer had thirty-two cases of trench foot reported.

On 18 December the battalion returned to the front line for what was a fairly peaceful two days. Lieutenant Henry Foley returned to the battalion on 16 December, having recovered from the injury he received on 16 September.[7] Lieutenant Foley said:

> In the evening of the first day [in the front line] an order came from battalion headquarters for a patrol to go out under an officer to find out all information possible about the enemy and his movements. As the most experienced officer up there, I took the job, but it was not likely to be a pleasant one, as snow had fallen during the day, and movement in no man's land would be precarious! However posts were warned and at the appointed hour I slipped over the parapet accompanied by Carr and Lance Corporal White, a man of steady nerve, and therefore suitable for work of this sort.
>
> The enemy posts were separated from ours by about a hundred yards. Hardly had we crawled twenty yards from our line, when to my surprise I heard a hoarse challenge, coming apparently from our left rear. Once more it rang out, and in a flash I realised that it came from one of our own posts which by some oversight had not warned that a patrol was going out. We were thus, to put it mildly, between the devil and the deep sea. To shout out 'friend' was to run the risk of bringing a hail of bullets from the nearest German post, and probably starting the whole firing line, while to stay quiet was to invite death at the hands of our own men. But we were not given much time to decide. Next moment I heard a dull thud, apparently very near us, followed by an ominous hissing noise. Getting no answer to their challenge our men had thrown a bomb. We had just time to flatten ourselves to the ground when it exploded with a terrible flash and bang.
>
> No one was hit, and we didn't wait for any more but scuttled back like rabbits over the parapet and into the piece of disused trench from which we had started. We were endeavouring to regain a little breath, when round the corner of the traverse came an evil-looking bayonet, followed by [Sergeant] Dawson, in charge of the post, his eyes flashing in anticipation of sticking the midnight marauders through their gizzards. His astonishment at finding one of his own officers was almost ludicrous. I am glad to say that I had the grace to congratulate him on the alertness shown by his men.

On 20 December the 7th Somersets were relieved, soon marching to Méaulte where the battalion stayed until 1 January 1917.

Lieutenant Jenks described Christmas:

> Luck unbelievable – relief in time to be out for Christmas Day. Taking a chance [2nd Lt John] Buckland was sent off some hours before the rest of the Battalion with instructions to take 'Saint' and buy up all the beer obtainable. Hence C company boasted 3 barrels for the feast – French beer, but still beer. Next RSM received orders for roast beef for the day. Groans of 'impossible' from the cooks. Threats of 'return to duty' and the impossible was achieved, field ovens were made and a real 'ration roast' was the piece de resistance.
>
> It is kinder to draw a veil over the hilarity that followed, and the Hogarth similitude al fresco concert in the candle lit barn. Kinder too, to forget the untimely end of the rooster who 'fell off a fence' and committed suicide to provide C Company officers' mess with a seasonable dish. The one draw back was the lack of fuel.
>
> Good food, good drinks, good smokes demand a good fire, but alas the R.E. were stubborn and we looked like shivering. List to the tale the wily batman who was told to procure fuel at all costs. He reported to the CSM and demanded a fatigue party of six men with sacks. These procured he marched to the R.E. yard reported to the R.E. corporal 'Fatigue party to carry coal, Corporal. Halt, left turn – fill sacks.' Exchange of cigarettes and small talk. 'Fall in, quick march. Goodnight Corporal.' and C company headquarters glowed with satisfaction and comfort. A merry Christmas indeed.

While out of the line two more men from the battalion died. On 21 December Private Henry Crawley died at home, and on New Year's Eve Private Harold Burnett died at the Northamptonshire War Hospital. He had sustained a leg injury and had been a patient in the hospital for some weeks with his leg having been amputated above the knee. He underwent another operation on New Year's Eve and, although it seemed that he had recovered from the surgery, he later that day. He was the 247th man from the battalion to die.

NOTES

1 On 30 September Private Ernest Hall was killed outright. Corporal Francis Williams died of wounds.

2 The dead were Lieutenant Steele, Private Charles Eason, Private William Gregory, Private William Satwell, Private George Harris, Private John Smith, Private Frederick Popham, Private Hedley Rugg, Private Courtney Isaacs and Private Albert Rees. Two men, formerly from the Devonshire Regiment, Privates Francis Whiddon and William Prowse were also killed. Three more men died of injuries received on 1 October – Private Joseph Chenaweth, Private Cephas Thompson and Private William Littlejohns.

3   Others killed were Privates Reginald Burge, Frank Rountley, Sidney Vaughan and Chester Vallance.

4   The other dead included a group of men formerly from the West Somerset Yeomanry, Privates William Creech, Ernest Bullock, Ernest Moore and Alfred Snow. Also killed were Privates Thomas Cole, Wesley Young, Joseph Matthews and John Routley.

5   Private George Rocen died on the 9th. Private Harold Nichols died on the 10th and Private Samuel Needs on the 11th. Private Arthur Moore is listed as being killed in action on 15 October 1916. This is unlikely as the battalion was not in the line at this time.

6   These were Sergeant Sidney Pitt and Privates Samuel Pope and John Sweetland.

7   While here on 19 December, Private Hubert Pedrick died (cause unknown).

CHAPTER X
Winter on the Somme

A new year

The winter of 1916–17 on the Western Front was the hardest for many years. It had started early and was to go on well into the new year. For the men of all armies camped out in the battlefields, in rain, snow and alternating mud and frozen conditions, the tours of duty in the front were almost intolerable even without the added ordeal of facing a sudden death. Nearly all of the belligerents on the Somme front were in a state of exhaustion following the mammoth battle that had raged for more than four months and which had caused more than a million men to be killed, wounded or to become 'missing'.

Lord Cavan, the commander of the XIVth Corps, had visited the 20th Division's brigade headquarters on 27 December at Méaulte. He told the assembled officers that the XIVth Corps would be holding the Sailly–Saillisel sector of the line. This part of the line was significant being along a ridge that flanked the enemy's positions at Le Transloy, the ridge also commanding the approaches to Combles, a now important position behind the British lines. Lord Cavan was acutely aware of the condition of the men and the very poor state of the front-line positions, but was at pains to point out the importance of the sector to be held.

For the men of the 7th Battalion Somerset Light Infantry the new year meant a return to trench warfare. After the battalion's welcome break for Christmas, they were to return to front-line duties – simply enduring and holding the front line from January through to the beginning of March when everything would change. The spell in early February was described as the worst that the battalion would endure in the war.

On 1 January 1917 the men of the 7th Battalion left the safety of Méaulte and marched to Combles. At this time Combles was full of heavy guns and was immediately behind the front line. Duck-board tracks led from Combles forward across the sea of deep sticky mud to the front-line positions, and on 2 January the battalion went forward through the ruined village and relieved the Irish Guards in positions just in front of the village. The duckboards themselves were extremely slippery and nearly every battalion suffered a few injuries moving across them when men lost their footing.

Between 2 January and 16 March the 7th Somersets occupied this front, or were camped near to it. Enemy snipers and shelling steadily took their toll on the battalion, while snow, frosts and mud made winter at the front the scene of terrible suffering. During this time twenty-six men were killed, or died of wounds or disease.[1]

The trenches only became usable when frozen which, due to the extreme cold, was quite frequent, especially in the first half of February. The cold and the mud were so bad that groups of officers and men were kept out of the front line so that they could rest, although most of the battalion would normally have to move into the front-line trenches. Notwithstanding the difficulties created by the conditions, the battalion was engaged in many of the usual activities; training in weapons such as rifle grenades and in tactics continued. Some of the officers also had to map the enemy positions.

One of the places the battalion stayed was in a camp at Guillemont. On 6 February Captain Jones returned to the battalion after recovering from his injuries received in the attack on Lesboeufs:

> The whole area wore a desolate aspect, and it was with sad feelings that I saw Guillemont again. Of course, there were no traces of a village to be seen; the ground was pitted with shell holes and thickly littered with the debris of the tremendous struggle which had been waged in the autumn. The site of Guillemont looked forlorn in the evening twilight, and it was sad to think of the men whose lives had been given to gain a village that did not exist.

Contact with home was maintained through post, parcels and for some lucky members of the battalion, leave. One concerned wife, Susan Hann, sent her husband Walter a bullet-proof waistcoat that he wore for the first time on 10 February in the front line when he was shot clean through the forehead by an enemy sniper.

Another event of note during this spell was a significant air raid that took place on 12 February when German aircraft flew over Carnoy where the Somersets were in camp and also Maricourt, dropping some two hundred bombs. The aircraft managed to set fire to a large ammunition dump that burned and exploded all day, flinging unexploded shells all about – some travelling up to a mile and a half.

In early February because of the conditions, the battalion would only spend two days at a time in the trenches. A typical journey to the front is related by Captain Jones:

> We walked, in parties at intervals, along the road to Combles, on whose outskirts we met our guide. Here we turned off to the left, and tramped in single file along a duckboard track to the trenches in front

of what had been the village of Morval. In the gathering dusk the appearance of the countryside was desolate. We were advancing in a wide valley, and never had a place looked so sinister. The only signs of life were the files of men making their way in a winding fashion towards the trenches. In front and behind we caught glimpses of small bodies of men like ours, while at the junction of the track other parties branched off along a similar meandering track which afforded the quickest approach to the line. Dark night had fallen by the time we arrived in the vicinity of the trenches which we were to take over. Now we advanced more cautiously; smoking and talking were forbidden. Once more we saw the coloured lights rising and falling in front, with the country stretching, vague and mysterious on either hand. The night was fairly quiet; occasionally a rifle shot broke the silence or the rapid chatter of a machine gun fell on our ears. Now and then a shell would burst in the empty wastes.

The hours of freezing endurance were punctuated by short violent events, two of which resulted in bravery awards for men from the battalion.

On 27 February Private Shaddick was killed when a 5.9 shell landed in his post, the blast injuring many others. Lieutenant Brown was with the men being shelled and, after initially helping with the injured, he quickly found that the field telephone line back to headquarters had been cut by the enemy bombardment. He promptly set off across no man's land under machine-gun and rifle fire to report the casualties and the situation to battalion headquarters. After doing this he returned across the bullet-raked open ground to his men's positions to reorganise the posts. He later received the Military Cross for his courage.

The second award was given to Sergeant Towler for his actions over four days that began at about half past three in the afternoon of 1 March. A German shell directly hit a post near to him. Sergeant Towler had seen that Lieutenant Buckland had been sitting in the post and that two men were standing outside – he rushed over to help them. The two men nearby had been killed by the blast, but Sergeant Towler thought that he heard Lieutenant Buckland call, and he started digging frantically to get him out. The blast had levelled the parapet and the Germans opened rifle and machine-gun fire on the spot which meant that Towler, and Corporal Robinson who had arrived, had to scrape away at the earth while lying down. The enemy shellfire continued, and twice Sergeant Towler and Corporal Robinson were buried and had to dig themselves free. It took three quarters of an hour to dig John Buckland's body out. He had been killed instantly. Lieutenant Buckland had joined the battalion in July 1916 and had fought at Guillemont. He was the son of a former Taunton clergyman and had joined the reserve officers where he had undertaken training before joining the battalion immediately after leaving school at King's College, Taunton.

Sergeant Towler and Corporal Robinson then took turns acting as sentry for the post and patrolling the area to raise the morale of the men there. The platoon had been badly shaken by the bombardment and the casualties that had occurred. The numbers in the platoon were low anyway because of illness amongst the men – three were sick – even before the casualties. Four men were killed that day.

The battalion remained in the front line until 4 March 1917, under repeated enemy fire during which time one man was killed and another twelve injured. On the morning of the relief Sergeant Towler's shelter was blown in by a shell that threw him yards up the trench. Miraculously he was not killed or seriously injured, although he remained unconscious for three hours. On waking he resumed command of his post and was fit enough to lead his men out when relieved. For his bravery in the line Sergeant Towler was recommended for the Distinguished Conduct Medal. Sergeant Towler had come to the Somersets via an unusual route, joining the Lancers in 1914 and then being discharged on health grounds. He then joined the North Somerset Yeomanry and had fought and been injured in the knee at Loos. On recovering he had been transferred to the Somerset Light Infantry with whom he had undergone a course in bombing before being posted to the 7th Battalion.

Casualties were not always limited to enemy action. On 10 March two men were killed through a British 6 inch howitzer battery firing short on the Somerset trenches before word could be got back to the gunners.

The personal loss of each casualty could be tremendous. On Wednesday 13 March a lance corporal from the 7th Battalion, John (known as Jack) Harris, died at Stockport Hospital aged 38. He had been severely injured in July 1916 by a piece of steel being driven into his temple and his recovery had never been expected. His family had been notified of his very poor condition and his wife, who had herself only recently come out of hospital, father and sister made the journey to Stockport to see him, but Jack Harris died before they arrived. His body was conveyed to Monkton Combe near Bath where he was buried after a procession from his home in Mill Lane to the cemetery, which was lined by eighty soldiers. The Union flag was a pall for the coffin that was covered in flowers and the man who had been a gardener for a local clergyman was laid to rest in the presence of nearly the whole village. As well as his wife he left a 10-year-old son.

On 12 March 1917 the battalion left these front-line positions for the penultimate time, returning to a camp at Carnoy. While the men were there on the afternoon of 15 March the camp was rent by a terrible explosion that had detonated between the officers' huts and the men's camp of the 12th King's Liverpool Battalion area. The whole of the 12th

King's camp was destroyed. Fortunately most of the men were away playing football or at the Verey Lights performance, although the blast still killed three officers and nine men from the King's. One officer and fifty-two men were injured.

The Verey Lights

Through the dreadful winter of 1916–17 the 20th Division formed a concert party that became established in a semi-official way at Carnoy. The division had built a large wooden theatre at the rest camp which was called the Coliseum after the London theatre.

The troupe called themselves the 'Verey Lights', after the illumination rockets used to light up no man's land. Captain Foley:

> The function of a Verey light was to turn darkness into day. When the 20th Division founded its own concert party there was a touch of genius in the inspiration that christened them the Verey Lights. For if there was one institution more than another calculated to brighten the darkness of our 'rest' periods it was that team of hard working and gifted artists.

The artists were certainly gifted. Their parodies and sketches, which nearly every man in the battalion at the time must have seen, not only made light of the terrible ordeal that the troops were experiencing, but managed to incorporate events from the recent fighting. Soldiers came away carrying the tunes and songs with them as they returned to the front line. The opening chorus summed it all up pretty well:

> Verey Lights, Verey Lights, V-E-R-E-Y,
> Carnoy Camp
> May be damp
> But the Coliseum's dry;
> Now you know, where to go
> To enjoy yourself at nights
> When you are near us
> Come in and hear us
> For we're the Verey Lights.

A memorable tune was the skit based on a revue song that was popular at the time, 'Chalk Farm to Camberwell Green'. The Verey Lights' version ran as follows:

> Up on the duckboards it's lovely to go,
> Specially when there is fog, rain or snow;

I met a Sapper, a terrible swell,
He said 'You're looking as muddy as hell'.
He said 'We're building deep dug-outs for you;'
I said 'That's splendid, if only its true!'
Down came a shell, and we gave a great lurch,
Lone Tree to Saillisel Church.

Chorus – Lone Tree to Saillisel Church
        All on a winter's day
        I stepped on to the duckboards
        And we started right away;
        When we got to the end of the boards
        He asked me to stop for a drink,
        But I said 'They're shelling the chateau,
        So I don't think'.

Men sometimes come up to me and enquire
When all this warfare is going to expire;
I am now in a position to say
The war will be over as soon as they lay
Right up to Berlin a new duckboard track,
It's a long way so don't carry a pack;
As it's hard work they are bound to give
It to the Twentieth Div.

Chorus – Lone Tree right on to Berlin
        We'll all be going soon,
        We'll step on to the duckboards
        And all be there by June,
        When we get to the end of the track
        Some fine lager beer we will drink,
        And the Kaiser and Willie we'll bring back as souvenirs,
        I DON'T THINK.

One sketch, performed by four men dressed up in German uniforms, would have been very familiar to some of the men from the 7th Battalion as it recounted an incident from the line facing Lesboeufs:

We're four German prisoners, as gay as can be,
There's Ludwig, und Heinemann, und Frederich, und me.
O where we were captured, it was at Lesboeufs,
Where the King's and the Somersets did give us such snuff,
And in the next war in the Hun A.S.C.
You'll find Ludwig, und Heinemann, und Frederich, und me.

The ASC (Army Service Corps) was correctly considered by infantrymen as being safer than their job.

NOTES

1   Nineteen-year-old 2nd Lieutenant William Ellis (killed by a sniper on 13 January), Private Samuel Linthorn, who looked after battalion pack animals (killed by shell on 14 January), Private Charles Death (died of wounds on 18 January), Private James Cox a battalion transport driver (killed 24 January), 34-year-old Private Arthur Rendell and father of three young children (died of bronchitis at a hospital in Rouen on 1 February), 26-year-old Private Walter Hann (killed by a sniper on 10 February), 40-year-old Private Edward King (killed 10 February), 37-year-old Private Richard Smith (10 February), 23-year-old acting Corporal Frederick Church (10 February), Private James Caddick died at a casualty clearing station (12 February), Private Samuel Criddle (killed on 13 February), Private Christopher Downton (died of wounds on 16 February), Private Thomas Singer (died at home on 16 February), Private Henry Cullen (died 17 February), Private Henry Hardy (died of wounds on 19 February), Private Fred Shaddick (died on 27 February), father of two Private William Pattermore (killed 1 March), Lance Corporal Albert Palmer (killed 1 March), Private Eddie Radford (killed 1 March), 26 year old Lance Sergeant James Vickery (killed 1 March), Private Arthur Southcott (killed 3 March), Private Arthur Henge (killed 10 March), Private Edward Thomas (killed 10 March).

PART THREE

1917

CHAPTER XI

Pursuit to the Hindenburg Line

The background to the retirement

On 24 February 1917, after careful deliberation and planning, the Germans began to leave parts of the front-line positions that they had occupied and fought so hard for through the Somme offensive. The first areas to be vacated were those in the northernmost part of the Somme battle area – the areas of Pys, Miraumont and Serre, that were now forming a German salient, given the successes in the southernmost part of the Somme offensive and positions already held by the British in the north. The Germans fell back in a planned move to new positions – the Hindenburg Line. It was known to the Germans as the Siegfried Line.

Erich Ludendorff, the German Quartermaster General and in effect the second in command to Hindenburg on the Western Front, later accounted for the retirement in his memoirs. He accepted that the decision 'implied a confession of weakness', but stated that it was 'necessary for military reasons'.

These comments after the war reflected the strategic reality on the battle front in early 1917. The ground so bitterly fought over and given up by the Germans in the previous seven months meant that the battered and hastily prepared German positions were unlikely to hold against a sustained attack in the spring. Better a retirement in an organised way to carefully prepared and defensible positions, than a forced retreat with all the risks that that entailed.

The retirement was explained to the general public at home in Germany in fairly frank terms. Herr Querl, correspondent to the *Berliner Tageblatt* paper:

> It was easy to understand that a good German front rank soldier was better pleased to undertake the most risky deeds of arms than to stay any longer in this morass and mud, in the rubbish and ruins. Modern weapons are such that in the long run, they overcome field fortifications, and that one day the whole area becomes so poisoned that only beasts can live in it. When matters have gone this far the

defender must be able immediately to seize the means and opportunities of regrouping.

The explanation carried with it the tacit admission that the Germans, on the Western Front at least, were on the defensive. Gone now were the ambitions to bleed France white on the fields of Verdun. The explanation also reflected the growing stature of the British and Commonwealth forces. Gone were the shell shortages and heavy gun shortages. Now the soldiers tramped past battery after battery of heavy guns on their way to or from the trenches and shell production meant that millions of rounds could be fired in offensives.

All of the combatants on the Western Front had suffered terribly in the preceding year, but the British and Commonwealth forces now had additional hope for the future. Tanks that could crush through dense tangles of barbed wire, creating passages for the infantry, were being produced in ever increasing numbers and quality. Many more Lewis machine guns, rifle grenades and Stokes mortars were available, and the infantry were being trained to use them to suppress or destroy strongpoints without having recourse to the artillery and communication problems this entailed.

The early part of 1917 would also bring with it two major world events that would have a big effect on the war. The first event, the Russian Revolution that took place on 9 March 1917, would later have a significant effect on the 7th Battalion when large numbers of German soldiers would be released for deployment on the Western Front in November 1917 and March 1918. The second, the American declaration of war on Germany on 6 April 1917, would eventually seal the fate of the Central Powers because of the inevitability of defeat once the huge resources of the United States were mobilised.

The retirement

The German retirement, that had started in the northern parts of the old Somme battlefields, gradually spread southwards. Throughout this time British and Commonwealth troops probed the German lines with patrols to see whether they were still occupied. At dawn on 17 March 1917 a patrol from one of the 20th Division's battalions probed the line in front of Saillisel and found that it was still occupied. The Australians who were on the left of the 20th Division reported later the same day that the Germans to their front had gone. Immediately patrols were sent out again in broad daylight across no man's land to the German trenches. The enemy had disappeared.

The 7th SomLI were at Carnoy when the retirement began, but quickly became involved in the pursuit. The next day the battalion marched out of the camp at 11am and took over the positions occupied by the 10th KRRC in the Le Transloy trenches. The 59th Brigade, of which the 10th KRRC was part, had quickly followed up the retiring enemy and the men of that battalion had occupied Le Transloy and had pushed forward outposts on the far side of the village. The Somerset's battalion headquarters was near Lesboeufs and the trenches were very quiet. The Somersets later advanced into the German trenches themselves. Captain Jones recalled: 'Night had fallen; it was pitch dark and wet. The mud in the evacuated enemy trench area was, if possible, worse than on our side, and there were no duck board tracks to show the way.'

On 19 March the 61st Brigade took the vanguard of the advance and the spirits of the advancing soldiers soared. Captain Jones:

> The day's advance had brought us through the shell pitted ground, and we had now reached country which had not been ploughed up by the blast of war. There were shell holes of course, and big ones at that, but they were not rim to rim as they had been further back. The spirit of resignation which had been so evident in the trench warfare of the preceding months was now chased away by the novelty of the situation and the spirit of adventure.

Captain Henry Foley said: 'The next few weeks were for all of us a time of pure and unalloyed delight.' To the left of the Somersets in the midst of some trees a ruined heap of what had been the village of Villers au Flos could be seen; a patrol found this to be held by Australians. As evening fell on the 19th the men could see the eastern sky aglow as the retreating Germans burned villages as they left.

Because of the difficulty in bringing up the guns through the mud and devastation of what had been no man's land, the British infantry advance was not as quick as it could otherwise have been, even though cavalry patrols found the Germans a long way off. Another reason for caution during the advance was the strength of the battalions. Winter casualties and disease had severely reduced battalion strengths. In the 7th Somersets, for example, the strength of D Company, which was to lead much of the early pursuit, was now only thirty-eight men. Many men were sick, like Private Follett who was hospitalised with pneumonia.

On 20 March D Company was ordered forward to occupy the village of Barastre. Captain Jones was with D company:

> We advanced in an approved text book style, point, van and main guard. We marched towards the southern edge of the village and then through the woods which bordered it. We took up our positions on the eastern edge of Barastre. As the weather became threatening we looked for material to make head cover. We wandered through

Barastre. Scenes of destruction met our gaze everywhere. The village had not been subject to intensive shellfire like Guillemont and Morval and had not been completely razed to the ground like those hapless villages. But there was a cruel perversity behind a great deal of the havoc which the enemy had wrought just prior to their retreat. There were two mighty craters near the church, but these craters were legitimate obstacles to the pursuit. But the enemy had committed acts of vandalism for which no excuse can be offered. The church and the houses had been destroyed and gutted. These villages had sheltered his supports and reserves during the Somme battle and he had decided that they should afford no cover for our pursuing troops. What exasperated us most of all was the deliberate cutting down or ringing of the fruit trees in the orchards, while the wells had been filled with debris and dung.

The advance by the Somersets continued on 23 March with two very weak platoons from D Company going into the village of Bertincourt. German barbed wire was used to set up improvised defences. The night's sleep was disturbed when a fire restarted in a house in the middle of the village, and the following morning a German patrol tried to raid the village. One German was shot dead and the others scampered away.

The battalion was relieved from the vanguard on 27 March; the men spent the next two days digging new trenches and occupying a defensive strongpoint.

On 29 March the battalion returned to the forefront of the advance with patrols being sent to Ruyaulcourt which they found unoccupied. They had been informed that the day before the village had been strongly held. The weather at this time was still cold and that night fairly heavy snow fell. By nightfall piquets had been established on the far side of the village and the night was spent on watch as snow drifted across the front. The next day the Germans started accurate shelling of the British positions and Lance Corporal Frank Shaw and Private Percy Tucker were killed and three men injured.

On the morning of 31 March two officer led patrols were sent out at night to discover the whereabouts of the German positions. Both contacted the enemy and, after short firefights in which both sides sustained casualties, they withdrew. The battalion lost four dead and eight wounded.[1]

Another patrol that was sent out at half past midnight on 1 April also encountered Germans about fifty yards from the Somerset positions. A short firefight followed which again resulted in both sides suffering casualties. The Somerset patrol retired leaving two injured men behind. Private Holvey had a shattered leg and Private Lancaster was incapacitated. Two men, Privates Walter Parsons and Herbert Willshere, were killed. Lieutenants Brown and Joscelyn, who had led the patrol, returned to carry back both wounded men, although both later died from their injuries. The officers were recommended for bravery awards by the battalion, but were eventually censured by Brigade staff for unnecessarily exposing themselves to danger. They were also criticised for retiring under enemy fire.

Havrincourt Wood

The battalion was relieved on 1 April returning to a snow-covered camp near Le Transloy for four days' rest. German resistance was stiffening and on 4 April the 59th Brigade captured the village of Metz-en-Couture by assault. The 5th, the day the 7th Battalion returned to the front at Lechelle, was officially the last day of the German retirement.

The battalion initially marched to Lechelle on 5 April, the same day that Private William Edmonds from Newton Abbott died of wounds. Captain Jones said: 'Nothing of general interest occurred for two or three days. Friday, April 6th, passed quietly and cheerfully until nightfall when snow and rain made everything miserable.'

The battalion remained at Lechelle until 7 April when they moved to the newly captured Metz-en-Couture. The 7th was 'Jellalabad Day' for the Somerset Light Infantry but the battalion was unable to celebrate because it occupied trenches that spread out across the new front near the village. The outposts faced Havrincourt Wood, a large imposing forest that stood between the advancing British and the Hindenburg Line. Later that day the battalion received orders to establish an outpost line within Havrincourt Wood if possible. Patrols were therefore sent forward to the wood where they encountered stiff resistance and the attempt to enter the wood was abandoned for the night.

Early the next morning the battalion received orders from Division to make another attempt at entering the wood. Colonel Troyte-Bullock queried the order which he considered a suicidal one, but was told to proceed with the attempt to get into the wood. The party of eleven men, led by 2nd Lieutenant Brown, moved out of the trench at 9 o'clock in the morning. They had no sooner left the cover of their trench than heavy rifle and machine-gun fire was opened on the squad. Lieutenant Brown was soon hit in the body, with three other bullets piercing the rim of his steel helmet. The remaining men were also shot down. Miraculously all survived and were dragged back into the trench.

Havrincourt Wood was beginning to cause concern to the higher commanders. The Germans had now shown no interest in retreating voluntarily from the wooded positions despite a number of patrols, and it was decided that on Easter Monday, 10 April, an attack would be launched to gain a foothold in the wood. The attack could not be supported by much artillery, as most of the guns had yet to catch up with the soldiers in advanced positions. This was despite three battalions from the 20th Division being allocated to help in clearing and opening the roads forward to allow supplies and guns through. The advance into Havrincourt Wood was to coincide with the Arras offensive.

The attack began at 4 o'clock on a cold but clear afternoon. The 61st Brigade deployed the 7th KOYLI on the left, three companies of the Somersets in the centre and the 7th DCLI on the right. The men left their trenches and moved quickly towards the wood. A feeble barrage was put down on the German positions and the Germans retaliated with whizz bangs which, although few in number, caused some casualties. Most importantly though, the defenders were caught completely unawares. The piquet positions were rushed, and although they fought back, were quickly overwhelmed. The Somersets rushed on into the wood causing the surprised occupants, who were in the middle of preparing their tea, to flee. By 7pm the battalion had fully obtained its objectives and a piquet line was established 300 yards into the wood. To add to the success the victorious soldiers were able to eat the food that the defenders had unwittingly prepared for them.

The battalion had only suffered two men killed. Private Sidney Guppy was shot in the side towards the end of the attack. He died a few hours later and the men from the battalion were able to bury him in a grave that they covered with moss and daffodils. Sid Guppy was 36 when killed and a bricklayer by trade. He had been with the battalion since the beginning of the war and was looked up to by others as a veteran. The other man killed was 26-year-old Corporal Stanley Hall, known as 'Bert'. He came from the village of Pill where he had been an assistant master at a school and a keen cricketer. He left a wife and three young children. Seven others were injured in the attack – a remarkably low number. One of those injured was Private Charles Nott, the former butcher's assistant from Bath, who having received shrapnel wounds to his thigh and left hand was happily back in a hospital in London with his Blighty wound within days.

The other two battalions involved in the attack had similarly achieved their objectives but at greater loss. On the left the 7th KOYLIs encountered strong opposition at a farmhouse which caused a number of casualties. On the right the 7th DCLI suffered many more casualties. Across the whole front the night was very quiet.

Captain Jones: 'At dawn on the 10th April, under cover of a thick mist, enemy patrols attacked D Company's sentry groups, but were repulsed. The first intimation of an attack that our men had was the bursting of bombs around their posts, but they quickly opened fire'. One of the German grenades was hurled into a post holding three men. The two closest to the bomb instinctively crouched in a corner while the third man, Private Beale, rushed up and tried to throw the grenade away. It exploded, blowing off his hand. Private Beale's actions had saved both his friends from almost certain death and he was later awarded the Distinguished Conduct Medal for his bravery. Captain Jones: 'The enemy retreated as silently as they had come and our patrols which pushed deeper into the wood failed to catch up with them. Except for this early alarm the day passed very quietly.'

The next few days were very quiet with the posts that had been made after the assault being consolidated. Because of the great distances between the wagon lines and the posts, supplies were carried forward by mule. On the evening of 13 April eight transport drivers brought up the rations by mule as had been expected and set about delivering the food in a heavy snowstorm. Later that evening Lieutenant Scott, who was in charge of the transport, came up to headquarters to make enquiries as only six of the transport drivers had returned. There had been no reported firing and it was surmised that the men had probably got lost in the wood. Later it was discovered that they had been captured by the Germans after getting lost. Captain Jones: 'There was a great deal of amusing talk among the men, some of whom opined that the Germans would conclude that the British cavalry were short of horses and were now mounted on mules'.

On 14 April the outpost lines were pushed forward a significant distance through the wood. Patrols were moving about in the rest of the wood and finding no significant German presence. When found the Germans seemed to have no interest in a fight. Havrincourt Wood was untouched by the ravages of war and, once the outposts had been pushed sufficiently forward, the men were able to wander safely among the trees.

A further advance was ordered and by 16 April the battalion had reached the middle of Havrincourt Wood, but were forbidden to advance farther. This same day Captain Henry Foley received a letter from his mother telling him that his brother Geoffrey had been seriously injured in recent fighting. Geoffrey Foley had recovered from the injuries he had received when serving with the 7th Battalion and had been posted to the 1st Battalion SomLI which had been heavily involved in fighting near Arras. He had now lost the lower part of a leg.

With the relative inactivity on the ground, the battalion's soldiers turned their attention to the world around them. Captain Jones: 'There was a great deal of activity in the air, where the Germans suddenly developed a temporary superiority. We used to feel very sad at heart as we watched the slow British machines being overtaken and shot down by the enemy.'

The battalion had set up an observation post in the roof of the brewery at Metz-en-Couture, hidden beneath its slates. From here they could watch the Germans move behind their lines preparing their defences. For most of this time the artillery had not been brought forward in sufficient quantities to shell these areas and the Germans were able to proceed unhindered. The 18pdr guns that had come forward hardly had the range of the area. This changed on the last day of the battalion's stay in this sector. Captain Jones wrote:

> On the 19th the artillery liaison officers provided a treat for us. They ranged their guns on a dump between Havrincourt and Flesquières, where the Germans used to congregate in the morning. The shooting aroused our admiration and chased away the monotony of our daily routine. Our shelling caused great surprise and confusion among the enemy who had hitherto been undisturbed.

After a short break from the front, the battalion returned to Havrincourt Wood where it remained until 19 May. The 7th SomLI alongside the other battalions of the 20th Division spent this time digging miles of trenches and wiring them for defence. The Germans were digging too, about four hundred yards from the British. Casualties during this time were extremely light with only four men killed in the three-and-a-half-week stay.[2]

During this time Captain Henry Foley received the sad news that his brother had died of his injuries. Septic poisoning had set into Geoffrey Foley's leg wound requiring first an amputation below the knee and then another above it to try to save the young officer. Captain Henry Foley wrote:

> Ready as I thought I was to bear it, the shock of the news when it came was almost unendurable. It was terrible to think of the poor bereaved home. How ill we could spare his sunny, boyish nature – his irrepressible laugh – his unselfish comradeship.

On 19 May the 20th Division was withdrawn from the line and re-introduced two days later about eight miles to the north-west in trenches near Favreuil. The battalion spent a glorious week in the reserve trenches there. The front was very peaceful as the opposing trenches were far apart. A week later the battalion moved into support trenches where shellfire injured two officers and three men and on 6 June, a hazy summer day, it moved into the front line. This area was overlooked by high ground behind the German lines, which themselves were heavily wired. This made any movement more difficult. No man's land was about 1,000 yards wide and covered with long grass that was largely undamaged by the war.

On the following day three men from the battalion were killed by an enemy sniper who was variously identified as operating from an advanced enemy post that was on the road to Pronville, or hiding in the long grass. Four other men were killed by shellfire.[3]

The raid at Lagnicourt

On the night of 8 June a patrol was sent forward to reconnoitre the enemy forward post that was thought to harbour the sniper. This was found to be concealed behind some trees that had been felled across the road. The patrol came across a party of Germans moving towards their post and opened fire. After this the patrol withdrew, the men claiming on their return to have killed at least four Germans as well as identifying the post's location. The following night a patrol by another company moved out and was able to identify the post's location by approach from a different side. Again an enemy relief was seen and fired on. No casualties were reported. On 9 June a decision was reached to raid the enemy post in the early hours of 12 June.

The planning for the raid was done on 10 June 1917, the same day that news of the great success in the attack on the Messines ridge on 7 June reached the battalion. That attack was to the south of the Ypres salient, where nineteen mines were exploded simultaneously beneath the German positions which were then assaulted and captured by English, Irish, Australian and New Zealand brigades. Captain Jones recalled: 'We were greatly elated by the news of the successful attack.'

On the night of the 10th a further patrol from Captain Foley's B Company was sent out. This patrol was led by 2nd Lieutenant Fry. Captain Foley said:

> Fry was out on patrol, and getting too near a German post was fired upon by a machine gun. He turned back, but had not gone far before noting that his runner Private McCardle, was missing. Sending the patrol on, he turned back himself and started shouting the man's name. This was the last the patrol heard of him.

Private McCardle did not return either, and the patrol the two men had been with returned to no man's land to look for their comrades until dawn when they returned without success. 2nd Lieutenant Fry and Private McCardle would spend two days behind German lines. They were both captured on 12 June trying to get back to safety.

Another patrol on the night of 11 June identified some enemy soldiers but returned without any exchanges of fire. Because of the proposed raid, Captain Jones, the intelligence officer, spent the following day watching the enemy lines and noticed parties of men proceeding in both directions indicating a relief in progress.

As midnight approached, the party led by 2nd Lieutenant Lewin, who had recently joined the battalion, waited pensively for the guns to open fire and signal the start of the raid. Captain Jones watched the beginning of the raid:

A box-barrage of 18pdrs was first placed on the enemy post. During the raid I stood on top of the bank near the signal office watching the shelling and the display of coloured lights which followed the opening of our barrage. There was a feeling of suspense, for it was impossible to see anything that was taking place in the enemy post.

The raiding party closely followed up the barrage and rushed the post with fixed bayonets. The post was surrounded with barbed wire which the men clambered through, entering the trench. The Germans at first stood their ground, but were soon overwhelmed by the suddenness of the attack, with those men who were able to fleeing into the box barrage. One of the wounded Germans tried to get away from the trench but was captured after having a greatcoat thrown over him. Nine Germans were killed where they stood, and another nine were shot down as they fled. The raiders suffered three casualties, all wounded, who were able to be brought out from the post. The captured German was brought back for interrogation.

Captain Jones said:

Major Preston-Whyte asked me to get some information from the prisoner and I proceeded to interrogate him in the best German at my command. I asked the prisoner what his formation was. He said that he belonged to the 9th Grenadier Regiment, 3rd Guards Division. Major Preston-Whyte phoned this information to Brigade. A little later the Major sent for me and told me that Brigade and Division staffs demurred to this identification, as this particular division had but lately been identified on the French front at the Argonne. I inquired of the prisoner the date of his arrival on our front. He said that his regiment [the equivalent of a British battalion] had only entered the line early that morning having detrained at Cambrai on the 11th. The 3rd Guards Division had been sandwiched between two average divisions to strengthen the front against possible attack. Soon after our division had entered this sector, one of the British units engaged in the fighting at Cheresy, a little further north, captured a German document in which reference was made to our coming into the Bullecourt area. Enemy GHQ referred to the 20th Division as an excellent fighting division, whose entrance into a sector heralded aggressive tactics on our part. The German divisions in the line were warned to be watchful of a resumption of fighting in this sector.

The raid was seen as a great success and 2nd Lieutenant Lewin was awarded the Military Cross; a Distinguished Conduct Medal was given to Lance Corporal Gibbs and the Military Medal to Sergeant Archie Hurley.

The day after the raid the battalion left the line and went back to a camp at Favreuil where the men spent their time training and supplying working parties for the construction of the new British line. On 21 June Private Stanley Wait was killed while on a Royal Engineer working party, and on 24 June three men working on the new front line were killed by trench mortar fire.[4]

On 24 June 2nd Lieutenant Betteley MC, who had previously commanded C Company, but who was then the Brigade intelligence officer, was killed while patrolling in no man's land in front of the 12th King's line. He had won his Military Cross in the attack in front of Lesboeufs on 16 September 1916. Lieutenant Jenks later wrote of him:

> Cap awry, ungainly step, ever smiling, on first rate terms with every French 'madame' – never a soldier, but always a pal – such was 'Bet'. Having 'mushed' with dog-teams in the frozen north, mined for nitrates in the thirsty wastes of Chile, and knocked about in the odd corners of the world, his vocabulary was polyglot and expressive when dealing with a 'cushy' sector like Morval. With him, the men's comfort came first – he was full of hair-brained schemes, such as treadmill duckboards to prevent trench feet. His utter contempt for red tape and brass hats made it inevitable that brigade should claim his services.
>
> Who will ever forget the picture of Bet and the Brigadier standing at the crossroads, lost in a heated argument, oblivious of a gorgeous strafe going on around them. Bet's especial gift was the ability to charm fresh vegetables from village housewives – oh! that I could tell you the tale of the celery. His epitaph could most truly be found in the words of the Brigadier's usual introduction – 'This is Betteley, my Intelligence Officer, a damned bad intelligence officer, but a ___ good mess president'.

In the early hours of 28 June the battalion left the front-line area. It was given three weeks' rest at Autheux where it was joined by three drafts totalling 254 soldiers and Captain Mills rejoined the battalion. Captain Mills had been one of the battalion's original officers, and had only now returned to it after recovering from falling off his horse shortly after the men had landed in France.

On 19 July the battalion marched to back to Doullens where they had originally detrained nearly a year before on their way to the Somme battlefields. This time they boarded a train that took them north towards the Ypres salient. The battalion detrained and marched to Haandekot, a collection of farms about five and a half miles north-west of Poperinghe, where time was spent assimilating the new drafts and in training and route marches.

NOTES

1   Those killed were Lance Sergeant George Dawson and Privates Francis Thorne, Ernest Palmer and George Hill.

2   On 1 May Private Edgar Chapman died. Two days later shellfire killed Private Frederick Brown and severely injured Private George Plin. He later died of the injuries sustained. Also killed was Walter Way.

3   The dead men were Privates Richard Soloman, Henry May, Griffith Jones, John Gunter, Alfred Trent and Lance Corporals Stanley Hall and Leonard Carr.

4   These were Lance Corporals William Smith and Walter Kelland and Private Robert Dunn. William Smith had previously been awarded the Military Medal.

CHAPTER XII
Langemarck

The Third Ypres – Passchendaele

The Third Ypres battle had been planned for a long time. Since April 1915 it had been Sir Douglas Haig's ambition to launch an attack from the northernmost part of the British line that would break through the enemy defences in the area of Ypres and then wheel north to the coast. The objective was to cut off a large German force that would be trapped without supply up against the sea, or at least force it back raggle taggle to new positions much closer to the German border. The second goal was the capture of various ports on the Belgian coast, in particular Ostend and Zeebrugge. Haig perceived that there would be great difficulties in effectively breaking through the now very deep defensive positions held by the Germans on a sufficiently broad front to get strategic results without a plan such as that envisaged in the Ypres offensive.

Haig's plans had been frustrated and delayed throughout 1917. Initially the need to co-operate with French attacks at the Chemins des Dames meant the British attacked at Arras in April 1917; and later the recently formed British War Policy Committee was slow in approving the operations because of fears of another Somme-length casualty list.

Prior to the War Policy Committee granting permission for the Ypres offensive, Haig had been allowed to continue preparations for the offensive, and had been allowed to launch the highly successful Messines attack. The attack that captured the Messines ridge on 7 June was intended to be the first blow in the Ypres area, to be followed quickly by successive attacks from the Ypres salient itself. On 20 July the War Policy Committee eventually gave Haig permission to launch the offensive, forty-three days after the Messines success, and three days after the commencement of the bombardment of the German defences had begun. The delay would cost the British dearly, particularly when summer turned to autumn and the rain started to fall.

From 17 July until the early hours of 31 July the artillery were the main combatants, firing the largest barrage seen so far in the war. More than four million shells were fired at the German trenches and guns, killing thousands of defenders and smashing in many of their defence works. The effect of this barrage was both numerically and effectively much greater than that fired on the Somme because of improvements in the quality of shells and artillery techniques. Not only did a far greater proportion of the shells fired in the Third Ypres offensive explode – an estimated third of those fired in the Somme offensive did not – but technological advances also meant that those shells fired would have a greater effect. Shell flight calculations had improved, which together with batching of shells by small weight variations meant far more accurate gunnery. Other innovations, such as the instantaneous fuse, enabled guns to deliver high explosive shells that would explode on contact with the ground, rather than after burying themselves deep in the mud. These shells were far more effective in clearing enemy wire than previous munitions, and the ground was easier to move across after a barrage. Specialist munitions, such as smoke and gas shells, were also in far greater supply, enabling more complicated fire plans to be evolved.

When it came on 31 July 1917, the first attack was carried on a fifteen-mile front. The French, now holding positions to the north of Ypres, were engaged in attacks along the Yser canal, but the main blow was delivered by the British on a seven-and-a-half-mile front from the salient itself.

At 3.50 on the morning of 31 July soldiers clambered out of their trenches and attacked the German lines. Sir Douglas Haig's dispatch:

> Preceded at midnight by discharges of thermite and oil drums, and covered by accurate artillery barrage from a great number of guns, the Allied infantry entered the German lines at all points. On the greater part of the front of the main attack the resistance of the German infantry was quickly overcome, and rapid progress was made.

The first assaults became known as the Battle of Pilckem which went on until 2 August, grinding itself out on the main defensive line that had been built just behind the front 'outpost' positions.

The rain started to fall on the evening of the first day of the battle; it would fall on and off throughout the autumn offensive. The rain often seemed to coincide with the main attacks, bogging down any early successes and helping the defenders immeasurably.

The second 'battle' of the Third Ypres offensive became known as the Battle of Langemarck. It began on 16 August and officially ended on 18 August. This attack was launched from the northernmost part of the salient and involved attacking German positions defended by trench works and reinforced concrete emplacements, soon to be called pill boxes because of their appearance.

In all there would be eight 'battles' in the Third Ypres offensive which ended on 10 November, but throughout the offensive smaller actions over

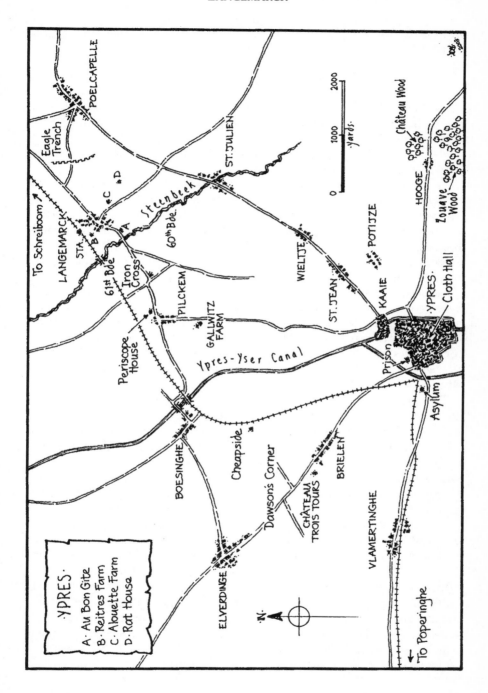

parts of ridges or small woods would be carried out independently of the other actions.

The 7th Battalion

Since 20 July 1917 the 20th Division had been attached to the XIVth Corps which had been concentrating in the Proven area. The XIVth corps was still commanded by Lord Cavan who led it through the Somme battles. The other divisions in the XIVth Corps at this time were the Guards, the 38th (Welsh) and the 29th Divisions.

While the Somersets were camped at Haandekot undergoing their final days of training, the XIVth Corps went into action on the first day of the offensive on 31 July. Both the 38th and Guards Divisions were sent into the attack in the Pilckem ridge battle. They both succeeded in capturing and holding their final objectives, the Pilckem ridge and a line up to the Steenbeek stream on the first day of the attack. The 20th Division was in reserve at this time.

On 1 August in pouring rain, the 7th Battalion marched about one and a half miles closer to the front to a camp at Proven where they stayed until 4 August. The village was a rail centre that housed hospitals, three casualty clearing stations and training areas. It was also a major billet area for soldiers and during the time the Somersets were there it was particularly busy with the offensive under way. The heavy rain continued throughout their stay.

The 20th Division was due to replace the 38th (Welsh) Division in the front line on 5 August, which meant a further advance for its elements on 4 August. The 7th Battalion moved up to a bivouac camp called Dawson's Corner. In preparation for taking over the line, advance parties were sent up to Pilckem to the newly captured positions that lay on the ridge. The whole ridge was under constant shellfire from the Germans who were trying to prevent the attackers from consolidating their gains and while involved in the reconnaissance Private Ernest Earner was killed.

The next morning the whole battalion advanced on to the ridge in broad daylight. The soldiers partially took over former German trenches which had been severely damaged by British fire and now afforded little cover. Three men were killed that afternoon. Captain Mills had stepped out of a trench on a visit to a company in another trench when a shell splinter killed him. He had just rejoined the battalion in July after recovering from the fall from his horse shortly after the battalion had landed in France. It was his first and last trip into the line. Others killed were a former cabinet maker from Bristol, Private Arthur 'Sandy' Hunt, and Lance Corporal James Mead. Captain Foley said:

Soon after dark we were led by guides up to our allotted positions.

My company was in support on the right in trenches near the cross roads known as Iron Cross, my headquarters being in the ruins of a building converted into a concrete blockhouse. These blockhouses, which stood some ten or twelve feet high were the feature of this captured country. They were very strongly built of reinforced concrete, and took the place of ruined dugouts, which would have been impossible here owing to the marshiness of the ground.

The front-line positions were a series of shell hole posts running from the railway to the Langemarck road along the main bank of the Steenbeek stream. The posts were slippery holes which were nearly impossible to improve. The bottoms were filled with liquid mud – a combination of the shelling and heavy rain. The Steenbeek itself would normally have been a stream about fifteen feet wide and about seven feet deep forming a natural defensive barrier. By the time the Somersets came upon it, the channel had been severely damaged by gun fire; its banks and bed had been turned into a near impassable barrier. The only way of possibly crossing it was where any vestige of a bridge remained. About 500 yards behind the shell hole posts was the support line – also a series of shell hole posts. The reserve positions were about one thousand yards behind the front line where the soldiers were able to shelter in the battered former German trench and the pill box described by Captain Foley. This fortification, a former German construction now called Periscope House, had a now inconvenient door that faced the wrong way.

The battle front at this time was subject to a fierce artillery duel between the two opposing forces. The British gunners tried to flatten the defences; the German guns engaged in a fierce counter-bombardment of British lines in an attempt to cause maximum casualties to the British soldiers consolidating for a new attack. Cover was sparse and casualties were therefore high. On 6 August a miserable and wet day dawned after a night of heavy rain and the soldiers huddled in whatever cover they could find under waterproof blankets. Throughout the day enemy artillery fire killed two men and injured eighteen others. Five of those injured were from D Company and were gassed by enemy mustard gas shells which were used for the first time against the Somersets.[1] By the evening Brigade headquarters took over Periscope House and the battalion headquarters were moved to a farmhouse called Stray Farm which was most unsavoury. The farmhouse had been used by the Germans as a soup kitchen for front-line soldiers. It had a cellar with bunks which were necessary as the floor was one foot deep in black slimy water that smelt awful whenever movements stirred it up.

The next day the battalion was again bombarded and by the end of the day the battalion had lost another thirty-five men. Twelve were killed outright or disappeared and were later assumed to have been killed.[2] 2nd

Lieutenant Paul and another twenty men were injured. Private Francis Keevil was one of those injured but he died a little while later. The rain continued adding to the misery particularly of those in the front and support positions, who found their posts gradually filling with sloppy mud.

Relief came that night. Men of the 11th Rifle Brigade came in and the Somersets were able to withdraw to Rousell Camp at Elverdinge where they remained until 14 August. Here the men were able to refit in those six days in preparation for their part in the offensive. The days were spent in detailed planning. Captain Foley who commanded B Company:

> With the help of aeroplane photographs and detailed trench maps, we worked out our plans for the attack. I had formed my company into three platoons, which were at this time commanded by Goode, Liddon and Phelps, a newly joined officer, quite a boy. A and D were to lead, C and B supporting them. I arranged that Liddon's and Phelps' platoons should form the first wave in my company, while Goode followed with his platoon to do the mopping up which was so essential after the leading waves had passed on.

The other three companies were also reorganised into three platoons.

Each of the lead platoons would attack with two sections of riflemen ahead of the platoon's Lewis gun sections. The third platoon was for mopping up any Germans the attacking waves had missed. The men were given instructions that:

> If any part of the line is held up, units on the flank of the unit held up will on no account check their advance, but will create an offensive flank and assist the troops held up with enfilade fire and by pressing around the flank of the enemy points of resistance. It is of vital importance that the barrage is followed closely by the infantry and that any 'nests' of Germans should be dealt with by reserves.[3]

Captain Foley recalled: 'Men were allotted to work every building and pill box which from the maps appeared likely to give trouble, and no efforts were spared to ensure so far as it was humanly possible, that the show, on which so much depended should be a success'. By the end of this period the battalion was estimated to have 470 men available as combatants amongst the four companies.

The plan to capture Langemarck

While the Somersets had been taken out of the line to 'fatten up' for the battle ahead, as Colonel Troyte-Bullock described it, men of the 10th and

11th Rifle Brigade battalions had pushed the outpost line forward about one hundred yards on the far side of the Steenbeek. This fighting was fierce and one of the battalions, the 10th Rifle Brigade, lost fifteen officers and 200 soldiers in the fighting.

Unsuccessful attempts were made on 15 August to capture or destroy the significant block house about 300 yards from the Steenbeek called 'Au Bon Gite'. These attacks employed one infantry company from both the 10th and 11th Rifle Brigade, six detachments from the 83rd Field Company Royal Engineers armed with explosive charges and support from machine guns and Stokes mortars. Au Bon Gite was perceived as the key to the defensive works in the area even though a number of pill boxes spread out behind this block house also covered the approaches from the river.

Despite the failure to take or demolish the Au Bon Gite strongpoint, it was decided that there was now sufficient land on the far side of the Steenbeek to enable an assault force to be deployed on there and from which a major attack could be made. It was decided to attack and capture the village of Langemarck on 16 August, the same date as a general offensive by British forces in the east and north of the salient.

The 20th Division was to capture Langemarck. The plan was for the 60th Brigade to attack on the right and the 61st Brigade on the left of the divisional frontage. The 59th Brigade was to be withdrawn into reserve, less the very weak 10th and 11th Rifle Brigade battalions who were to remain where they were in front of the Steenbeek as covering troops. Two battalions from the 38th (Welsh) Division were attached to the 20th Division as a divisional reserve. To the left of the 20th Division the 29th Division were to attack and to their right the 11th Division.

The attack was to be made in three bounds. The first objective, the Blue Line, was the capture of a road 'line' that ran along the western edge of the village. The second objective, the Green Line, was a line on the far side of the village on its eastern side about 500 yards on from the Blue Line. The third objective, the Red Line, was part of the German defensive line just beyond Schreiboom, approximately 600 yards on from the second objective line on the eastern edge of the village.

The front occupied by the 60th Brigade was narrower than that of the 61st Brigade. The reasons for this were three-fold. First, the attack by the 61st Brigade could encompass the whole of the village of Langemarck; secondly, the attack was to be delivered in a north-easterly direction, which meant that the 60th Brigade would most likely encounter the main counter-attack by the Germans who kept their local reserves at Poelcapelle, a village a little over 2,000 yards to the east of Langemarck. The third reason was that it was envisaged that if the 61st Brigade were held up, the 60th Brigade might be able to partially encircle the defenders of Langemarck and take the positions from behind or flank. The 60th Brigade would attack on a one-battalion frontage, with one battalion to be used for each objective line, leaving one battalion – the 12th RB – in reserve.

The 61st Brigade, with a wider line to attack, was to attack on a two-battalion front. The 7th KOYLI on the left and the 7th SomLI on the right were allotted to capture the first and second objectives. The 7th DCLI and the 12th King's were allotted the third objective. For the Somersets, A and D Companies were given the first objective line to take, and C and B Companies were to follow and take the second line.

Special arrangements were made to deal with Au Bon Gite. The company of the 11th RB that had made the unsuccessful attack before, together with a party from the 83rd Field Company Royal Engineers, were to advance with the first wave of the 60th Brigade. Their sole objective was the destruction of this block house.

Supporting the infantry was the artillery of the 20th and 38th Divisions and the heavy guns of the XIVth Corps. Three distinct artillery barrages were to be fired – the first a creeping barrage moving at twenty yards per minute which the infantry were to follow as closely as possible. The second was the standing barrage, a series of which would fall upon definite positions as the battle progressed. The first objective line was to be subject to a standing barrage for twenty minutes as the creeping barrage approached it. The second objective line was then to become subject to a one-hour-long barrage, to catch retreating enemy soldiers, damage the defences of the second objective line and suppress any enemy in this area. Both creeping and standing barrages were fired by the divisional gunners. The third barrage, a back barrage, was fired by the Corps heavy guns. This 'searched' the area from 300 yards to 1,500 yards ahead of the advancing soldiers, to prevent machine guns placed behind the attacked area from interfering with the attack. Smoke shells would also be used to curtain the battlefield between the phases of the attack to prevent the enemy from interfering with the attacking soldiers as they regrouped on the objectives.

A barrage would be fired by forty-eight machine guns from the Division to help cover the attacking infantrymen. Half of the machine guns from the 60th Brigade and 61st Brigade machine gun companies would advance with the attacking infantry to add to their firepower to fend off any counter-attack. Additionally, low flying aircraft would attack any targets that presented themselves.

One feature of the attack was that the soldiers were to cross from the west to the east bank of the Steenbeek into their assembly positions overnight, across wooden bridges that were put into place by the engineers on the night before the attack. The British forward positions on the far side of the river ranged from approximately eighty yards from the Steenbeek in front of parts of the 61st Brigade area to 150 yards at most from the river in respect of the 60th Brigade.

There was no possibility of establishing aid posts on the east bank before the attack, other than the regimental aid posts that were to be established by the battalions themselves as the attack progressed. All casualties would either remain where they fell in the deep mud, or would have to walk or be brought across the Steenbeek. The advanced dressing stations (ADS) for the walking wounded were at Elverdinge and Cheapside – approximately 8,000 and 6,000 yards from the front line respectively. Stretcher cases were to be carried to an ADS at Gallwitz Farm, about 3,000 yards from the front line, and 200 men were detailed by Division as stretcher bearers to cover the front it was to attack. The plan was to evacuate casualties from Gallwitz Farm by a light rail system, although when the attack commenced, enemy shellfire quickly broke the rail link and the wounded had to be evacuated using wheeled stretchers and hand trolleys. The ADS at Gallwitz Farm was also abandoned because of enemy shelling.

The Battle of Langemarck

Early on the morning of 14 August the 7th Battalion marched to Magenta Farm where they remained for the rest of the day. Ammunition, bombs, flares and tools were issued to the men while they waited in preparation for the battle. While there they saw an enemy aeroplane swoop down and attack an observation balloon, sending it to the ground in flames. Two parachuting figures floated down to safety in its wake.

Captain Henry Foley said:

> At 7pm we fell in, preparatory to moving up nearer the line. My platoons were in line one behind the other with a gap of about 30 yards between each. I had left the centre platoon, and was walking towards the front of the company, when a 5.9 shell screeched down apparently just over my head and burst with a deafening crash behind me. Swung round, and saw that where but a second before had stood some thirty men, chatting and joking as they slipped on their equipment there was now an appalling shambles. The shell had landed right in among them. Many men were simply blown to pieces. Those who still writhed on the ground were carried into an old trench nearby, and tried to dress their wounds. The poor fellow I was carrying, Liddon's servant, kept saying 'It's no good, sir, you can leave me. I know I'm done'. He was terribly hit in the back and soon died. All told, this one shell cost us 26 casualties – practically a whole platoon gone.

The shell that caused such destruction had been aimed at a nearby British 8 inch howitzer battery. Eight men were killed, the other eighteen injured.[4]

After this brief incident, the battalion continued towards the front line where the men remained on the west bank of the Steenbeek until after nightfall. The conditions were not at all pleasant. Sergeant Dolman wrote: 'We did 24 hours in water up to our knees on August 15th the day before our attack.'

As soon as night fell on 15 August, the 83rd and 84th Field Companies of the Royal Engineers started their essential work of bridging the Steenbeek. Canvas-covered wooden bridges were thrown across the muddy, banked stream to enable the attacking battalions to cross later that night. Other elements of these engineer companies moved across the stream with the difficult task of laying tapes on the east side to mark the forming-up areas for the attackers. The work had to be carried out as quietly as possible, as discovery of the assembling soldiers would have spelled disaster for the whole attack. Even though apparently unaware of the imminent attack, the Germans kept the assembly area to the west of the Steenbeek under sporadic artillery fire and occasionally a burst of machine-gun or rifle fire would issue from Au Bon Gite or other German posts. The Germans were alert and often sent up flares.

A and D Companies crossed the river first, making their way forward about 100 yards on the far side of the river to the outpost line occupied by the 11th RB. Here they dug to improve their positions. The banks of the stream were boggy and flooded, making the relatively short journey forward very difficult. Sergeant Dolman of A Company: 'In single file we passed over a plank, and having gone about 100 yards beyond the brook we lay down in the open, waiting for the eventful dawn.' After the advanced companies were across, both B and C companies followed, taking up their positions in fairly open ground that lay between the forward shell-hole posts and the Steenbeek. Lieutenant Jenks of C Company: 'We crossed on a single swaying plank and lay in the open until dawn. To those in the vicinity of Au Bon Gite, however, the period of waiting, lying without cover, was distinctly harassing.'

Captain Foley of B Company had gone forward to reconnoitre the way ahead. He had found that the position of B Company, in support of A Company on the right flank of the battalion, was perilously close to Au Bon Gite and its occupants were nervously shooting up SOS rockets and Verey lights at the slightest movement.

Captain Foley recalled: 'East of the Steenbeek we were so close to the enemy that we were immune from their shells but back where I had left the company they were falling thick and fast.' Captain Foley returned to his company and waited with them under a fierce barrage for half an hour. When it eased he led them across the Steenbeek.

One by one the men slithered across the flimsy wooden bridges, some losing their footing and falling off when they would sink up to their armpits. By 3.30am the whole battalion, less a few casualties, were across the Steenbeek and drawn up ready to attack. D Company was in the front to the left. A Company, now led by 19-year-old 2nd Lieutenant Claude Lewin, after acting Captain Ledsham received a serious injury from a shell as the company was crossing the river, was in front on the right. C Company formed up behind D Company on the left and B Company in support of A Company on the right. The battalion headquarters found a ruined farm from which to operate, which was in the area held by B company.

Because of the proximity of headquarters to B company, Captain Foley and Colonel Troyte-Bullock were able to meet before the attack. Captain Foley:

> For a long time I sat with him and we talked of the former shows we had been through. At times like these he was at his best – perfectly self possessed, ready with shrewd advice in all our little difficulties, eager to go through any danger and discomfort with his men. Before I left him, as zero time drew near, he told me that A Company had been weakened by casualties and might be slow in starting, in which case I was to do my best to get them on the move myself.

Little was known of the exact German positions. The shelling had been so heavy in recent times that photographs were of little value. The pill boxes could be easily seen, but otherwise all that was known was that the enemy front line of shell-hole posts was about 150 yards from the British front line.

The countdown to the attack was a pensive time for all concerned. Captain Foley recalled:

> Four thirty, thirty five, forty; how many anxious eyes glanced in the first blush of dawn at watches so carefully synchronised that they beat as one? And then like a clap of thunder above the raging storm, burst out the deafening roar of our opening barrage, that curtain of flying steel and smoke that was to creep slowly forward across the unknown before us. The excitement of that moment was intense. In a twinkling I was on my feet, urging on the men of A Company. So thin was their line that my leading wave overtook and intermingled with it.

Sergeant Dolman of A Company:

> Then just before dawn the barrage opened and away we went. There were a good many lads from Bath and Bristol in our battalion, and they went forward splendidly towards Langemarck. It was a wonderful sight as we went over. Right and left we could see our

battalion going strong. My four company officers were casualties in the first five minutes; and then as senior sergeant, I had to take command of the company.

The German counter-barrage was swift, falling harmlessly on the far side of the Steenbeek within thirty seconds of the British guns opening fire. The fire from Au Bon Gite was equally prompt, although more deadly. Machine-gun bullets swept the right flank of A and B Companies and accounted for many men of A Company within minutes of the attack starting. 2nd Lieutenant Lewin, A Company's commander, was injured soon after the attack started.[5] 2nd Lieutenant Kinsey, the only other officer left in A Company, was killed. A Company's attack faltered until the men of B Company came up with them.

Captain Foley of B Company:

> I had hardly gone forward 50 yards, when I felt a sharp pain in my left arm. At the moment it seemed nothing and I ploughed on. In another minute, however the gauntlet glove I was wearing was full of blood; I pulled it off, and found that blood was pouring down my arm. I saw this must be stopped and at once went over to battalion headquarters where [2nd Lieutenant] Rich soon had the wound bound up with my field dressing.

Second Lieutenant Goode took over B company.

It was quickly recognised by 2nd Lieutenant Goode that A Company was losing direction and that Au Bon Gite was holding up the attack. Even though it was outside the 61st Brigade's line of attack, he led B Company against the block house. Men of the 11th Rifle Brigade had crawled up overnight to within yards of it, and they threw smoke bombs from the shell holes in which they hid. The smoke covered the advance of the Somersets who were able to storm Au Bon Gite from the flank after a short fight, capturing the one officer and fifty men who had held it. The way was cleared for the battalion to advance on the first objective line. This was the road and trench system on the west side of Langemarck which was protected by a line of pill boxes in the vicinity of Reitres Farm and Langemarck station on the left-hand side of the 7th Somersets' line of advance and in front of the 7th KOYLI.

On the left side of the battalion attack, although the mud and shell-hole-broken ground quickly disrupted the formation, D Company remained in front of C Company. On the right side, both A and B Companies were partly intermingled, although part of A Company – the remnants of two platoons – lost direction and veered off to their left. As the men advanced behind the creeping barrage they overran the shell-hole posts which contained the odd enemy sniper. These were dealt with by rifle fire and the bayonet. The ground throughout had been very boggy, but this got worse as the men approached the German defensive line on the western side of the village; the Somerset men were increasingly getting stuck at the same time that enemy fire increased as they advanced. The only protection afforded here was the shell-cratered ground and a line of battle-shattered trees. Sergeant Dolman: 'We got along fairly well but the going was very hard, as there was so much mud. We had to help one another out of the mud very often, for we sank above our knees in the marshy and rain sodden ground.'

Captain Jenks of C Company: 'Tim Hill [leading D Company] was the first officer casualty I actually saw. He lay on the lip of a shell hole, beckoning the men on with blasphemous words of encouragement and waving off all assistance – irresponsible as ever but game to the end.' 2nd Lieutenant Hill had been hit in the face and leg by machine-gun bullets.

Captain Jenks continued:

> A few short minutes later and Liddon was down; leaving him with what assistance was available I pressed on, and with the lifting of the barrage events crowded themselves thick upon us. A bad check on the left – flank in the air – Boche machine gun holding up the line – Sergeant House and Lewis gun section rush to cover us. A splendid young NCO was House – later he discarded his useless gun and carried on with a captured German gun.

The little cover there was proved fortunate as heavy machine-gun fire from the pill boxes in front of the 7th KOYLI held up the Somersets' advance and caused many casualties. The delay was about fifteen minutes while men from the 7th KOYLI attacked the pill boxes. One man, Private Edwards from the KOYLI, was awarded the Victoria Cross for rushing a pill box at Reitres Farm and subduing it by throwing grenades through the firing holes. A Lewis gunner from the 7th KOYLI did similar work by firing his machine gun through the loophole of another pill box.

Once the fire from the left diminished, the Somersets attacked again. The time was about 5.15am when the 7th Somersets and the 7th KOYLI captured their first objective line. Sergeant Dolman was with the group of A Company that had veered off to the left:

> The worst things we had to deal with were the pill boxes, full of machine guns. Yet although they were very strong it was surprising how they were presently silenced, the enemy being bombed out of them, and then surrounded and taken. Men who had been firing at us with their machine guns to the last minute came running towards us with hands up shouting 'Mercy, Kameraden'.

D Company together with two sections of A Company then set about consolidating the line. This group was still being led by 2nd Lieutenant Hill MC with his serious facial and leg injuries. He remained with his men until the positions were secure and later got a bar to his Military Cross. While this consolidation was taking place, the men of C Company and B Company were preparing to capture the village and take their second objective line. The attack so far had resulted in many casualties both dead and injured. Among the dead were Private Charles Caperton, a father of two and a pawnbroker from Bath. Only two weeks before he had narrowly escaped death and lost an ear lobe to a shell splinter.

One of the sergeants from the group of A Company that had lost direction was Sergeant Dolman. The platoons had lost their officers, but having gained what they believed were their objectives, started to consolidate. Sergeant Dolman said: 'I had very few men left. I fell across a sergeant from number 2 platoon, and he had a few men so we decided to join forces and make one company of it.'

At 5.35am the men of C and B Companies passed over the first objective line to attack the village. Captain Jenks of C Company:

> My own task was to advance along the centre with C Company, throwing out a section of bombers to clear the village street. That section consisted of eight stout hearted Welsh miners, game for anything. We never saw them again – neither did we ever see the 'village street'. The broken nature of the ground soon reduced our line to knots of struggling units, and from fragments of A and B Companies I discovered that Ledsham had gone from A, and Foley from B, and it was a case of 'carry on sergeant'.

Enemy pill boxes situated at the north-western edge of the village were still active, and these opened heavy machine-gun fire on the attackers. Captain Jenks recalled:

> Almost there! Then – the first of the famous 'pill boxes'. How to deal with the unknown? Goode [from B Company] and a section round to the left; myself with Sergeant Major Hill to the right. A preliminary bombing at any likely looking hole and a rush. Round the corner comes an iron helmet – an arm – a stick bomb – and Hill and I are on our backs; he with a chunk in the thigh and myself nothing worse than a bruised knee. Another rush, and we were in – eight machine guns and a crowd of 'Jerries' were ours – including a wounded Yorkshire boy they were holding as a prisoner, from two days previously.

Some of these pill boxes were by-passed once they became silent, the attackers carrying on through the village, where the men came under rifle fire from German soldiers to their right. Battalion snipers were told off to deal with these men, and effectively stopped this fire. Meanwhile the two attacking companies moved from shell hole to shell hole through the village dealing with enemy strongpoints – often concrete-reinforced houses – by laying covering fire on the strongpoint with Lewis guns while parties of infantrymen would close and attack at short range with grenades. Both Lewis gunners and bombers suffered heavily. Private Henry Purchase, a married man from Hardington Mandeville in Somerset, was one of the Lewis gunners killed. Private Jack Cummins, a bomber, was involved in an attack with three colleagues before being blown up by a shell and killed. He was a married man aged 34. Captain Jenks:

> Yet another pill box, and a sergeant hammering on the iron door with a Mills bomb, excitedly shouting 'Come out you ___ , or I'll ___ well blow you out', and we realised that our objectives were reached. Hastily improvising cover behind a hedge we took breathing space, and with relief watched the King's go through to carry on the good work.

This was at about 7am.

As the King's attacked, a group of about seventy Germans ran from Alouette Farm, across the right flank of B Company in a desperate effort not to be cut off. B Company Lewis gunners opened fire and accounted for more than fifty of the fleeing soldiers.

Captain Foley, with his arm now dressed, decided to rejoin his company but fainted shortly afterwards:

> On regaining consciousness I realised that reaction, following the bleeding and the strain, I suppose of the last few days, had thoroughly set in; I felt like nothing on earth, and about as much use as a sick headache. In a dazed way I looked around for some convenient refuge, and eventually wandered off towards a large pill box. The one thing my soul craved for at that moment was sleep. Outside the pill box were several Tommies. I remember wondering why they stayed on the outside, instead of taking shelter within. The reason was soon apparent – it was full of Boches. I felt perfectly furious with these inoffensive Huns for being in the pill box. I called loudly through the low doorway for them to come out. The thickness of the walls made it impossible to see into the interior. At the sound of my voice the babble within only grew into a roar. I tried in English, French and German but with no effect. At last a brain wave seized me and I yelled 'kamerad' at the top of my voice. The result was magical.

A perfect shriek of joy came from the lusty defenders and one after another they bolted out, while I leaned against the wall of the pill box, revolver in hand dizzily trying to count. I next remember waking up on a chair inside the pill box, and finding that my wound had been redressed.

Consolidation

By 7.15am the 7th Battalion had reached all of its allotted objectives, and contact was made with battalions on both flanks. The southern portion of the village started to be heavily shelled with trench mortar bombs and 5.9 shells landing in the ruined carcasses of the houses and on the land about the scattered trenches. The shellfire was falling on the area occupied by A and D Companies, but was largely ineffective as by this time the men had dug themselves in. Parties from the Royal Engineers had moved up through the morning with the aim of building strongpoints – efforts which were frustrated by enemy fire.

Captain Jenks of C Company was in the Somersets' forward positions:

Rapidly traversing the sector, and allotting posts to NCOs, I realised how few of us had got through. Goode, Joscelyn, Checkland and Bussell were all I could find and almost immediately Bussell was hit by a sniper and though we got him into company headquarters he was gone before we could get him back. It took us all day to find that sniper – he was within our lines and took a deadly toll – but his end was sudden and sure.

Colonel Troyte-Bullock soon arrived at the front, which was now under fire from 5.9s. Enemy aircraft had also appeared and were trying to machine gun the forward British soldiers.

The King's attack ahead of the Somersets had not fared well; it had been unable to capture the Red Line objective, suffering heavily from machine-gun fire in the process. The King's in the end had dug themselves in about 200 yards short of the German defences, and because of their heavy casualties, Colonel Vince, their commanding officer, had requested help from the Somersets at about 2pm. As night closed, Colonel Troyte-Bullock ordered Captain Jenks to take C Company forward to reinforce the King's. At the same time D Company and what was left of A company was brought forward to reinforce B Company at the second objective line.

The Germans counter-attacked the boundary between the 61st and 60th Brigades at 4pm after creeping up on the British soldiers who were seeking shelter behind some hedges. The counter-attack was partly successful, driving the King's and the 12th KRRC battalions back up to 200 yards in places. The counter-attack was eventually contained, although the 12th KRRC lost almost an entire company on its left flank.

Captain Jenks:

> All was not well in front. Messages told of sections falling back in the front line. I went forward to investigate and discovered Colonel Vince in conference with a gunner major who had come along the line and informed us we were 'in the air'. I sent forward Joscelyn and a platoon to strengthen the line and join the King's.

The night of 16 August was relatively quiet with only intermittent shelling in and around the village. Assistance arrived in the shape of Welshmen from the 38th Division who moved up behind the Somersets, bringing water and ammunition with them which was distributed to the grateful men from the 7th Battalion. The British had captured Langemarck in a day. The 20th Division took about 400 prisoners, between twenty and thirty machine guns, a battery of four 4.2 inch howitzers and a 7.7cm field gun in the process. Significantly too, the Division had held on to most of its gains despite fierce counter-attacks.

As dawn broke on 17 August the enemy could be seen massing for a counter-attack on the front right of the 61st Brigade. An SOS rocket was sent up requesting a defensive barrage, to which there was a quick response by the divisional gunners. The barrage effectively dispersed the massing enemy and no attack came. The rest of the morning was spent in further consolidation of the newly won ground. The battered trenches were deepened as artillery duels were fought.

Orders were given as the day progressed to recapture the ground given up in the German counter-attack. The attack was to be delivered mainly by two and a half companies of the 12th Rifle Brigade of the 60th Brigade, together with the 12th King's; three companies of the 7th Somersets and one company from the 7th DCLI were in support. The hour of the attack was fixed for 7pm.

As well as supporting the attack a raid was planned. Captain Jenks said:

> Next day [17 August] I got orders to carry out a daylight raid and dislodge a 'strongpoint' at the cross roads. The task fell to Checkland on the right. Without barrage and with what small cover fire we could give they made the attempt. The job was never likely to succeed and Checkland fell shot through the head in getting out of the trench.

At 7pm the barrage was put down to support the King's attack, and C and D Companies were ordered to move forward to support the King's and occupy their former positions as they advanced. By 7.30pm a report was received which said that the 12th King's had taken their objective, but had suffered heavily in the process. A request for more assistance was sought and B and D Companies were sent forward to help. These men found the King's in a very boggy spot and unable to advance. Orders were eventually received to dig in where they were, there being little other option.

In the raid and supporting the King's attack the battalion suffered a number of casualties. Sergeant James Llewellyn was shot dead by rifle fire, and Privates Avery, Read and Edward Fullbrook were also killed in action. Private Samuel May died of wounds.

Captain Jenks: 'Quite exhausted after forty eight hours endless scrapping, our only hope was to hold on, and at nightfall we handed over our positions, intact, to the incoming relief. With Goode alone left (Joscelyn being still with the King's[6]) I brought out the remnants of our command.'

On the night of the 17th the battalion was relieved by men of the 38th (Welsh) Division, the relief being completed by 1am on 18 August. On the way out to their camp at Dawson's Corner Private Henry Jones was killed. The battalion left the battlefield where forty-one men were known to have been killed and 148 injured. Eighteen men were still unaccounted for. The final casualty figures were forty-four killed and 226 injured.[7]

The battalion remained resting at Dawson's Corner where they were visited by Lord Cavan, commander of the XIVth Corps, who congratulated them on their part in capturing Langemarck. He told the assembled men that they would be taken out of the line for a month for a rest, and that evening the battle-worn soldiers boarded a train to a camp at Proven.

The fighting strength of the battalion had been sapped by the attack. Of the 470 men available to fight before the battle, the battalion fighting strength now stood at about 250. Reinforcements and reorganisation were needed. New Lewis gunners and bombers were found to replace the casualties amongst the specialists, and a draft of ninety men who arrived on the 24th were assimilated.

Deaths continued from the fighting as severely injured soldiers succumbed. On 19 August Private Martin Wallace died. He had been an original volunteer and had survived being wounded on two previous occasions. Private William Winslade's parents were sent the news by a hospital chaplain that their son was dangerously ill. A short while later, after 22 August, they received another letter from the chaplain saying that their son had sunk very rapidly towards the end, becoming semi-comatose before he died.

In Bath the 7-year-old daughter of a former furniture packer, Private George Price waited eagerly for the post on her birthday. When none arrived she asked her mother: 'I wonder why Dad hasn't sent me a birthday card?' The answer came in the later post with a letter from

Lieutenant Spark: 'The brave fellow met his death in an attack on enemy trenches from a shell. He died almost instantly and suffered no pain. He is buried in the village he helped to capture and a cross marks his grave. The Regiment has lost a good soldier.' George Price left three younger children.

Apart from a short spell at Herzeele, the battalion remained in the Proven area until 8 September. The early time was spent in earnest training, but towards the end of the 'rest' the men entered brigade competitions in football, Lewis gunnery, stretcher bearing and cross country running. A further nine men from the 7th Battalion died of injuries during this time.[8]

One of them, a former coachman Private Robert House, had received gunshot wounds to the face, left leg and arm and was treated in the No 14 General Hospital at Wimereux in France. Robert House's wife was written to by two nursing sisters, one of whom assured her that although severely wounded, 'He was very patient and in time would probably get on. He had a very good night the previous night, and was quite cheery in the morning.' Reverend Jones, the hospital chaplain, also wrote to Mrs House:

> I was by his side when he came around from the chloroform. I spoke to him to help him realise where he was. I told him I was a Baptist Minister. I hardly expected him to grasp it but he did. 'Do you know Mr Wyatt?' he asked, and on answering that I did he said 'Dear Mr Wyatt' and then fell to sleep. I was with him last night, and before I left I prayed for him and stroked his dear hair from his forehead. 'What a friend you are to me' he said. Then with his hand in mine he asked me if I would be good enough to write you a few lines on his behalf. He wants you to write to him as soon as you can. He is so anxious to know how you all are. It is unnecessary for me to say that I shall keep in the closest touch with him while he remains here.

Mrs House received the terrible news by telegram three days later; her husband died on 25 August aged 30.

Reporting of the battle was widespread in the days that followed. This was particularly the case as the 20th and 29th Divisions attacks were the only ones where the enemy counter-attacks were contained. The national and local papers repeated variations on a common theme. *The Bridgwater Mercury* for example:

> One young officer of the Somersets knew most of what happened, and his own adventures that day would fill a book if told in detail. He took me to his tent and showed me how his kit had been pierced by a bullet and torn by the blast of shellfire, and he marvelled that he had no more than a hurt hand cut against the teeth of a German sniper and

a body bruised all over but with a whole skin. 'A bit of luck' he said. Some of the strangest episodes happened between the village and a point called Schreiboom. There were two more block houses on the Langemarck road girdled by machine gun fire. The first was rushed by twenty men, led by this young officer I have been telling about and bombed until 30 Germans tumbled out and surrendered. Beyond was the other block house on which this officer advanced with six men. A machine gun was firing from the right of it and it was a strong place with no open door. The seven Somersets went straight for it and the officer flung two bombs through the loopholes, but they did not seem to take effect. Then he hurled two more at the iron door but they did not burst. With his fists he beat the door shouting 'Come out you blighters, come out'. Presently to his surprise they came out forty two men and a wounded Yorkshireman.

The account is undoubtedly based upon Captain Jenks' actions. He later commented on a similar article in the national papers: 'For pictorial illustration of this little fracas, see Caton Woodville's picture, where "a gallant young Somerset officer" is complete with Army Service Corps badges (but not rations).'

Analysis

Tactically the Battle of Langemarck is interesting in a number of respects. The battle had a number of features some of which were not new. First was the employment by the Germans of the 'deep' battlefield, where their forward posts were merely meant to impede the advance of the enemy who would be drawn into the main battle zone – in the case of Langemarck the village and fortifications on either side of it. It was here that the defenders planned to stop the enemy. A nearby reserve position, holding the majority of the defenders, would stand by to expel the British from any ground captured after the main attack had been stopped. The main reserve for Langemarck was correctly identified by Major General Douglas-Smith as being held in the Poelcapelle area. The 'deep' defensive pattern was by no means new, and had been very effectively employed in the later Somme fighting one year earlier.

The British plans for dealing with the deep battlefield were interesting. The attack, in theory, was to be conducted in a familiar three stages. Because of the availability of a variety of munitions, the gunners were able to deploy a far more complicated fire programme than they had done in any battle fought by the 7th Somersets to that date. A number of features were re-runs of the old battles. A creeping barrage moving towards each objective line was now commonplace. It proved successful in suppressing the defenders until the attackers were close enough to assault the defending infantrymen without suffering serious harm. Despite the extremely boggy ground, the barrage advanced sufficiently slowly for the attackers to keep up with it in this attack. A new feature that no doubt saved many lives was the introduction of smoke shells into the standing barrages that fell as a stationary barrage on the next objective line to the one being attacked. This had a dual effect of masking the attackers from observation from long-range enemy machine gunners and from artillery observers.

The Divisional Commander, Major General Douglas-Smith, also employed an unusual plan of attack in that the line of advance was at an angle to the main defensive lines. He envisaged that the 60th Brigade, on the right of the 61st Brigade, would attack on a north-easterly 'line' that would bring it between Langemarck and Poelcapelle, effectively severing the German battle zone in Langemarck from the Poelcapelle reserves intended to protect it. While this was not a strict encirclement or envelopment attack, it nevertheless had the same effect, while retaining a simple attack direction for the men of the 60th Brigade. In the actual attack the plan worked. The Somersets were left fairly untroubled and in possession of the village despite the strong enemy counter-attack. The attack plan was able to rely upon the now predictable German defensive tactic of absorbing the attack and then mounting a strong counter-attack using local reserves.

Another defect inherent in the German defensive plan was that their artillery was limited in where it could fire. In front of Langemarck the British troops formed up so close to the German positions as to be within the German gunners' defensive fire plan. So long as they were able to advance fairly rapidly, which they were despite Au Bon Gite, the casualties from defensive artillery fire were minimised. It is always difficult to surmise, but the casualties caused by the heavy artillery barrage on the British side of the Steenbeek as the men waited in shell holes to cross suggests that the attack would probably have failed if the attackers were required to move through a proper defensive barrage.

Another striking feature of the attack were the tactics used by the infantrymen. Although the battle plan was of necessity drawn with companies occupying given positions and advancing on given objective lines at certain times, three features are evident. The first is that for the first time the planning was objective-led at a platoon and section level, with men being assigned to deal with particular known strongpoints so far as they could be identified before the battle. The second is the introduction and co-ordination of the engineers with the infantry in a combat engineering role, bridging obstacles and assaulting the Au Bon Gite strongpoint. The third, and most significant, is the manner in which the infantry were organised to deal with the unknown. The four companies were reduced to three platoons each – two assigned to lead and the third for 'mopping up'. The orders given to the infantry were essentially infiltration tactics where the lead platoons would bypass any resistance and attack from the flank and rear (as the battalion did at Au Bon Gite and other strongpoints) and where the assault momentum would be maintained by the foremost soldiers leaving the mopping up platoons to deal with bypassed points of resistance. Within the platoons there was a reorganisation too. Lewis gun teams were assigned to provide suppressive fire on an objective, while infantry squads ahead closed upon it with grenades and rifles.

This is the first example of the 7th Battalion (an average British infantry battalion) using modern infantry squad tactics. It was extremely successful. The battalion suffered 270 men killed and injured, but had been in the forefront of an attack that was carried through knee-deep mud against machine guns in concrete emplacements and against an enemy who were alert to being attacked.

NOTES

1   Those killed were Corporal Henry Short and Private Henry Whitehorn.
2   The men killed were Lance Sergeant Cecil White, Lance Corporal Walter Talbot and Privates Frederick Wooley, Sidney Counsell, Henry Hexter, William Chitten, Tom Tucker, Herbert Grant, William Board, Joseph Spicer, Charles York and Joshua Vincent.
3   Notes on 38th Division Orders for the Attack – 20th Division No G484. It would appear that these orders were copied by the 20th Division from 38th Division orders.
4   The dead included 19-year-old Lance Corporal Arthur Davies, Private Arthur Tanner – a father of three and chemist – from Bedminster in Bristol, 36-year-old Private Edward Fisher, 35-year-old Lewis Gray and 25-year-old Frank Candy. Soldiers who died from their injuries were Privates Albert Kingston and William Foxworthy, and Lance Corporal William Brown who died in an advanced dressing station nearby aged 32.
5   2nd Lieutenant Claude Lewin received the Military Cross for his brief involvement in the battle.
6   Joscelyn was subsequently killed by a shell in Poperinghe as he went to go on leave. He had remained with the King's.
7   The dead were Private George Baber, Private John Bazley, Private Frederick Bone, Corporal William Briggs, Sergeant Albert Burgess, Private Charles Caperton, Private Albert Carter, Private Allan Cox, Private John Cummings, Private Frederick Cutler, Private Henry Dutton, Private Samuel Fevin, Private Frank Foley, Private John Gammon, Private Charles Gingell, Private William Hamlin, Lance Corporal William Harding, Private William Hayball, Private Reginald Heal, Private William Hillier, Private Edwin Hippard, Corporal Francis Hutchison, Lance Corporal Charles James, Private Sidney Jordan, 2nd Lieutenant Albert Kinsey, Private John Knight, Private Ernest Lay, Private George Marchant, Private Arthur Merry, Private Frederick Moran, Private George North, Private Thomas Painter, Private Albert Perry, Private Richard Phillips, Private Archie Portingale, Private George Price, Private Henry Purchase, Private Harold Seuse, Private Frank Shaw, Private

Edwin Taylor, Private Percy Thomas, Private Frederick White, Private Alfred Widlake and Private John Winter.

8   On 18 August 1917: Privates Frederick Davey and William Conday. On 24 August: Private Percy Harper and Private Albert Vowles. On 25 August: Private Robert House. On 26 August: Private Wilfred Cox. On 27 August: Private George Bellamy. On 3 September: Private Edward Warner. On 4 September: Sergeant Cyril Ashley.

CHAPTER XIII
Eagle Trench

Pilckem Ridge

On 9 September 1917 the 7th Battalion returned to the dugouts along the banks of the Ypres canal. These positions were now relatively safe as most of the enemy artillery fire was directed at the soldiers farther ahead, although the weather cleared allowing better artillery observation.

Although the Ypres area was familiar to most in the battalion, for Lieutenant McMurtrie, a new officer, it was his first tour to the front line. McMurtrie wrote:

> On the way, I saw for the first time ruined houses and just before reaching the canal we passed several batteries. We got the men into dug-outs by the side of the canal and then after having some food, had a look around. There was a little stagnant water in the canal, which smelt abominably and all around could be seen nothing but shell holes, barbed wire, odd duds and here and there dead horses. All night there was a continuous rumble of guns and we found it very hard to sleep because our guns were firing just behind the canal and the rats were a little too near to be pleasant in the dug-out, which I shared with [Lieutenants] Smith and Langdon.

On the night of the 10th the battalion returned to Langemarck. Lieutenant McMurtrie:

> Every man wore a haversack on his back instead of a pack, the usual equipment, rifle and also about 120 rounds, 2 mills bombs each and either a shovel or a pick. I wore a pack, revolver, compass and revolver ammunition. Each man had in his haversack, one or two pairs of socks, shaving and washing materials, waterproof sheet, oil bottle and pull through. We left the canal in single file just as it began to get dusk.

The battalion tramped along the now improved although still dangerous duck board pathways over Pilckem Ridge and crossed slippery bridges

167

over the Steenbeek, where they were to meet guides to take them to the front line. Pilckem Ridge was under constant harassing fire, as were the 18pdr batteries that had been hauled through the mud across the Steenbeek.

Lieutenant McMurtrie recalled:

> As we got to the top of the ridge the Germans opened fire with their guns at the corner of the road and managed to set an ammunition dump on fire, which was only about 150 yards from the duck boards, up which we were going. Shells were exploding everywhere and several of the men in headquarters company were wounded; meanwhile no guides had turned up. We went forward away from the danger zone and then got off the duck boards into shell holes. We waited for an hour or so watching the glowing of the exploding ammunition dump. It began to get cold which was not very pleasant as the shell hole I was in was half-full of water and there was a distinct smell of dead Boche, which did not improve matters. After a long wait, the guides at last turned up, and we began to go down the slope towards Langemarck.

In the barrage twelve men were injured, including 2nd Lieutenant Malpas, the battalion adjutant, whose tote had come unstuck at the race meeting in November 1916. Private Reginald Whiting was killed.

The battalion quickly settled into their new positions in the front line which was frequently subjected to enemy fire. Most of the men occupied shell-hole posts because of the impossibility of digging proper trenches in the marshy ground. These posts would be reinforced with sand bags and pieces of wood or metal that could be found lying about or brought up the line. Some of the officers had shelters within the posts and the headquarters staff were able to use a captured block house, now called the 'Pig and Whistle', for cover.

In two full days at the front the battalion suffered ten fatalities from shellfire and twenty-one injured.[1] One of those badly injured was 32-year-old Private Frederick China, who suffered severe spinal injuries. He had worked as the manager of the Twerton Co-operative Society in Bath before joining the colours in June 1916. He had been initially sent to the 3rd Battalion at Plymouth and then to the 7th Battalion in October 1916. Within days of his injury he had been transported to the King George's Military Hospital. There it was diagnosed that should he survive he would never be able to walk again. He died on 21 September with his wife, Lucy, and his mother present. He left a small son.

It is noticeable that the battalion's casualties had started to come from areas with a wider geographical spread by the time of Third Ypres. Although most of the men were from Somerset, casualties from the previous two days included men who had prior military service with the Worcestershire Regiment, the Devon and Dorset Regiments and also the Royal Berkshire Regiment. This reflected the increasing flexibility in where drafts were drawn from to make good losses.

The battalion had two days out of the line constantly engaged in carrying parties. There were no proper roads forward, and because of the heavy casualties among supply animals they were only used to deliver their loads to the rearmost areas; the supplies were then carried forward by the infantry. Everything that was required by the soldiers at the front had to be carried there along muddy duck boards that wound their way around the shell holes. Trench boards, salving equipment, ammunition and food and water were carried forward by parties of men, hidden from the enemy only by the darkness of the night.

Lieutenant McMurtrie later recalled the salient:

> Always on the Ypres salient there was a huge amount of salvage lying about – old rifles, Lewis guns, steel helmets, boxes of small arms ammunition, box respirators and unused shells. By degrees these were in part collected and sent back to be repaired and reissued. Whenever I went up the line in the Ypres salient and saw all this carnage and wasted material, a dead horse here, a broken limber there, bits of wood all around and one vast bleak country of shell holes, barbed wire and wasted material, I could not help thinking what a worthless waste of time, human life, energy and material war was. I also thought of all the families without a father or a son parted perhaps for a time or killed in the war. No, war causes much hardship and anxiety at home and is not a pleasant experience.

On the night of the 14th the battalion returned to the front. The first day in the line was quiet, but at dawn on the 16th a heavy barrage was put down on the British front line. The Germans attacked the 12th King's to the left of the Somersets and also the Guards Division front line to the left of the King's. They were beaten back. Germans were also seen massing ahead of the Somersets, but were prevented from attacking by a prompt artillery barrage on their positions. Despite the lack of an attack, five men from the battalion were killed by the estimated 400 shells fired into their area during the day.[2] The battalion was relieved that evening and the exhausted men returned to the reserve area to the west of the Steenbeek. Just before the relief a machine gunner from the battalion, 26-year-old Private Arthur Brown, was shot and seriously injured. He was taken to one of the Mendinghem casualty clearing stations where he died three days later.

Once again the time out of the line was not one of rest. The men carried munitions forward for the Royal Engineers. This work was carried out for the 'Z Special Company' of the Royal Engineers, who were part of the Special Brigade; their expertise was in the launching of gas attacks on the enemy. At this time Z Company specialised in attacking the enemy using Livens projectors which were large mortar-type devices that would fire a gas canister at an unsuspecting enemy.

Lieutenant McMurtrie:

> Langdon and I had to take a carrying party of 100 men up the line. We reported to the R.E. officer at the dump and there each man was given a 60lb gas shell. The 100 men were divided into three parties of 33 each and Langdon went with the first party. A sergeant was put in charge of the second party and I brought up the rear with the third party. There was also a guide for each party. The night was pitch dark and it was no easy job carrying these heavy shells along shelled duck boards. This was the worst carrying party I have ever been on, a great many men felt tired and did their best to dump their shell, others got very scared when a shell exploded near them and it was only by bullying them that I could make them get on with the job. I must say of all line work except an attack, working and carrying parties were the worst. Just before we arrived at Alouette Farm, I met Langdon with the first party going back having taken the shells to the dump. The dump was a little distance beyond Alouette Farm and as the rear of the third party reached the farm, the enemy commenced to heavily shell a spot on the duck boards about 100 yards beyond the farm. The front men of the third party came running back and all the men got in an awful state of panic. Two or three had got shell shock and were gibbering about people being killed in large numbers in front. I got all the men into shelters behind the farm and then asked for two volunteers to go out with me and find the wounded. I then went up the duck board track with these two stretcher bearers and found one man terribly mangled by a shell. He [Private Henry White] died in my arms and then we took his identity discs and belongings and went further up and found one man badly wounded in the leg. We got him on to the stretcher and looking around and finding no other men returned with the stretcher case.

The party led by Lieutenant McMurtrie found that the Royal Engineers guide had disappeared, and the gas shells were left at Alouette Farm. The working party returned to the reserve area. Private White was a married man from Aston in Birmingham; his body was never identifiably found after the war possibly because of the removal of his identity discs.

Up until 23 September 1917 the battalion remained at Dawson's Corner supplying carrying parties in support of offensive operations in the area of Eagle Trench which lay ahead of Langemarck. On the 20th itself the men of the battalion could hear the guns booming in support of the attack. Lieutenant McMurtrie said:

> There was heavy artillery drum fire the whole morning but we could get no news at all. I cycled over to the Chateaux at Elverdinge to the field cashier to get some money for the battalion and there found out that so far the news was very good, we had advanced a good distance but Eagle Trench was holding us up.[3]

The time in reserve did not pass without loss. Enemy aircraft had been active for most of September as the weather had improved, and the Germans held a temporary air superiority. Utilising their advantage German aircraft dropped two bombs on the Somerset's tent camp on the morning of 22 September. Eight men were killed and another twenty-two injured.[4]

Eagle Trench

On 20 September the 59th and 60th Brigades of the 20th Division attacked Eagle Trench, a defensive system east of Schreiboom, which included a main trench with an eight-foot embankment built on either side and a central strongpoint. The two attacks had succeeded in capturing the northern and southern parts of the trench system, but the stronghold had withstood the onslaught.

A further attack, to be supported by two tanks, was planned for the 22nd, but when both tanks bogged down in Langemarck it was postponed until 23 September. The difficulty in attacking the strongpoints was that the artillery were unable to support the attack – other than by firing smoke – because of the closeness of the British soldiers to the north and south of the point to be attacked. The attack was therefore to be made with the support of Stokes mortars and rifle grenades firing at the defended positions as bombing parties closed from both northern and southern flanks.

On 22 September Lieutenant Colonel Preston-Whyte who was temporarily in command of the 7th Somersets, called all of the officers of the battalion to a meeting at the headquarters mess.

Lieutenant Chappell recalled the meeting[5]:

> We knew something was on when all officers were ordered to rendezvous at the headquarters mess. Here Pip W [Lieutenant Colonel Preston-Whyte] explained that we were to relieve the front line at Eagle Trench on the night of the 23rd/24th September – optimism was rife these days, because at that moment the whole of Eagle Trench had not been taken – straighten it out and generally act

like the heroes and maneaters the 7th SomLI were known to be. He certainly gave us the idea that there was dirty work in the offing and the air was a little electric, as we weren't sure if it meant a man's war, or just a finicky trench affair.

On the morning of 23 September, just before the British attack was due, the Germans counter-attacked the British-held part of Eagle Trench which was still held by men of the 59th and 60th Brigades. The attack was beaten off. Despite the disruption caused by the German attack, the 59th and 60th Brigade assault was still able to go in against the strongpoint. It completely surprised the defenders who had just stood down for the morning. The Stokes mortars were very effective, and the bombers closed along the trenches from north and south. At the last moment, one company of the 10th Rifle Brigade stormed the strongpoint frontally and after a short fierce fight captured the position, clearing the whole of Eagle Trench.

The Somersets left their camp at Elverdinge at 7pm on the 23rd and started their journey to the front to relieve the 10th and 11th Rifle Brigades. The platoons marched along at 200-yard intervals because of the enemy shelling. The journey required the battalion to once again cross the hated Steenbeek stream.

Lieutenant Chappell:

> The very thought of crossing that miserable, pestilential, stagnant streamlet, the Steenbeek produced a sky high wind-up and terror within me. At every storm of rain the wretched thing would overflow and make the surrounding country into mud-heaps – slimy, soft mud heaps; I only knew of one bridge, and on either side was a large R.E. dump where there seemed to congregate thousands of unfortunate soldiers doomed to carry trench boards and what not up to the front; on relief nights these carrying parties would get seemingly inextricably mixed up with working parties, guns and gunners, infantry, and transport all queued up waiting to cross, the whiles the Hun would drop salvos of 4.5s around at regular short intervals, with an occasional 8 inch howitzer, the more completely to destroy one's morale. It was not unusual for a pair of mules attached to a wagon to imagine themselves at the Royal Tournament and attempt a flying leap of the ditch, and then the waiting P.B.I. [poor bloody infantry] would be called on to retrieve the situation and haul out tons of wagon, stores and mules from the sticky, filthy mud.

One of the platoons was hit by a shell, although fortunately suffered only a few minor injuries. While the men were being attended to, the rest of the battalion filed past towards the Steenbeek. Lieutenant Chappell continued:

Such was the Steenbeek which faced us as darkness fell, and as soon as it was sighted I began to time the salvos falling around the bridge, being greatly assisted in this by the lurid and fervent exclamations from my platoon. At last the bridge was only 100 yards away and we were overjoyed to find the road 'cleared' for relieving units. Pausing for the inevitable salvo to drop, we completely forgot we were the bright lights of the British Army, and rushed with unseemly haste over the bridge to Au Bon Gite and safety.

The battalion moved into Langemarck to await guides who never came. Lieutenant Chappell:

> Heavens knows how long we waited there, but no guides turned up, and at last, in desperation, we decided to find the way ourselves. We eventually arrived in Eagle Trench, but only after strolling round the whole of the Salient or so we thought, and falling into every possible shell hole. I know I arrived there looking as much like a British Officer as Bairnsfather's 'Old Bill' looked like a Field Marshal! The 10th Rifle Brigade were really glad to see us and hopped it without delay – small blame to them, as the poor devils had had a rough time – and there we were in Eagle Trench ready to live up to all that was thought of us, but not having the foggiest notion of the job required, except to straighten the line.

As dawn came the Somersets found themselves in the deep trench between the eight-foot earth embankments that had in places been reinforced with concrete. The occasional machine-gun emplacement – with the door facing the wrong way – providing cover for the company and battalion headquarters. The men from the battalion had been told by soldiers they had relieved that the enemy were anything from 100 to 1,000 yards away.

The morning found the Flanders countryside shrouded in a very heavy mist, which did not help at all, especially when word came that the battalion might be attacked that day. The recently captured trenches had not been prepared for defence and it was found that there was no wire at all in front of the Somersets' trench which added to the nervousness of the men. Grasping the nettle, the battalion sent out a number of patrols into no man's land to locate the enemy and to identify strange noises coming from there. Lieutenant Chappell took a corporal out to patrol:

> We advanced into the mist and no man's land to find what we could. The noise guided us to some 60 or 70 yards in front and there we discovered a badly wounded German officer who was just able to ejaculate 'Kamerad'. I found he was shot through the body.

After rendering first aid, and losing an automatic pistol and a pair of binoculars as souvenirs to the eagle-eyed corporal, the officer was carried back to Eagle Trench where he was left at Captain Peard's headquarters. More patrols recovered another three injured Germans, all from a storm troop unit that had been used to counter-attack Eagle Trench the previous morning. British soldiers from the 59th and 60th Brigades were also found and brought in.

The mist remained all day, which the men spent trying to improve their defensive positions using odd bits of wire and rubbish. The enemy sent over the occasional random shell. It was clear that their gunners had no idea where the British were.

On the night of the 24th the men received their orders. The battalion was to push forward some outposts overnight, up to 500 yards in front of Eagle Trench if possible. Lieutenant Chappell:

> My platoon was to establish two posts, one section in each, and as my prowling during the day had given me a very good idea of the lie of the land, by 'stand to' on 25th – that is, a good night's work – we had our posts dug, manned and taped to my own headquarters. It was not a pleasant prospect for the sections manning the posts; they took food and water with them for 24 hours and no matter what happened, it was impossible for them to come back to the front line until darkness set in.

Soon after dawn on 25 September the Germans put a heavy barrage down just in front of the support line. 2nd Lieutenant Smith:

> At the time I was supposed to be in charge of the support trenches. Peard and Spark were in a pill box (company headquarters) a little way in rear. The German barrage was principally on or in front of the support line, though it must have been pretty bad behind too, as I remember Peard and Spark describing either how they had swallowed or contemplated swallowing (I forget which) some secret orders which were not supposed to fall into Boche hands. Why they couldn't have put a match to them is always a puzzle to me.

Farther ahead, Lieutenant Chappell watched the barrage falling behind his front-line positions:

> I watched it for a bit and then wandered along to Peard and said 'What about it?' He replied, as I thought, very morningish, 'You'd better hop back to your platoon, as it looks like a big attack.' I hopped it, thinking that as the Huns want a scrap (I surmised this from the fact that the barrage was well behind our line and not on it.) It was,

perhaps, just as well we were the heroes and maneaters Pip W had said we were.

Tension mounted amongst the waiting men. 2nd Lieutenant Smith recalled:

> Anyway the Boche shells rendered our posts in front of me invisible, and the idea occurred to me, 'What about our jolly old SOS rockets?' I held a small pow-wow in the trench with a junior officer and senior NCO and pointed out that, having lugged the darn things into every trench we had occupied during the last six months, it appeared to me that now was the time to 'poop off'. They concurred. We 'pooped off'. I had always envied the Boche his superiority in the matter of pyrotechnical displays, but I'm bound to say our old SOS came up to the best the Boche standard and our guns almost immediately started to paste the stuff over in no uncertain fashion.

Lieutenant Chappell, was ahead and to the right of Smith:

> Fortunately, C Company on the left possessed the real hero in 2nd Lieutenant Smith, who, without orders or advice, sent up the SOS rocket. This was instantly replied to by the gunners, a result which, as was afterwards proved, completely smashed a big attack just commencing. For this action 2nd Lieutenant Smith was, and is still, known as SOS Smith.

The enemy barrage petered out as the day progressed. Remarkably the Somersets had no casualties. The night of the 25th enabled more work to be done to strengthen the defensive line, although little wire was available. It had been promised. That night efforts were also made to find the enemy front line, with patrols moving about in the mist-shrouded darkness. An enemy machine-gun post was located in a battered house some way ahead, and the next day heavy artillery fire was used to smash it to pieces. The enemy could not otherwise be found in the 800 yards ahead of Eagle Trench until another stream was found. No efforts were made to cross.

The 26th was a fairly quiet, mist-covered day, and the men received the news that they were to be relieved that night. The quiet was broken at about 8pm when the Germans dropped a heavy barrage on the front-line posts. Lieutenant Chappell said:

> All heavy stuff, too, with nothing less than a 5.9 Crash! Crash! Crash! All along the line they continued to burst; we stood with Peard, a very silent group; he, in his curt manner said 'What's up now? Is the

promised attack coming off?' No one replied, each being too much engaged with his own thoughts, mine being more concerned with my posts than an attack, as I knew by the line of fire that the barrage – for barrage it surely was – must be perilously near them. As we watched and the minutes slowly sped, dusk began to creep in and the flashes of bursting shells grew brighter. Then to our utter astonishment from out of the inferno in front walks a man in khaki, unsteadily, and without equipment. For some moments we could do nothing, but as he came nearer I recognised him as one of my platoon from the right advanced post.

Good God, what had happened? I ran forward and asked him the reason he had left his post, but all he could mumble was 'All gone. All gone'. His very helplessness and inability to tell me anything seemed to smother all sympathetic feelings and I furiously cursed him for leaving his comrades, and realising the futility of this and the need for immediate action, called for a volunteer stretcher bearer, who was instantly forthcoming. We made our way back to the post. What a sight! Large calibre shell had burst right in the post, which was now strewn with the remains of six soldiers, the sole survivor being blown a considerable distance and eventually wandering into company headquarters where we first saw him, suffering from shell shock.

Lieutenant Chappell and the stretcher bearer could do nothing; later the post was filled in – bodies and all – and a new post was dug nearby. Seventeen others had been injured in the barrage.[6]

The battalion was relieved by the 12th King's at midnight and moved back to the piece of land that lay between Langemarck and the Steenbeek. While out of the front line, Corporal Villis wrote to the parents of 23-year-old Private Wilfred Bawden, who had been killed in the post that received the direct hit:

No doubt you will be surprised to receive this letter from an utter stranger, but I have a very painful subject to write to you about. It is a task I do not relish, but having given my promise to write to you I will carry it out. The task I have to perform is to inform you of the sad death of one who is no doubt dear to you. I mean Wilfred Bawden. He was killed by a shell a few days ago. Perhaps it will be of some consolation to you to know that he suffered no pain, for he was killed instantly. It was strange that he should ask me to write if anything happened to him this last time in the line. He had never done so before, but perhaps he had an idea he was to meet his death this time. I know of many who have had the same feeling. All his friends and I feel his loss greatly. He was liked by everyone, for he was cheerful and willing at all times.

Wilfred had worked at his parents' farm, Elm Tree Farm at Woolavington, before joining up.

While stationed between Langemarck and the Steenbeek the men were unable to rest; the area was subjected to occasional shelling, and carrying parties were needed. On the morning of 28 September, the battalion's last day in the Ypres salient, their area was heavily shelled, killing 46-year-old smelter Private Joseph Cox who had served with the battalion since the beginning of the war. Eleven others were wounded, some seriously. One of those, 20-year-old Alfred Gay died in the nearby Mendinghem casualty station. That night the 7th Somersets were relieved and within five days had travelled by train and foot to a bell tent camp near Peronne.[7] It was the battalion's last involvement in what was later called the Passchendaele offensive.

NOTES

1   Those killed on 11 September were Privates Cecil Tilley, John Hammon, Edward Batley and George White. Private James Randall, a 21-year-old married man who had worked in a brick yard before the war, was also killed instantly after being blown up by a shell which dropped into the post he was in. On 12 September Lance Corporal Albert Chorley and Privates Thomas Shanklyn, George Spear, Arthur Dancey and Ernest Monckton were killed.

2   Those killed were Private Thomas Winter (who had been with the battalion for fifteen months, during which time he was allowed to return home on leave in June 1916 after his wife had died), Lance Corporal Halroyd Hamblyn and Privates William Kirkwood, Henry Cook and Thomas Slackstone.

3   On 18 September 33-year-old Private Charles Cook died at Wimereux hospital near Boulogne.

4   The dead were Privates Wilfred Shier, Frederick Gillett, Harry Haines, Charles Jarris, Wilfred Chamberlain, Ernest Price, Frederick Daymond and Harold Callow.

5   Lieutenant Chappell, although new to the 7th Battalion, had served with the 1st SomLI as a sergeant major since the beginning of the war. He took part in the attack on the first day of the Somme offensive and was the most senior officer to cross no man's land to survive uninjured. A good account of this appears in Martin Middlebrook's book, *The First Day On The Somme, 1 July 1916.*

6   The six men blown up in the post were Privates Wilfred Bawden, Edward Smart, William Marshall and William Davey, Lance Corporal Daniel Thomas and Sergeant William Fry. Only William Davey's body was ever identified after the war. Dan Thomas from Pentre in Glamorgan was only 22 years old and had been with the battalion since the beginning of the war. He had joined with his father who had recently been discharged from the battalion after three years' service.

7   On 28 September 1917 Private Edgar Palmer, a 20-year-old policeman's son who had worked at the Asiatic Petroleum Company in Portishead, died of wounds in a hospital in Rouen, and Private William Vickery, a 42-year-old veteran of the Boer War and holder of the Military Medal, died of wounds at Etaples where he was buried. The following week Private Alfred Diaper also died of wounds.

CHAPTER XIV
Cambrai

Preparations

The withdrawal of the 20th Division from the Ypres salient was a welcome relief for all as the move south brought them to a very quiet sector of the line. The 7th Battalion, with the rest of the Division, had moved into the vicinity of Havrincourt Wood where they had been promised one month's rest. The area was familiar to many of the battalion who had been involved in the spring advance. The Division now faced the Hindenburg Line; a series of deep trenches and bunkers, dotted with strongpoints – sometimes a whole fortified village, and protected by dense barbed-wire entanglements, six feet high and ten feet deep.

Because of the heavy fighting in the Ypres area that had worn both British and German units to the bone, the quiet sectors were normally very quiet. Many of the units there, like the 20th Division, had been taken away from the titanic struggle in the north to recuperate. However, because of the near total collapse of the Russian efforts, the Germans were beginning to transfer relatively fresh units from the Eastern Front to the Western Front.

Unknown except to a few, for it was initially a closely guarded secret, Haig was planning a surprise attack in an area the enemy did not expect. The planning at that time envisaged an attack in the direction of Cambrai that would break through the Hindenburg Line and either capture or menace Cambrai, which was an important communication centre for the Germans six miles behind their front line.

The attack would involve the use of 400 tanks and a preparatory artillery barrage would be dispensed with, in order to maintain surprise for the assaulting soldiers. A feature would be that the artillery would not even be able to pre-register their guns, a process whereby spotting rounds would be fired, observed, and the fall of the shells corrected. This would have given away the intention to attack.

Arrival at the new front

On 8 October the 7th Battalion travelled by bus from their camp at Haut-Allaines to Heudicourt where they stayed in huts in the ruined village for the day. The next day the battalion went into the line near Villers-Guislain. Captain Spark said:

> The contrast was remarkable. To those who have not seen a modern battlefield, the conditions are almost incredible. The utter desolation, sense of unreality and smell of decay are indescribable. A journey to the front line at night in the Ypres Salient was a nightmare. The greasy, broken duck-boards; the sweating, heavily laden men; shrapnel, HE. and gas shells; occasional glimpses given by the Verey lights of a sea of slimy mud, tree stumps, stagnant water, broken wagons and dead mules. These were the surroundings in which we had lived for months, and the sight of the green rolling downs, hard dry roads and unshelled trenches was a very welcome change.

The battalion had by now been brought up to a front-line strength of twenty officers and 560 other ranks through the arrival of more men in drafts, and they occupied trenches that were in excellent condition. The front and support lines had duck board throughout and the trenches were well drained. The Germans were very quiet with occasional sniping activity, and only around twenty light shells per day were fired into the battalion's area.

The dugouts were deep and comfortable. These shell-proof structures contained beds made from wood frames and wire netting, utter luxury for men who were accustomed to living in water-logged shell holes or damp and heavily shelled pill boxes. Despite the generally good trench conditions, there was always the problem of rats, which would especially frequent the gloom of the men's shelters. Soldiers would return to find their packs and other personal effects gnawed through. Rat hunting therefore continued to be a frequent pastime in which the men would equip themselves with strong sticks and set about hunting down their elusive quarry.

The Somersets' positions overlooked a valley, at the bottom of which lay the St Quentin canal. The men directly faced the village of Honnecourt which straddled the canal, and to the north-east lay the village of Bantouzelle which was also overlooked. With field glasses or telescopes officers were able to watch the Germans moving about and working in these villages that lay behind the front of the Hindenburg Line defences. During the day the officers were also able to hunt partridges behind the lines.

The battalion could exploit the quiet by dominating no man's land with frequent patrols at night. Up to four ten-man patrols were sent out. Although no enemy were encountered, the Germans were often heard working in their positions. Between two and four pairs of snipers would also be deployed at night into no man's land where they remained

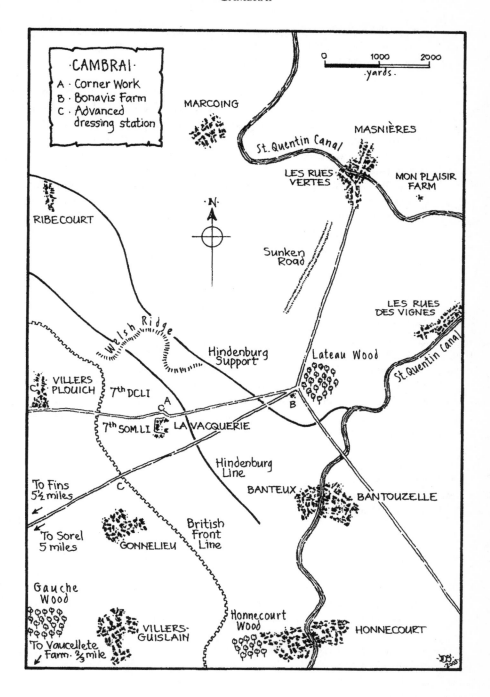

·CAMBRAI·
A · Corner Work
B · Bonavis Farm
C · Advanced
  dressing station

throughout the next day. Opportunities to shoot were very rare and many snipers did not fire at all because the enemy were so far away.

Lieutenant McMurtrie described life there:

> The ordinary trench routine in quiet parts of the line and whenever it was possible was as follows. You always relieved at night. At dusk everyone in the front and support lines 'stood to'. After it was quite dark the company commander would pass along the word to 'stand down'. Night sentries would then be posted and all the rest of the men would be able to get off the firestep and sit or lie in the trench, but no NCO or man was allowed in any dugout or shelter except for special purposes during darkness. Soon after 'stand down' hot tea or soup would come up and be sent around. After this, some of the men would be nominated to clear up the trenches, altering them or putting up more wire in front of the trench, going out on patrol etc. After midnight another lot of soup or tea would be issued. Just before it began to get light every one would again 'stand to'. When it was quite light 'stand down' would be sent along, rum would be issued by an officer, tea would be issued, day sentries posted and after having breakfast, all the men not on duty would turn into their shelters or dugouts to sleep. At 1pm every man had to be washed and shaved and from 1pm to 3pm everyone would work on the trenches. Just before 'stand to' in the evening, all the trenches were tidied up, all the paper, tins, odd scraps of wood would be buried, all the latrines would be disinfected. This was the routine every day for all days, and it can be seen that the men only got about six hours sleep and were at work all the rest of the time.

The battalion remained in these trenches until 15 October mostly following the same routine. The only event of note during this time was an unfortunate incident with a patrol on 12 October.

Lieutenant McMurtrie:

> A patrol went out from a certain post and as usual warned the whole front line that they were out. It came in too soon and was sent out again by the second in command, but did not warn the rest of the front line. When they came in the second time, the sentry not knowing that a patrol was out saw them coming towards the front line, did not wait to challenge, but fired and killed one of the patrol.

The dead man was Private Milton Parsons.

Between 15 October and 10 November 1917 the battalion was rotated at six-day intervals between the front-line and rear positions. Training behind the front line included rifle range firing, Lewis gunnery, engineering and medical training for stretcher bearers. Large working parties of up to 200 men at a time were also drawn from the battalion. Five men per day were also given leave in Amiens which was reached by light rail.

The tours at the front line remained very quiet with only occasional incidents breaking the routine. On 25 October a sniper shot a German about 800 yards ahead of the British line and an unsuccessful attempt was made to recover the body that night: at 3am on the night of 27 October the brigade to the right of the Somersets opened fire with all of its guns, mortars and also used gas projectors to attack Honnecourt Wood, a small wood on the western approach to the village. The Germans did not retaliate. On the night of 6 November a party of Germans crept up on a post and threw a smoke bomb which landed outside. The whole battalion stood to, but was soon allowed to stand down after the perceived danger passed.

Early on 10 November the battalion was relieved by the 12th King's. It had started to rain at 'stand to' that evening and the soldiers marched overnight to Fins in the rain and growing daylight. The next day they boarded a train to a secret destination. In the month that the battalion occupied the line it had suffered one fatality, from the accident with the patrol. Only three men had been injured. It was a very pleasant contrast to their experiences of the Ypres salient. The day the battalion was relieved, 10 November 1917, was the last day of the Passchendaele offensive.

Training with tanks

Some of the men of the battalion had hoped to spend the winter in the luxury of the deep, well built trenches they now occupied. Others had noticed ominous signs: work was being done to improve the roads, and ammunition dumps were slowly starting to be formed in the area. Information was also trickling down the command chain that a large raid would soon be taking place. Certainly Colonel Troyte-Bullock knew this as he passed the information on to his subalterns that the battalion would be part of it.

The secretive train journey carried the men through gloomy, rolling countryside until daylight started to reveal the rolling grass-covered hills and late autumnal trees. The train eventually arrived at Bray at half past seven in the morning and the men were quickly marched to a camp close to the railway where they had breakfast.

Lieutenant McMurtrie said: 'We paraded at 10am and were then marched to a small valley where many tanks were moving about.' Captain Spark: 'After a hasty breakfast [we] had our first sight of the tanks. It is true that we had seen them in ones and twos on the Somme, but now we saw them in scores! They seemed to be on every road and hill for miles!'

The men were allotted to a group of tanks. Three were assigned to each company and the men quickly started to practise with them. Captain Spark described the training:

> At first we all felt rather sceptical. In our experience tanks had been a failure and had usually stuck in the mud. But after we had seen them flatten out belts of wire six feet high and ten feet thick and had followed them for three miles across very rough ground and deep trenches, we began to change our opinion. The district was of course ideal for their use: the ground was undulating and firm; it had not been shelled to any great extent and the only obstacles were the trenches. To meet this difficulty the tanks carried large bundles of faggots on their bows, which could be dropped into a trench and so form a bridge. In practice these were quite successful.
>
> We were told that we were to attack the village of La Vacquerie, and trenches had been dug to represent the German trenches we had to take. Soon we had complete confidence in the tanks and knew how they manoeuvred in every circumstance. [Captain] Peard, who had just taken over command of C company from me, was the only sceptic. When I asked him what he thought of it all, he curtly replied – 'C'est magnifique, mais ce n'est pas La Vac'. [It is magnificent, but it is not La Vacquerie] (A French general said of the charge of the Light Brigade, 'C'est magnifique, mais ce n'est pas la guerre'. [It is magnificent, but it is not war])

Two days were spent practising tactical manoeuvres with real tanks after which the battalion was sent to Sorel-le-Grand for five days where the details of the attack on La Vacquerie were rehearsed. The tactical planning involved the three tanks attached to each company attacking in a triangular formation, with one tank 100 yards ahead of the other two. The infantry were trained to follow the tanks 100 yards behind. They were to advance by sections in short rushes, seeking cover when not advancing.[1]

Lieutenant McMurtrie:

> We were at Sorel for 5 days and during the whole time had grand weather and a very enjoyable time. All the morning and part of the afternoon were given up to carrying out the attack with tanks, by platoons, by companies and by the whole battalion. Bivouacs were being put up in scores, all sorts of dumps were being formed, Indian cavalry was said to be at Peronne, Staff officers were all over the place. Several times the battalion attacked Sorel; our part in the attack was to take La Vacquerie; Sorel was made to represent this village. Over and over again we practised attacking it. All the German trenches were marked with tape and the R.E.'s constructed a model

of the whole ground we were to advance over. It was about 50 yards wide and 30 yards long and very well made. All the roads, canals, villages, railways and light railways, tracks, trenches and hills were shown, the hills being modelled correctly. We spent a whole morning on the model, the officers were shown where we were to attack first and then every NCO was shown what to do. The officers went to see the model every day to make sure they knew the exact lie of the ground. By now we understood this attack was a big affair and not a raid as we had at first thought.

During these five days the officers were also given detailed instructions at Fins. Captain Spark recalled:

We went back to Fins and studied trench maps and plans until we knew by heart every detail of the trenches opposite us. This knowledge proved invaluable. During the actual attack I never once looked at my map. We even selected a particular dugout for our company headquarters.

Lieutenant McMurtrie:

On November 18th, [Lieutenant] Wild, [Captain] Andrews and I had a bath at the Fins baths, and collected chocolate, candles, tobacco and cigarettes etc, for everyone was preparing his kit. We had to parade at 2pm and about half an hour before that time one of the sergeants was found drunk and put under arrest. This was a very serious offence for at that time any NCO or man who through drunkenness was unable to go into action was liable to be shot as a deserter.

We left Sorel at 2.30pm in fighting order. Every man wore his webbing equipment with a water bottle filled. He had his 170 rounds of ammunition and had a haversack instead of a pack, wire cutters, wire snippers, wire breakers and SOS rockets were also taken. I was in charge of the company as Andrews had gone ahead in the morning to take over the line. On the way, one very old man fell out, I took him to the medical officer who sent him back to details. We passed through Heudecourt and then the sugar factory and branched off cross country. At about 5.30pm the battalion fell out under cover of a wood, and the cookers which had come with us had tea for the men. After a short while we went forward once more, it was beginning to get dark and we were also getting tired. We met guides at Cemetery Road and from here onwards we had a rotten journey, the path was slippery and was just on the edge of a steep cutting. One man fell over and broke his thigh, a commotion ensued and as our company was in the rear it was disastrous. It was a pitch dark night, there was a good sprinkling of oldish men, who couldn't see or march well in the dark. Everyone began to spread out, some began to curse and we stood a good chance of losing touch with the company in front. Luckily we just managed to keep in touch.

Captain Spark:

> Having made all of the preparations, we again went up to the front line on November 18th, armed with aeroplane photographs, plans and maps and a strong conviction that now, at last, we were going to see a 'real good show'. I had never been in a really big attack and, from what I had seen and heard had no wish to be. Many men looked forward to a 'Push' as an escape from the stagnation of trench warfare, but I admit that I dreaded 'going over the top'. To me the idea of hand to hand fighting was worse than any amount of shelling. In addition, the possibility of being wounded and helpless in no man's land was a nightmare. In trench warfare one was tolerably certain of medical attention within a few hours, but I had seen (or rather heard) men taking days to die in no man's land and I still feel this was the worst fate a man could have. But even I began to feel excited at the prospect of taking part in what we hoped would be the most sensational and bloodless battle in the whole war.

The eve of the attack, 19 November, was cold and a thick fog began to form as the officers went forward to their company assembly positions. Here they met up with the tank officers and the start positions of the tanks were shown to the Somerset officers. Arrangements were made to fill in parts of trenches to allow the tanks to cross in the morning. Big trees that the Germans had felled across the road in their spring retreat had been sawn through during the preceding day and night, so they could be easily rolled off the roads. After the final preparations the officers returned to their companies to wait. Lieutenant McMurtrie remembered that wait:

> Imagine our feelings that night. Andrews and Cox had been in other attacks before but this was to be my first 'stunt'. The three of us were in the dugout together, candles lit it up partially, it was fairly warm as we had a big brazier going. We all talked of our chances the next morning. Should we be killed? Should we get a good 'Blighty' wound and then go back to England away from this rotten show, or should we get through without a scratch to carry on this rotten business of sitting in a trench and freezing, of dodging 5.9s in a communication trench, or having the fear of God put into us when going up duck boards and running for dear life like scared rabbits, from machine gun fire?

186

The plan

The essence of the Cambrai attack was surprise. The enemy would be attacked and overwhelmed by a sudden rush of tanks and infantrymen, who with careful preparation were assembled secretly in front of the Hindenburg Line. This is why the 7th Somersets, like all the other formations involved, had been withdrawn far behind the front line to train.

The attack was to be carried out on a front of approximately 11,000 yards and would involve nineteen infantry divisions, four cavalry divisions and three tank brigades. The front-line attack was to be carried out using six infantry divisions. From north to south the attacking formations were the 51st Division, the 62nd Division, the 6th Division, the 20th Division and the 12th Division. Behind the 20th and 12th Divisions was the 29th Division which would pass through the gap created by them.

The role of the 20th Division was to break through the Hindenburg Line and Hindenburg Support Line, in an attack that would be delivered in a north-easterly direction on the front of La Vacquerie and Welsh Ridge. The 61st Brigade would attack the La Vacquerie area and the 60th Brigade the area to the north called Welsh Ridge.

The German front-line defences were a series of well constructed trenches set around, and running north and south of, the village of La Vacquerie. This village protruded from the main defensive line at the top of a small hill; it had been turned into a strongpoint with redoubts on either side. The whole front was protected by a number of lines of barbed-wire fences often up to ten feet deep.

The 7th Somersets were to lead the attack and were given the task of capturing La Vacquerie. The 7th DCLI on the Somersets' left had the task of capturing a redoubt called the 'Corner Work' with two companies, then to advance through the north of La Vacquerie with the remaining two companies and with the 12th King's to attack the main defensive trench works that lay behind the village. The 7th KOYLI together with the 12th King's were then to attack the Hindenburg Support Line. If all went to plan the whole of the Hindenburg Line would be pierced in one sudden blow within a matter of hours.

To the north of 60th Brigade and 61st Brigade was 59th Brigade, which was to wait until the front line had been captured (by elements of the 29th Division) and then attack through the gap and head towards Masnières.

Sixty tanks were allotted to the 20th Division, and these were allocated to the first two assaulting brigades. Thirty-six were allotted to the 61st Brigade – three tanks for each infantry company. The remaining twenty-four tanks were allotted to the 60th Brigade. The tanks were mainly the Mark IV version that had great improvements on the tanks initially used on the Somme the year before. They no longer had a steering wheel trailing behind them which had been vulnerable to enemy fire. The armour was improved to be resistant to armour-piercing bullets, which were now widely available to German infantrymen. The fuel tank was armoured and placed externally and better escape hatches had been fitted. Also, a vacuum fuel feed system had been introduced which allowed the tank to manoeuvre over rough ground reducing the chance of engine failure. The Mark IV tanks came in two versions at this stage of the war. 'Male' tanks were equipped with two six pounder guns and four Lewis guns. 'Female' tanks were given six Lewis guns. The top speed of these tanks was still only 3.7mph, although over rough ground the speed would be far slower.

The other critical arm in the attack was the artillery. In preparation for the attack, batteries of guns had been secretly brought forward to just behind the front line. They were camouflaged so that the Germans were unaware of their presence, and would remain so until the attack began. This had taken place on the four nights before the attack, and by the night of 19/20 November only two of the 20th Division guns were left in their original positions covering the British front line.

By this stage of the war gunnery was a science. As guns were moved forward, their positions were calculated using trigonometric calculations. Known points on the map would be used as a reference and the exact location of the guns could be worked out using the angles and mathematics. Together with this, the battlefield which the assaulting soldiers would pass over had been mapped in detail using pre-existing maps together with updates provided by aerial photography. Aerial photographs were adjusted to accommodate factors such as the curvature of the earth and the angle of the photograph. Using the known position of the British gun, and the map position of the target, guns could be effectively targeted in what was called 'predicted' fire. Two more factors were central to these calculations: the guns themselves and the shells that they fired. It had been found that as artillery pieces were fired, barrel wear would differ for each gun, and this would cause a variation in the fall of shell for each weapon. The characteristics of each gun had to be added into the calculations for predicted fire to work properly. So far as the shells were concerned, increasing standardisation and quality in production methods meant less variation in accuracy of the artillery caused by the shells themselves, although there would always be small variations.

Plans were made by the Divisional Signal Company to run out ground lines as the attack progressed, so that effective communication could be maintained with the advancing soldiers. In practice, the lines were often to be severed by the tanks, and in the end recourse was made in the early stages to overhead cables to maintain communications.

Other preparations included the establishment of an advanced dressing station and walking wounded collection post at Gouzeaucourt. Also, advanced posts were set up near Villers Plouich and on the Gouzeaucourt–Bonavis road just behind the front line. As the battle progressed, provision was made for dressing stations to be established in the La Vacquerie valley in the direction of Marcoing and also later in Les Rues Vertes.

Throughout the night, as the tanks moved forward into their starting positions, and the men laboured filling in trenches, clearing the roads and generally preparing for battle, the odd burst of machine-gun fire attempted to cover the inevitable noise. As dawn approached the Royal Flying Corps was also involved and aeroplanes were flown low over the German lines so that the engine noises would muffle those of the preparations.

The battle was due to commence at 6.20am.

Ce n'est pas La Vac?

Lieutenant McMurtrie recalled the wait:

> At 1am on the night of the 19th/20th we heard the tanks being moved up into position and soon after that the King's relieved us in our support line. At 3am we all went round and issued rum to the men; most of them were pretty cheery but all of us felt very cold and I shall never forget that tot of rum. It warmed me up and improved my morale.

At 4am the men were got out of their shelters and moved forward in platoons to their assembly positions just behind the front line. C Company was on the right, B Company in the centre and D Company on the left. Each was formed up with three tanks in support. A Company, with no tanks, started about 150 yards behind B Company in the centre. The whole front occupied by the battalion was approximately 500 yards.

Captain Spark was with C Company:

> The night was clear and cold with a slight mist on the ground. An occasional rifle shot or the 'tap-tap' of a distant machine gun alone broke the silence. One could almost feel the excitement in the air. For miles along the British front gunners and tank crew were working hard, and thousands of infantry were wondering what awaited them. One felt sure that, so far, the enemy were entirely unsuspicious, as very few Verey lights were being sent up and their guns were silent. The tanks had lumbered up to within a short distance of our front line and by 5.50 am [I believe this to be approximately 5.20am] the company was drawn up behind them in the open. We then had an hour to wait – a somewhat nervy hour. However by issuing the rum

189

and visiting the tank officers inside their machines (where they allowed us to smoke!) we passed the time and all remained quiet.

The infantrymen waited, so far as possible, in the occasional shell holes about the front line in an effort to afford some protection should they be detected.

Lieutenant McMurtrie was with A Company:

> Soon the C.O. and [Major] Chappell turned up. The C.O. was very bucked with life, full of confidence and came around with a cheery word for everyone. At ten minutes before zero [6.10am], the tanks started and we got up and on the move, thankful to be able to do something at last.

The men moved out on to the damp misty grass in no man's land and started up the long slope towards the fortified village of La Vacquerie.

Company Sergeant Major Bulson was with D Company on the left of the Somersets' attack:

> At dawn we had the signal to move forward and who can forget the boom of the big gun away back which was the signal and how it relieved us from the suspense of waiting. It was one of the grandest sights of an advance ever witnessed. Looking to the left and right so far as one could see was a double line of tanks, 'females' in front, supported in each case by two 'males' and they were in turn supported by a bombing section. From D Company's position especially, looking to the left, one got the view of a double line of tanks with supporting infantry creeping forward, stretching away into the distance as the day was breaking.

Lieutenant McMurtrie: 'We had formed up in artillery formation and when we came to the gap in the wire, each section and each platoon ran through the gap and took up the same formation on the other side. This manoeuvre we had practised over and over again at Sorel.'

Captain Spark was with C Company on the right of the Somersets' attack:

> This was the worst part of the attack, for the tanks seemed to be making an appalling noise and every moment we expected the German barrage to crash down on us. Over our front line trench we went and still no sound except the tanks infernal noise; then carefully through the gaps in our own wire; the tanks were now rattling and grunting as they increased their speed; we cursed them in whispers in fear of being heard by 'Jerry'. When not under fire, silence in no

man's land had become a habit which not even a clanking tank could break. Suddenly with a deafening crash our guns opened the barrage. For a moment the enemy made no sign; then inquiring lights went climbing into the sky; they seemed to be trying to discover the meaning of this extraordinary affair. Behind those lights was an inferno of bursting shrapnel, brilliant high explosive and heavy clouds of smoke.

Now it was getting light, and tanks, followed by small parties of infantry, could be seen on either side. Soon German shells began to scream and moan overhead, and looking back we saw them bursting on our own front line which we had crossed only moments before. Then I heard the rattle of machine guns and the sinister noise of bullets whipping past. From this point everything seemed unreal to me. I felt no fear but only a vague curiosity. It all seemed impersonal and as if I were only a spectator. I had no conscious thought, but little scenes impressed themselves on my mind. I noticed neither time, space, nor noise, but only incidents. The next thing I remember was finding the Colonel [Troyte-Bullock] at my side; he shouted in my ear and I could just hear 'Why don't the damned things go faster?' I think this is the only time I ever heard him use a 'big, big D'. As he had a broad grin on and was obviously in high spirits, may it be forgiven him? He then hurried on to visit the other companies.

As, from left to right D, B and C Companies advanced towards La Vacquerie, A Company which had so far taken the most casualties, took cover in a sunken road and a slight hollow in the ground on the slope that led up to the village. A Company was held back to assist the attacking companies should the Germans counter-attack. The plan was to keep these soldiers out of the initial assaulting groups.

Lieutenant McMurtrie with A company:

All the German shells landed on spots which our men had just left, a few came unpleasantly near and, the German machine gun fire was pretty hot so that we were not at all sorry to get down into the valley, into dead ground. There was a sunken road in the side of the hill leading to La Vacquerie. At this road, we got the men to take shelter. A few men had been hit, there we bandaged up and sent back to the dressing station. We got the men to dig themselves into the bank for by now the enemy had got over the surprise and their machine guns were beginning to be effective; bullets were whistling over our heads and we had to keep pretty low to avoid being hit. Several men were hit while we were here by machine gun bullets. I shall never forget a lance corporal who had come out and joined the battalion the same time as I did [just after Langemarck] – he was crying like a frightened

191

baby and asking to go home or some such rubbish. He got home but not in the way he wanted, for at that moment he was shot through the stomach.

The three assault companies were meanwhile closely following their tanks and were by now approaching the German wire in front of La Vacquerie. The enemy fire on the leading parties was far less than that falling on A Company. Most of the fire directed at the front three companies fell on the rearmost sections as the German gunners shortened their range too slowly.

Captain Spark, of C Company on the right said:

Suddenly there was a crash in front, which at first I thought was a shell bursting. On investigation I found it was my tank's gun firing at an enemy machine gun. After firing four or five rounds it seemed to silence it. Soon after this I realised that my tank was going too much to the right. Now loss of direction was the one thing to be avoided. Not being able to attract the attention of anyone inside, I had to run round in front of it (passing in front of the gun as I did so), and wave to the driver. Luckily he saw and understood at once, and after that managed to 'keep his course'.

At last we were close to the German wire and the tanks started to crash through it. It was at this moment that a company runner yelled at me that Peard was wounded and that I was to take command. I had been so fascinated by the scene around me and by the tank's solemn and dignified progress, that I had almost forgotten the men behind me. Now turning, I saw the whole company with their rifles slung on their shoulders, their hands in their pockets and smoking cigarettes! In the act of shouting to them to get their bayonets ready, I felt a strand of barbed wire catch me in the small of the back and slowly pull me forward. On turning, I was unable to get free and immediately saw that I should be pulled over the top of the tank, which was pulling the wire over one of its 'treads'. My orderly quickly borrowed some wire cutters and cut the wire just before this happened.

At last through the smoke we saw the front line trench and, leaving the tanks we went forward. Just before reaching the trench, I caught sight of a pile of timber and sandbags, which had been a machine gun emplacement before a tank had crushed it. I wondered vaguely if the gunners were underneath it and passed on. At last the trench – unoccupied except for a few dead bodies. I then watched the platoons pour into the trenches and go forward to their various jobs. Each platoon had its own sector and 'mopped up' dugouts. The final objective was reached in a few minutes without opposition and we were 500 yards beyond the front line.

CSM Bulson with D Company on the left recalled:

> The tanks and front of the company had got through, but our rear sections were caught, and that was the first cry for stretcher bearers. On reaching the village the enemy had skedaddled, so we only stayed there long enough to drink some hot coffee just made by them, and left behind in their hurried departure.
>
> The only occasion I knew during the whole time out there of a bayonet being used in real anger, was that morning. A German who was left lying wounded had not been disarmed by an oversight, and he grabbed his rifle as a last effort and shot one of our fellows in the back. This so incensed his pal that he immediately turned around and bayoneted him.

The forward men of the battalion immediately set about consolidating in the village, taking souvenirs, tending to the injured and sorting out the prisoners.

Captain Spark described the scene:

> Leaving my Company Sergeant Major at the dugout, I went forward and found my men consolidating on their objective. They were all very cheerful except a small group I found standing round poor [2nd Lieutenant] Rice, who had just been mortally wounded. He died almost immediately without regaining consciousness. A merciful end.

Second Lieutenant Rice was 26-years-old. He had gained his commission in the Devonshire Regiment, and had been seconded to the 7th Somersets just prior to the Cambrai attack. He had been struck by a machine-gun bullet in the last moments of the Somersets' attack.

As the soldiers moved through the village, small groups of Germans were found huddled together in dugouts and trenches; these were disarmed and sent to the rear. One group of eight Germans was found in a trench with three men in very dirty blue overalls. These were tank crew, the survivors of a nearby disabled tank that had been hit by a shell. They had run into the German trench for cover whereupon the Germans, although heavily armed, had surrendered to the unarmed crew.

Still in front of the village the men of A Company waited in the sunken road. Lieutenant McMurtrie:

> Very soon the first batch of prisoners were seen coming down from La Vacquerie. They all had their hands up in the air and were running as fast as they could. It was one of the funniest things I have ever seen, these poor devils running along, their heads bobbing up and down

and their eyes starting out of their heads, running for dear life and not knowing where to go or what to do. We sent out two men with fixed bayonets who brought them to the C.O. When I saw them closer, I felt very sorry for them, but they seemed very pleased that we had not shot them as they expected.

Consolidation

As the tanks and infantry of the 12th King's could be seen moving forward from the new front-line positions towards Cambrai, the men gathered together in and continued to organise the newly captured village. The battalion had suffered one officer (Lieutenant Rice) and four soldiers killed in the immediate attack. These were 24-year-old Sergeant Ernest Turner, Lance Corporal Frederick O'Donnell and Privates Thomas Ince and Arthur Harding. About thirty-five men had sustained wounds which were treated as far as possible in the dressing stations, either behind the lines or within the village itself. Private Frank Tooze, a 21-year-old man, was severely injured and was taken to Ytres where he died at a casualty clearing station.

Very quickly the detailed planning of the attack started to prove its worth. From the village of La Vacquerie the men saw horse artillery batteries move forward, unlimber and open fire on the enemy. Pioneers were quickly hard at work opening up the roads forward, so that ammunition columns could advance; and, thousands of cavalrymen passed through or near the village following up the attack. A constant stream of prisoners could be seen returning from the front. In the village itself while some bunkers were still burning from the attack, signs were put up pointing to canteens and tea for the wounded, and Battalion headquarters set out the canvas ground-to-air communication sheets, so that the RFC could assess the extent of the advance.

The men went through the enemy bunkers eating any food they found and collecting portable souvenirs like cigars, caps, bayonets and anything else that could be easily put into a pack. A more sombre task was also required with some men detailed to find and bury the dead. They were buried in La Vacquerie cemetery, although curiously none of their bodies was ever found to have a known grave after the war.

Retrospective

Throughout Britain the church bells were rung to celebrate the success of the attack at Cambrai. Within three days of the attack, Lieutenant General Sir Julian Byng, the commander of the Third Army which had carried it out, had been promoted to full general. After the months of fighting and dying in the Ypres salient, where the British Army had inched its way forward, the carefully prepared defences of the Hindenburg Line to the south had now been shattered in a sudden and unexpected blow.

In one day more than 10,000 yards of the Hindenburg Line and slightly (but not much) less of the Hindenburg Support Line about a mile behind the German front line had been captured. Approximately four miles of a third defensive line had also been taken. About 9,000 Germans had surrendered and many had also been killed. The casualties in the initial attack were generally slight and the morale effect at home and amongst the army was terrific.

It is fair to say that, by November 1917, the British Army had refined its ability to attack to a science. Cambrai was a fine example of what was possible when an attack was planned and executed properly, even where this had to be done in a very short space of time.

The keys to success were numerous but arguably three factors were critical. The first was surprise. The effect of the crushing and unexpected artillery barrage, followed up by tanks and infantrymen appearing through the mist at dawn on that Tuesday morning were enough to make the enemy flee or surrender in most cases.

The second was the co-operation between the various arms in the attack. The artillery fire plan was an extension of the creeping barrages that had evolved during the Somme offensive of the year before, supplemented by predicted fire barrages. The co-operation between tanks and infantry was also critical to the success of the attack. Infantry attack tactics were adjusted to take into account that the tanks would be able to drive through the ten-foot wide and six-foot high barbed-wire entanglements and then themselves suppress the defenders as bombing sections that followed immediately behind the tanks went to work. The remaining sections would follow the bombers, help clear the trenches and defend them.

The third factor was the sustained evolution of low level infantry tactics. As had occurred at Langemarck, but to a greater extent in this attack, officers and men knew exactly what they were expected to be doing and when. They also knew what the other men in their battalion would be doing. Once into the enemy positions, the teams of bombers, rifle men and Lewis gunners knew which stretches of trench and which dugouts they had to clear. The effect of this co-ordination in battle cannot be overstated, as it meant that once resistance had been encountered, the men at platoon and section level would act together against the obstacle in a cohesive way.

The combined effect enabled the 7th Somersets to attack up a fairly open slope and capture a heavily fortified strongpoint which held machine guns in bunkers, concrete reinforced buildings and protected by thick belts of barbed wire, in the process losing only six dead and thirty-four wounded. The battalion were not specially trained storm troops, and they had had little more than a week to prepare for this assault. In land which was suited to such an attack what positions could the Germans now build to stop the British?

NOTE

1   Notes on Tank and Infantry Training SG 192/93 JFC Fuller.

CHAPTER XV
Counter-Attack

Masnières

As soon as the immediate consolidation had been carried out in La Vacquerie, the men of the battalion were ordered to rest by Brigadier General Banbury, the brigade commander, when he arrived in the village. Most were quickly asleep, some using the German-built dugouts and beds. Those who remained awake were treated to the unique spectacle of the Cavalry Corps deploying forward towards Masnières in the early afternoon. The cavalry had orders to push forward to Cambrai if possible.

While most of the men were asleep, the battalion received orders at about half past two in the afternoon to move up to the Masnières area . The majority of the men set out shortly afterwards. Captain Spark's company received the orders later:

> I found that the other companies had already moved off; in fact we could see them about a mile ahead. Collecting the company as quickly as possible, I followed. The rain became heavier, darkness was falling, and the mud became thicker every minute. We soon found a guide who had been left for us and he told me that the CO had decided to leave the direct lane to Masnières and make a detour over high ground in order to avoid the mud and confusion in the sunken lane. The only cheering sight was the large number of French civilians who were coming back. These were all in high spirits and kept shouting as they passed; 'Les braves Anglais,' 'Vive L'Angleterre,' 'Vive La France,' and 'Les sales Boches – Bah!' They were a pathetic sight; some with bundles of clothes, several with wheel barrows and bird cages, and all apparently with dogs and children. The long walk in the thick mud of the lane did not seem to depress them in the least.

The mud and confusion in the sunken lane was a collection of broken down tanks, and also artillery and infantry trying to move forward. At about half past eight the battalion arrived at its allotted position, some level ground in front of Les Rues Vertes, where they were told to dig a defensive trench. The ground was hard and it took nearly all night to complete. As the men worked in the steadily falling rain, rifle and machine-gun fire could be heard about a mile ahead. The fire was from cavalrymen, soldiers of the 29th Division and men of the 59th Brigade (20th Division) who had crossed the canal and were trying to defend their positions on the far side.

Captain Spark said:

> At dawn on the 21st we were wet, cold and exhausted, and when orders came to stand by to counter attack, no one felt very enthusiastic. However, it turned out to be a false alarm and just as I was settling down to get some sleep the Colonel [Troyte-Bullock] came along and said he wanted me to come for a walk down to Masnières 'To see what was doing!' He also had had practically no sleep that night and was wet through, yet his manner reminded me of an energetic American tourist who was determined not to miss anything worth seeing! I did not share his enthusiasm.

The lack of enthusiasm was no doubt compounded by the fact that Masnières was not completely clear of enemy soldiers, and an attack was made by men of the 29th Division later that morning, substantially clearing the village. As Captain Spark and Colonel Troyte-Bullock reached the village, they encountered groups of civilians who had come out of hiding and were now fleeing the fighting. The Germans had started shelling the road into Masnières and some of the civilians were later caught in the shelling as they hurried away from the fighting. Captain Spark:

> We walked through the village as far as the canal and there saw the notorious tank which had smashed the main road bridge. It was said that this bridge had been deliberately weakened in order to trap a tank but I think it much more probable that the Germans had not had time to destroy it.

On reaching the bridge, the two Somerset officers met the brigade commander of 88th Brigade of the 29th Division, who were fighting for the rest of the village. The 7th Battalion had been put under his command, and a request was made for one company of Somersets to move up through Les Rues Vertes and protect the pontoon and trestle bridges that spanned the canal. Captain Spark and C Company were assigned to this task. They crossed a firm track that passed through some swampy ground to the south of the canal and then crossed a foot-bridge into the cover of the houses, walled gardens and cellars on the other side. The enemy, having seen the movements, responded by firing machine guns and artillery at

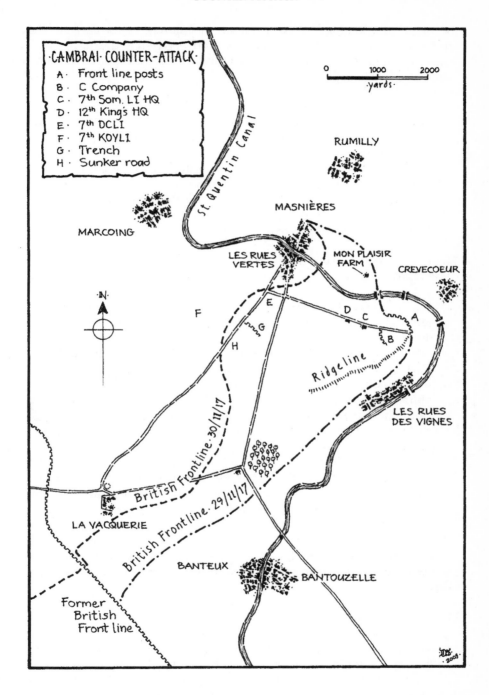

·CAMBRAI· COUNTER-ATTACK·
A · Front line posts
B · C Company
C · 7th Som. LI HQ
D · 12th King's HQ
E · 7th DCLI
F · 7th KOYLI
G · Trench
H · Sunken road

RUMILLY

MASNIÈRES

MON PLAISIR FARM

CREVECOEUR

LES RUES VERTES

MARCOING

St. Quentin Canal

Ridgeline

LES RUES DES VIGNES

British Frontline. 30/11/17

British Frontline. 29/11/17

LA VACQUERIE

BANTEUX

BANTOUZELLE

Former British Front line

the men. The shelling caused a number of injuries, particularly to the stretcher bearers and runners who were more exposed to the fire.

The rest of the battalion was ordered forward a little later that morning into Masnières to support the 87th Brigade in the village in case of enemy counter-attack. Major Chappell described the manoeuvre:

> To reach the canal a piece of open ground about five hundred yards wide had to be crossed in full view of the Hun and this was done by lines of platoons in extended order at two hundred and fifty yards' distance. It was a pretty sight to watch this manoeuvre carried out: there was an entire absence of bunching, almost invariably noticed and cursed on battalion field days – and this was probably due to some extent to the whizzing and zipping of machine gun bullets. Marvellous to relate, no one was hit.

There was no counter-attack and the Somersets were eventually stood down. Captain Spark was with C Company guarding the crossings:

> The men stayed at their posts the whole time, but I of course had to move about the village visiting them. This was most unpleasant, as apart from the shelling, one was sniped at in the most unlikely places. Going about at all became a really nerve wracking business and after having two or three very narrow escapes, I took to doing my business rounds entirely at night. The curious thing about this sniping was that although we were quite half a mile behind the front line and the German trenches were out of sight, the shots were obviously fired at close range. During the first day in the village sniping on the far side of the canal was constant and during the afternoon we heard that two companies had been ordered to clear out every house in Masnières. I should have explained that Masnières was on the far side of the canal and we, on this side, were actually in Les Rues Vertes, although the village was really all one. Later we heard that several snipers had been caught and the village was clear. However the next day the sniping was just as bad and we made some nasty remarks about companies that did not know their job! Again we heard that they had been cleared but the next day I was nearly hit directly I got near the canal.

Lieutenant McMurtrie recalled:

> There was a good deal of mysterious sniping in Masnières at that time but no-one could tell where it came from. One day about lunch time [Captain] Andrews rushed in to say that a man, most likely a German dressed up in our clothes was firing down the street. I went out with

him and no sooner had we got into the street than a bullet went whizzing past us and we saw a man in khaki clothes without a tunic kneeling in the middle of the street, reloading his rifle. We collected about five men and went round some houses to a small lane which led to the spot where the man was. I got there first and got behind a house just as he sent two bullets after me, which luckily did not reach their mark. After a great deal of shouting and firing we at last surrounded and disarmed him. He was carrying several bandoliers of ammunition and some field glasses and was unshaven and an awful looking sight. We sent him under escort to Battalion headquarters. Later we found he was a company sergeant major from one of the battalions in the front line and from continual shelling had gone insane. That afternoon the whole battalion turned out and searched all the houses in Masnières for German snipers, with fixed bayonets but none were found.

The mystery of the ever present but invisible snipers was soon to be solved by the French authorities who disclosed that the village of Masnières had a number of tunnels underneath it. A search was quickly ordered to locate the tunnel entrances. This was assisted by the 88th Brigade brigade major who produced an Alsatian prisoner who thought he knew where one of the tunnel entrances was.

Captain Spark said:

He [the 88th Brigade major] asked me if I could give him a bombing section, as he wanted to investigate. I was able to produce a very good section under Lance Corporal Edmunds, who had come out with the battalion in 1915. I asked if I could come too, as it sounded interesting. He agreed, and we started off in the following order: the prisoner, an interpreter, the major and myself, two other officers of the 29th Division, and Lance Corporal Edmunds with his section.

The nervous group stopped at one point after Edmunds saw some figures moving in a garden. Farther on some more figures were seen in shadows. They were covered with rifles and challenged, when it was discovered that they were a party of Newfoundlanders from the 29th Division. From speaking to them it was discovered that the group seen in the garden where most likely to be Germans.

The Alsatian prisoner identified a house which was entered with revolvers and Mills bombs at the ready. Captain Spark:

The major then kicked the door open violently. Inside was a typical French kitchen, a kettle boiling on the stove, and sitting in armchairs – two charming French girls! Both sides were equally taken aback and

201

the girls were naturally scared until the interpreter said 'Good evening' in a very matter of fact tone of voice. They recognised the prisoner and greeted him by name.

The interpreter started questioning the girls about their presence in the village. They told him that they were not afraid of the shelling as they had a good cellar, which they then went on to explain was more like a tunnel than cellar. While the major engaged the girls in conversation, Captain Spark and another officer started to explore the cellar, finding a timber-lined tunnel seven feet high and four feet wide with German painted signs disclosing various tunnel exits.

Captain Spark continued:

> It was rather nervy work I found. Moving forward with an electric torch on, you would be an excellent target for anyone who saw or heard you. When I was in front I held my torch about two feet to my left and had my revolver in my right hand. Of course we constantly used to switch off the light and listen but, even so, we always felt at a disadvantage.

The discovery of the tunnels led to a more thorough search the following day and night and five marked entrances were found. From the numbering of the exits it was known that six existed. There were also a number of unmarked entrances, such as that in the back of a dugout covered by a curtain that was discovered by Captain Spark:

> Going slowly down one passage, I caught sight of a light ahead. Creeping forward as quietly as possible, we found the light was shining round a blanket which was hung up across the passage. We could hear nothing except snoring, but could smell tobacco smoke. With revolvers and rifles ready we pulled back the blanket. Four men were sitting in their shirt sleeves playing cards and for a moment we did not know if they were English or German. However when one of them indignantly remarked: 'Ere, what the 'ell are you doing in our dug out?' we saw that we had again drawn a blank.

That the tunnels had been used by snipers was apparent as one of the entrances came up in a garden of a house, near to which stood a ladder. Climbing the ladder a small battlement-surrounded roof was found, as well as a pound of tobacco and about fifty spent cartridge cases. The tunnels also led to the basement of the commandant's house, and some speculated that this was the missing entrance. The tunnels were deemed generally safe, although a guard of Somersets was put at each known entrance, just in case.

On 23 November, the day after most of the tunnel clearing had been done, the enemy continued to bombard the village. Private Joseph Lye, a 38-year-old man was killed. The battalion was 'handed over' to the command of the 87th Brigade which had replaced the 88th Brigade. By now the men had managed to explore most of the village.

Captain Andrews said:

> It is rumoured that one company has 'borrowed' a derelict piano with which to enliven the tired troops, another has 'captured' a stray pig to supplement the army rations, whilst yet another has 'scrounged' a first rate cow which will supply much needed milk to sustain a delicate company commander and his staff.

On Saturday 24 November the constant shelling of Masnières continued, and a ration party was caught by the fire killing three men.[1] At the end of the day the battalion went into brigade reserve where they would remain until 28 November. The movement of the battalion out of Masnières was a relief as the German artillery was becoming increasingly active. It became apparent that their guns were being registered on the British front line near the canal bank. Major Chappell: 'During the relief I was very tickled at the sight of a headquarters runner solemnly leading a milk cow into reserve. The cow being used as a beast of burden and carrying several packs, a mattress, cooking pots and pans and a Hun helmet slung over one horn'.

The men came out of Masnières with sandbags filled with as many trophies as they could find. Their home for the next few days was a series of German trenches, some of them covered, from where they could see the spires and towers of Cambrai. Some of the battalion – along with the cows that had been found – were housed in old gun pits. All of the positions were very cramped to the extent that not everyone was able to lie down to rest and the weather had turned very bad, with either rain or snow falling. Near to the Somersets' positions were three knocked-out tanks that Lieutenant McMurtrie explored:

> It seemed that a German officer had single-handed drawn out one of his guns into the open and fired it until he was killed, but not before he had knocked out three tanks. I looked into these tanks – in all of them were the charred remains of the crew. All that could burn had been burnt inside, the aluminium parts of the Lewis gun had been burnt, the wooden handles, everything. Fire was the greatest danger to the crew of a tank. A tank was a hard object for artillery to hit but if it was hit, the petrol which was carried both inside and out, was almost certain to become ignited and though every tank carried several fire extinguishers, the inside of the tank became a furnace

almost immediately. So that when going into action in a tank, your chances of getting through were greater than with the infantry but if you did get hit, it was a horrible death.

During the time in brigade reserve the men were put to hard work digging and improving the new front-line trenches, dugouts and shelters. They were also constantly required for carrying parties while many officers were involved in the administrative tasks of logging casualties, checking munitions and equipment and writing reports on 'the lessons to be learned from the attack'. Although nominally out of the front line, most of the men through their work remained exposed to enemy shelling every day.

On 28 November Lieutenant Colonel Troyte-Bullock, along with many other battalion commanders, was given leave and Major Preston-Whyte assumed command of the battalion. The same day Major Chappell trod on a nail protruding from a broken duck board and was sent back to the field ambulance for a tetanus injection; an accident which might have seemed unfortunate at the time, but which would eventually prove a lucky one.

The men had hoped that after ten days at or near the front line under almost constant fire, they would be withdrawn for a complete rest. They were disappointed. Orders were received for the 7th Somersets to return to the front line and relieve the 7th KOYLI. Captain Spark: 'There was a good deal of grousing. We felt we had done our share.'

The 7th KOYLI were relieved by 9pm in the front line to the south of Masnières facing Crèvecoeur. The Yorkshiremen were themselves exhausted from constant shelling and digging. When relieved they were half way through excavating some new positions on a stretch of grass on the western side of the canal. The Somersets set to work deepening the holes and covering the earth with dried grass as camouflage from the enemy who were not yet aware of their location. The line held was a series of outpost trenches on the side of a hill that sloped down to the canal. Three companies were in the front line and one in reserve. The hill also sloped up to the right of the Somersets' positions and then fell away so that the posts of the battalion to the right of the Somersets – the 12th King's – could not be seen.

A defensive battle

On 29 November the 20th Division was disposed between the 29th Division to its left (in the Masnières area) and the 12th Division on its right. The 20th Division had two brigades in the front line, the 61st Brigade held the left sector and the 59th Brigade the right sector. The 60th Brigade were in reserve. Colonel Troyte-Bullock was given command of the 60th Brigade as its commanding officer was sick.

The 61st Brigade had the 7th Somersets and the 12th King's in the front line. The Somersets were on the left, holding positions between Masnières and up the slope facing Crèvecoeur. To their right the 12th King's line bent back sharply to the right following the curve in the canal, just over the crest of the hill, so that its men faced Les Rues des Vignes. The 7th DCLI were in support of the forward battalions and the 7th KOYLI were in brigade reserve. Orders were received on 29 November that the next day the brigade was expected to occupy an additional 1,000 yards of front to its right.

So far as the 7th Somersets were concerned, the battalion had three companies in the front line and one in reserve. D Company, commanded by Lieutenant Tawney, held the front-line posts on the left along the canal from Masnières; B Company, commanded by Captain Wild, was next in line and finally on the right was A Company, commanded by Captain Andrews. C Company, commanded by Captain Spark, was in reserve. The Somerset positions were quite good considering the amount of time that had been available to make them. The front line was a series of outpost trenches with a good line of sight down to the canal in front.

The only problem encountered by the men occupying their new trenches was an enemy machine-gun post in a small brick house near the canal. Through the day bursts of machine-gun fire would issue forth whenever a target showed itself. A Company was ordered to organise a raid on the post to destroy it on the night of 30 November and preparations were immediately put in place. To plan the raid, Captain Andrews went back to the battalion headquarters on the night of 30 November in order to liaise with brigade headquarters over artillery support for the attack.

Throughout 29 November the men generally kept their heads down in their trenches and for the first time since the attack on 20 November they received post. Some necessary functions had to be carried out, such as bringing up water for the men, and one party including a corporal went down to the canal to fetch the water for A Company. The Germans were shelling sporadically throughout the day and as the party passed near to the battalion headquarters a shell landed and exploded right between the legs of the corporal. Lieutenant McMurtrie: 'But in some extraordinary manner he just got a nice 'Blighty' wound instead of being blown to atoms as one would have expected.'

Major Preston-Whyte, now in charge of the 7th Somersets, ordered the battalion to push forward the outpost positions by 100–200 yards overnight. By now the men were exhausted.

Lieutenant McMurtrie:

> All that night I somehow felt very uneasy, the Company Sergeant Major felt the same thing and Bristow [the Company Quartermaster

Sergeant] noticed that we were rather nervy. Here we were with a company holding a ridiculously broad front, we were all tired out. We had had all the strain of an attack, we had been shelled day and night in Masnières, always standing to on some alarm or other, we had been in the line for twelve days and had dug in two nights running. If the enemy attacked we had no barbed-wire, we seemed to get no support from the RFC or artillery and we were all dead tired. No wonder we felt uneasy.

During the night the officers went about their business, organising their men and positioning the new posts. These were dug in a chequer pattern to provide mutual support, three posts per company. Company headquarters were dug in behind them. At dawn the officers toured their new lines checking on the men's positions in the early morning light. One of those was Captain Spark:

As everything was quiet and normal, [I] returned to my company headquarters, and waited for breakfast. Soon the very moderate amount of shelling began to increase and I put on my boots (which I had just taken off) and went to the door of the dugout to see what was happening.

The front line

While Captain Spark returned to his dugout at C Company for his breakfast, Lieutenant McMurtrie was settling down to eat some cake and Devonshire cream that had arrived in a parcel the previous day. It was just then that a very heavy bombardment commenced.

Lieutenant McMurtrie was with A Company on the right of the Somersets' defensive line:

Luckily for us they did not know that we had dug in the night before in new positions and so we watched in comparative safety all their shells dropping on our old posts. Andrews had not returned from Battalion headquarters and so command of the company fell on me. I immediately got everybody standing to. After about fifteen minutes shelling, we saw Germans advancing. We had plenty of ammunition and so opened fire on them. We soon stopped them as they were being killed in huge numbers and we had all our Lewis guns firing in a most perfect manner.

Company Sergeant Major Bulson with D Company:

Lieutenant Caulfield, myself and two sections of D Company were holding the left hand post of the battalion nearest Masnières, and close to the bank of the canal. The ground rose sharply on our right to a brow, out of sight of the next post. A mile away to our front we could see hordes of Germans moving seemingly across our front and to the right. Enemy aeroplanes were flying low overhead and artillery were shelling a bridge across the canal just to our left rear. Asking the Lewis gunner if his gun was ready for action, I tried it but found the spring too weak, so I put that right and hung on to the gun.

The attack that had begun along the front of A Company on the right also closed on B Company in the centre and parts of D Company. All were able to keep the attackers at bay, shooting down two waves of attacking Germans who advanced shoulder to shoulder. A third wave materialised after this, although events prevented the defenders from causing too much damage to this line. The defensive plan that had been arranged for the battalion was that the outposts were to be held for as long as possible. If these positions became untenable, the men were to fall back to a main line of defence which was to be held at all costs, and which was to be reinforced by the support and reserve soldiers. Initially there was no thought of withdrawal as the Somersets' line was holding against the frontal attack, but all this would soon change.

Lieutenant McMurtrie was with A Company on the right of the defensive line:

> I held on in our posts firing away at the Germans and for the time being stopped them. Soon however the battalion on our right [the 12th King's] withdrew and thus our right flank was threatened. Almost immediately the Germans started working round my right flank and so I gave the signal to withdraw. At the same time German aeroplanes began coming over, flying about 60 feet above us and firing their machine guns into us as we withdrew. Men were falling right and left, the Company Sergeant Major fell and I thought he was shot through the head. I sent a runner to battalion headquarters to tell the CO that we had withdrawn.

Headquarters and C Company

The 12th King's, to the right of the Somersets, cannot be unduly criticised for falling back as the positions they occupied were almost impossible to hold in the face of the attack against them. Unlike the Somersets, because of the convex shape of the ground ahead, they had no clear line of sight to their front. The Germans of the 30th Division were able to form up in this dead ground and advance rapidly against them. Like the Somersets, these men also had no wire to impede the enemy advance and no artillery support. The enemy barrage fell accurately on their defences. They had little opportunity to hold the attack.

Captain Spark had been recalled to battalion headquarters by Major Preston-Whyte: 'When I got there, I asked if there was an attack going on. P.W. said that he had no information but "was anxious". He then sent me back to watch from the entrance of my dugout for an SOS signal or any other indication of an attack.' Captain Spark then returned to C Company in the reserve positions to wait. He did not have to wait long. To his surprise a runner came up with orders from Major Preston-Whyte at battalion headquarters to 'stand to' and 'get outside somewhere'. Immediately after this a heavy barrage fell upon the C Company positions preventing any movement.

Major Preston-Whyte:

> I could not see too well what was happening on our front; however, it seemed to me we were maintaining our positions, and I was of course unaware that the enemy were through to the south of us. The phone to brigade was out of order; anyhow, I could get no reply, and so I got no information that way. In fact I did not realise the enemy were through until I saw movement up in my own front line. From what I could see this movement was from right to left, and so I fancy the battalion was caught by a strong flank attack after the King's had been rolled up, and under those circumstances they had little chance of holding their positions.
>
> When I saw this I ordered the battalion headquarters out to their battle station above the road, and I sent an orderly to C Company headquarters to see if anyone had been left there, and if so, to tell them to 'stand to' and 'get out of the dugout'. This was not a message to the company commander, whom I did not expect would still be at company headquarters. I was afraid that servants might get trapped, and as the dugout was not far from the battalion headquarters I sent an orderly along to clear it out.

Major Preston-Whyte had no doubt assumed that Captain Spark was aware of what was happening to the battalion, and that he would be following the battalion defence scheme and be moving his men to the main support line. Captain Spark, who was confused by the order he received, had to wait two or three minutes while the barrage passed by:

> Directly it did so and the smoke had cleared away, I saw small parties of men coming towards me from the direction of our front line. Immediately afterwards a line of men shoulder-to-shoulder appeared on the skyline about half a mile away. These were unmistakably Germans in great strength. It is true that the morning was misty, but

even so, it is very remarkable that we saw no SOS and did not even hear rifle fire.

Captain Spark gathered his company and headed for battalion headquarters where he found Captain Andrews, who said:

> Through the smoke it [was] difficult to see exactly what [was] happening, but almost immediately numbers of our men [fell] back on battalion headquarters in front of swarms of the enemy. An attempt [was] made to stem the advance by mustering the remnants of several different battalions, but this [was] foiled by the arrival of several enemy aeroplanes flying very low, which caused a large number of casualties owing to the absence of trenches or cover of any kind.

Because of what Major Preston-Whyte had seen, he left battalion headquarters before the arrival of C Company to investigate his right flank:

> When I got to the right of my line I saw troops retiring on our right, not far from my flank, and thinking these must be the King's, and seeing if they continued to retire my battalion would be cut off, I told the officer who was with me, Jenks, I think, to hold on where he was as long as possible. No attack was developing against us yet, and I went across with my orderly to stop these retiring troops and to order them to make a stand, so as to prevent our position from being outflanked.
>
> The smoke prevented me from seeing too well, and I was within 50 yards of these troops before I saw by their helmets that they were Germans. I leave you to imagine my feelings. Well, I had my rifle with me, and I let go the magazine into them. I do not think they had seen me before, as they halted; they were too close to miss, and I fancy they were not quite sure where the shots came from. I then slipped off to rejoin the battalion headquarters but now the Germans saw us and started to let fly. I was unable to get back as before I had gone far, I got one through the right elbow which smashed up my arm badly and put an end to my active participation in the battle.

The fighting withdrawal

While battalion headquarters staff and the men of C Company were trying to work out what was happening, the front-line companies were being rolled up by the German attack. After Lieutenant McMurtrie ordered A

Company, on the right of the Somersets' front line, to withdraw, this opened the way for the Germans to flank D and B Companies who similarly started to fall back. The Germans were in close pursuit.

Lieutenant McMurtrie retired with groups of men from A Company towards the main defensive line:

> After an awful race, we at last got to the main line of resistance only to find that we were almost surrounded and there were no other troops to reinforce us, so I gave the order to withdraw still further back as we had no chance of doing any harm to the advancing Germans and it was simply a waste of life to remain there. We went a little further back and came across some more men.

These men were in the area where Major Preston-Whyte had left Lieutenant Jenks. He had evidently managed to round up some of the retiring British soldiers and now this group of men were the right flank of the battalion. There were no other cohesive units to their right in their immediate area. Panic was taking hold.

Lieutenant McMurtrie continued:

> I turned round to try to stop them all. Everyone wished to clear out, everyone was out for himself and his own preservation. It is extraordinary what one thinks of at such moments as these and it is marvellous what a difference one strong, brave man makes in situations such as this. I remembered a lecture that we had had at Sandhurst by a Staff Sergeant and he had told us that if withdrawing the men tried to run away, then get out your revolver and threaten them and if that was not enough, shoot some of them. This was a similar situation, all the men had panicked and just commanding them was not enough. The place we had got to was quite a good place for making a stand and so I cocked my revolver and started threatening them with it. Immediately they turned around and faced the enemy and began firing away again. I saw Jenks doing the same thing further down on the left.
>
> For a time this was alright but the enemy kept on advancing, their aeroplanes were firing down on us, they had their machine guns playing on us unmercifully and to make matters worse, they once more started getting round our right flank. Jenks and I talked it over and decided to withdraw further back, hoping that reinforcements would turn up. We gave the signal to withdraw and we went back, across the La Vacquerie valley to some half dug German trenches and here we made another stand. Jenks was hit I believe through the chest and so I helped him along till some stretcher bearers took him away. I saw Paul, the Signals Officer, firing away just by the light railway.

There were some Cornwalls in the trench when we got there and soon a Major turned up and took command. Across the other side of the valley we saw the Germans advancing in huge numbers and they soon got round our right flank once more. We therefore, had to withdraw under very heavy machine gun fire. We went back several hundred yards to a sunken road which we lined and here we brought the enemy at last to a stand still. By this time I had lost all my men and so went around looking for them. There were no signs of any near me and so I reported to the nearest company commander who happened to be in the 11th Rifle Brigade. [The 11th RB were the reserve battalion of the 59th Brigade – to the right of the 61st Brigade when the attack commenced.] About this time, I saw one of our observation balloons come down in flames and I also saw the observer come down in a parachute. Almost at the same time one of our aeroplanes was shot down and crashed to the ground.

So far as D Company was concerned, the retirement of A and then B Companies to their right opened the way for them to be overwhelmed too. The right-hand posts of D Company quickly fell back in the face of the attack, leaving the one post held by Lieutenant Caulfield, Company Sergeant Major Bulson and two sections of D Company. CSM Bulson:

Our first sight of the enemy at close quarters was when they appeared over the brow where the next post was, coming at us sideways and less than fifty yards away. We could not shoot at them over each other's heads and Mr Caulfield asked me what we had better do, so I yelled to our fellows to hop out of the trench and line the road behind us, which would allow us to face the enemy. I was one of the first to get there and turning saw the Germans running after us, thinking they had us on the run, with our last couple of chaps still scrambling out of the post. Not stopping to think I ran back towards them a couple of steps and with the Jerries coming on in a bunch fired at them with the Lewis gun from the hip. They went down like rabbits and we never had a casualty at that particular moment although the enemy were throwing bombs as they ran.

From where this group now were they were able to see that the battalion front line had collapsed and that the Germans were engaged in a bombing attack on battalion headquarters about half a mile behind. The only way back lay between battalion headquarters and the canal, and luckily for them most of the party were able to get through. The rest of D and B Companies had fallen back in groups across the front they had occupied, closely followed by the Germans. Anyone injured was quickly captured or killed by the advancing enemy.

Meanwhile, at battalion headquarters Captain Spark and Captain Andrews made a decision that they would be unable to hold off the two or three thousand Germans they could see about 600 yards away. Both decided to take their men back to the reserve line where the DCLI were believed to be. The retreat was very costly as the Germans set up a heavy machine gun that opened fire on the Somersets on a road. Captain Spark described what happened:

> Men fell fast until everyone got off that deadly road. Enemy could now be seen on our left, and as they seemed to be cutting us off, we had to hurry on and leave the wounded behind. As we passed through the main Gouzeaucourt–Cambrai road we passed through a fairly heavy barrage and again lost heavily.

The retreating men were then attacked by enemy aircraft. Captain Spark: 'This was most unnerving, as concealment was impossible, and any sort of cover entirely absent.' The retreat continued, with the survivors encountering stragglers from the 61st Brigade and men of the 29th Division that was fighting to hold on to Masnières. The men then came across a company of the 7th DCLI drawn up in platoons and ready to advance. The dismayed DCLI Captain, when told that the Germans would be there within five minutes, agreed that the whole group should retire to a trench about a quarter of a mile behind to make a stand.

Captain Spark:

> The whole crowd (it was really nothing more) went back in a rough line but did, gradually, extend into 'open order'. When we reached the trench, the men were spread out over several hundred yards and began jumping over the trench and going on! This would never do and I suddenly thought of a way of stopping them. I blew my whistle as loudly as I could and signalled 'Halt' with my hand. They all stopped instantly and gradually got into the trench. Surely an example of the uses of drill and discipline. Just as I was getting into the trench, Sergeant Major Bulson of D Company arrived carrying a Lewis gun and some drums of ammunition. He had carried these from the front line, a distance of about two miles, and anyone who has carried a Lewis gun will know what determination and strength are needed. He quietly mounted the gun on the parapet and loaded it.

CSM Bulson's account of their meeting is somewhat different: 'Keyed up with excitement, he [Captain Spark] spotted me, and waving a revolver said, "Hello Sergeant Major, I don't care a ___ now, I've shot two of the blighters".'

The half-dug trench proved an indefensible position as the Germans had already worked around the right flank and began to fire a machine gun along the trench from long distance. Behind this trench lay a sunken road, and the order was given to retire to this position which would provide cover from enemy fire.

Behind the road lay a hill and the route up was two-fold, either straight up the hill, which was under machine-gun fire, or along a sunken road that ran around the bottom of the hill. Sergeant Major Bulson:

> Myself, I took the quickest way of getting to the top by going straight up the hillside, running a few yards at a time and falling down as though hit every time I saw the spurts of earth hitting up around me from machine gun fire. My proverbial luck held and I was able to get to the top.

The majority of the men who chose the cover of the sunken road were cut off. There was a short but fierce battle from which only a few Somersets escaped. Lieutenant Caulfield was killed there as well as Sergeant Major Bulson's batman, Harry Channing, who was shot in the stomach dying a short while later. CSM Bulson: 'Poor lad, he was only a youngster, not really big enough to carry a pack, and known amongst his comrades as "Piccanin".' The fight for the sunken road saw the Somersets at a distinct disadvantage as the Germans continued to enfilade their positions with machine-gun fire and clearly they had the upper hand in numbers.

Captain Andrews managed to get back to the sunken road on the higher ground with about fifty men and decided to launch a bayonet charge counter-attack against the Germans now occupying the recently vacated trench. Andrews was quickly hit by a machine-gun bullet from an enemy aeroplane as was Lieutenant Paul who was shot in one arm. The counter-attacking party engaged the Germans in a short hand-to-hand battle entering the trench and then retreated back to the sunken road, leaving Andrews and Paul as prisoners. Both were captured when they sought refuge in a German dugout to dress their wounds.

Captain Spark found his way up the bullet-swept slope being shot at by a German machine gun nearly all the way and eventually reached the KOYLI, who were just standing to after their breakfast. He spent the next few minutes dashing up and down the trench they were in to find the brigadier to try to get the KOYLI to advance and help in the fighting for the sunken road. The battalion would not move without the brigadier's orders. Spark was unaware that the sunken road had already fallen.

The KOYLI and remnants of other battalions that had fallen back now lined the trench and the men slowly started to spread along the defensive line to prevent the Germans from flanking this trench too. The Germans probed these defences with a skirmish line that was soon repulsed with rifle and Lewis gun fire. A few small rush attacks were also tried but were similarly dealt with.

Captain Spark said:

> During this time three Germans with a light machine gun came forward, planted the gun in the open about 400 yards from our trench and solemnly swept our parapet with fire. This went on for a few minutes and as no one seemed to be firing back at them, I and [a] DCLI officer began sniping at them between the bursts of fire. After three shots he hit the gunner and knocked him over backwards: after two more shots, I hit the second man who had continued to fire the gun: the third man then picked up the gun and calmly walked back over the skyline and out of sight. We fired one or two rather half hearted shots but were really glad that he had escaped. Those three were very brave men. It is rather interesting to note that although I was in the trenches for about two years, the German I hit then is the only German I am sure that I killed in the whole time. I am sure that he was killed because we watched both the bodies later with field glasses and neither moved at all.

The attack was stopped for the day. Slowly small groups from the different battalions grouped themselves together. Sergeant Major Bulson found twenty-seven men and took them to brigade headquarters where he met Lieutenant Jones, formerly of the 7th Somersets and now brigade intelligence officer. Captain Spark arrived a little after this with another seventeen men he had found after searching for hours along the trench.

In one day the 7th Battalion Somerset Light Infantry had been destroyed as a fighting force. At this time the extent of the damage was uncertain because of the confusing front-line situation, but the battalion had been reduced from a ration strength of 744 men to an organised group of about fifty in the front line (although many remained behind the line with the transport, cookers etc.).

The night was very quiet. The men had their first meal in twenty-four hours and they took only half-hour turns on watch because they were so tired and officers were fearful that they would fall asleep. In the night there were three or four false alarms but no enemy attacks, and daylight came to relative peace.

During the night Lieutenant McMurtrie had found the party of now about sixty Somersets, who were surprised to see him as they had been told that he had been wounded. McMurtrie and Spark were the only two officers left unhurt of those who had been in the front line. Captain Andrews and Lieutenant Paul had been wounded and captured together. Lieutenant Paul, who had been hit in one arm was unfortunate to be hit in the other by British fire while being led back in captivity. The acting

Battalion CO, Major Preston-Whyte, had been injured as had Lieutenant Jenks and Lieutenant Stoker. The battalion's doctor, Captain Pickup and Reverend Hines had also been injured along with another 158 men. It was later established that 116 men had been captured, most of whom were wounded. Captain Wild as well as Lieutenants Caulfield, Cox, Pearcey and Robert Tawney MC had been killed. Another seventy-two men had died.[2]

The peace of the early morning of 1 December was used to gather up stragglers bringing the total battalion strength up to twelve officers and 332 men. Among the men in the front line there was little cohesion as a fighting force. Only about eight of them were bombers. About half of the remainder were runners, servants or stretcher bearers, who were not used to fighting in platoons.

The morning calm was short-lived as the Germans decided to turn some captured 18pdr guns on the British trenches, the guns impressing the recipients with their speed and power of explosion. Captain Spark recalled: 'The shells come over as fast as whizz bangs but burst with an explosion more like a 4.2 shell.' The enemy activity only killed one man, Private Robert Rowsell, although another four men died of wounds on 1 December.[3] The day was spent with the exhausted survivors checking equipment and replenishing ammunition. Those men from the front three companies had used up most, if not all, of their ammunition. On 2 December Major Chappell took command and the remaining two officers and seventy men were relieved and marched to Sorel-le-Grand.

Retrospective

The Cambrai counter-attack was the first battle in which the 7th Battalion were confronted by a large-scale, co-ordinated German attack. In a matter of two hours the battalion's positions had been overwhelmed and more than half of its men were killed, captured or injured. The scattered remnants had been forced back to trenches in the former Hindenburg Support Line.

Not only had the German offensive driven in the right wing of the salient, it succeeded in capturing the formerly British-held villages of Gonnelieu and Villers-Guislain which lay to the south and from which the Somerset men had looked over the German defences before the Cambrai offensive began. In the following days the German attacks continued and La Vacquerie was recaptured. The British were eventually forced into a tactical retirement from much of the land captured because of the precarious position that had been created by the German gains. The British government set up a Court of Enquiry to look into how the 20th, 55th and 12th Divisions had been overwhelmed.

An analysis of the battle from the 7th SomLI perspective is enlightening.

215

The original battalion defensive positions were the shallow trench works which it took over from another battalion late in the day on 28 November, a little more than one full day before the attack. These positions were no doubt registered by the German artillery in the days preceding their occupation by the Somersets, as was demonstrated by the accurate and heavy barrage that fell on them on the morning of the 30th. Although Major Preston-Whyte had ordered the deepening of the original trenches on the 28th, he ordered new posts to be dug in front of the original line on the night of the 29th. These positions were the chequer board posts which were eventually attacked. None of the positions were protected by barbed wire.

The Germans employed three main elements: infantry, artillery and aeroplanes. German artillery commenced the attack with the very heavy and accurate barrage that fell on the Somersets' former positions at 7am. This lasted for fifteen minutes and was quickly followed by the appearance of at least three lines of attacking infantrymen. Because of the overnight move of the battalion, the accuracy of the German guns counted against their effect, and the new Somerset posts were left unaffected. The Germans did not use any type of creeping barrage or smoke, both of which were well tried by the British by late 1917, to cover the advance of their soldiers. Either of these would have greatly improved the chances of the frontal attack.

The frontal attack was shot to pieces by the Somersets. At least two lines of Germans advancing 'shoulder to shoulder' were shot down as they made the long advance up the slope from the canal to the posts. There is no evidence that at this time the Germans were using any developed low-level tactics which is curious given that the attack was in November 1917. The simple, early war tactics of advancing in lines used by the Germans on this occasion can be starkly compared to the tactics used by the Somersets in Langemarck. The defending Somersets in this case occupied nine front-line posts spread far apart, and it should have been relatively easy to suppress and attack these posts using modern infantry tactics.

The German attack succeeded by rolling up the 7th Somerset's line from the flank. This was achievable because of four factors. The first was the collapse of the battalion to the right of the Somersets. The 12th King's were overwhelmed by a rapid attack on their front because of the impossibility of their location. The ground to their front was convex in shape, which provided ample opportunity for the Germans to form up very close to the British line and rush the defences as soon as the barrage lifted. The 12th King's also had no barbed-wire or artillery support to slow down an attack.

The second factor was the lack of any proper defensive positions to which the men could retire. There simply had not been enough time or manpower near the front to dig them. The effectiveness of the enemy aircraft on the retiring troops who had little cover was tremendous, although, had the men been able to seek shelter in trenches, it is unlikely that the effect of the aeroplanes would have been so great.

The third factor was the almost complete lack of artillery support. Guns had not been properly registered for defensive support along the attacked front. Finally, the lack of proper communications between battalions and brigade headquarters meant that the defence was not properly co-ordinated. The inadequate communication systems available to the British Army in the First World War prevented a more flexible response to the attack.

At a higher level the German tactic of reinforcing success and flanking temporary defences was very effective. The other imaginative feature was the use of aeroplanes in a ground-attack role and in dropping smoke in the latter stages of the advance to cover their infantry.

NOTES

1   The dead were Privates William Ransome from Taunton, Fred Robinson from Chester and James Snell from Langport in Somerset.
2   The dead were Private Francis Adamson, Private Cyril Andrews, Private Edward Bath, L/Corporal Frederick Bool, Private James Bounsall, Private William Branfield, Private George Bray, Private Isaiah Carter, Private Harry Channing, Private William Chivers, Private George Clark, Private Ernest Cleaver, Private Frederick Clift, Corporal Gilbert Coles, Private Reginald Coombs, Private George Cooper, Private William Cottle, Lieutenant Cox, Sergeant John Dawson, L/Corporal William Dennett, Private Arthur Dommett, Private Ernest Dunn, Private William Fitzgerald, Private Frank French, Private William Friendship, Private Frederick Gale, Private Harold Gallop, Corporal Arthur Gay, L/Corporal Henry Goodman, Private Alfred Green, Corporal William Greenslade, L/Corporal William Hall, Private Charles Hannan, Private George Harris, Private Hugh Hayman, Private George Hemmens, Private James Hodge, Private Frederick House, Private David Hughes, Private Richard Hughes, L/Corporal William Hunt, Private Ernest James, Private Charles Jay, Private Edwin Kelly, Private Ernest Lawrence, Private Frank Lessey, Private Frank Lonnen, Private Fred Manning, Private William March, L/Corporal John Metherell, Private Stephen Millard, L/Corporal Charles Miller, Private Charles Notley, Private Charles Nott, Private Frank Parish, Lieutenant Pearcey, Lieutenant Rice, Private Edward Richman, Private Albert Rogers, Private Samuel Scolding, Private Arthur Simmonds, Private Herbert Smitheringale, Private Walter Stacey, Private Arthur Stevens, Private Arthur Stuckey, Private Charles Stutt, Private George Sussex, 2nd Lieutenant Robert Tawney MC, Private Edward Thrift, Private William Trueman, Corporal William Turner, Private Sidney Uphill, Private Andrew Urquhart, L/Corporal Albert Warner, Private Edwin Welch, Captain Lionel Wild, Private Joseph Woodward, L/Sergeant William Woodward.
3   Those who died of wounds were Private Michael Greedy, Private William Lewin, Private Christopher Ridgewell and Corporal Edward Shaddick. On 2 December Private Frederick Alden also died of wounds.

PART FOUR

The End

To sleep the sleep of victors whose duty is done

Anon of B Company 7th SomLI

CHAPTER XVI

Re-formation

Relief and rebirth

The initial route of the 7th Battalion survivors was from brigade headquarters to Gouzeaucourt Wood where they met the guides and cooks
who had been sent up to meet them.

Captain Spark:

> Just after we could see the wood ahead, someone shouted: 'Who are
> you?' I answered: 'Somersets'. The next question: 'Which company?'
> only produced in answer a few curses and some cynical laughter
> from the men. However we found that they were our own guides and
> cooks and our first touch with the outer world for two weeks. They
> told us that the cookers were only half a mile further on, and we
> managed to reach them somehow.
>
> I can still remember standing by the cooker drinking hot tea and
> talking to the cooks. It seemed like entering another world. I had felt
> that we were the only Somersets left anywhere and it was quite a
> shock to see there were others. At such times a barrier seems to come
> between those who have 'been through it' and everyone else. I think
> we all felt that these men were somehow strangers and not really in
> our battalion. They were horrified when they realised that we were
> the only survivors and they were quite sympathetic, but somehow we
> felt we could not answer their questions. We seventy men had been
> through something which no one else could share or even under-
> stand.

After drinking the tea and talking for a while, Captain Spark and
Lieutenant McMurtrie were given a horse to ride and the officers and men
moved back to the Fins–Gouzeaucourt road where motor lorries and
general service wagons waited to carry the infantry away to Sorel-le-
Grand to join the rest of the battalion. Lieutenant Scott, who had been in
charge of the transport, and who had worked tirelessly throughout the
German attack in bringing up supplies, was there, as was Major Chappell
with his injured foot who was now given command of the battalion.

221

Lieutenant Berry, the battalion's quartermaster, and the Reverend McKew were also there.

Lieutenant McMurtrie:

> After a long talk, we at last turned in and I was very soon asleep. The hut I was in had about ten valises belonging to DCLI officers who were being relieved that night and would be returning. They turned up about 3am and woke me when they came in. I woke in an awful fright, perspiring all over – I had dreamt the attack over again and when I awoke was being pursued by huge Germans.

The next day was beautifully warm and the relieved Somersets were able to get a change of clothes, their first for two weeks. The German counter-attack had stopped, and peace prevailed after some of the bitterest fighting of the war. There was a large amount of mail for the officers to censor as it was the first real opportunity for the men to write home after their ordeal.

On 4 December the remnants of 7th SomLI were driven by bus to a hutted camp near Bouzeacourt, and then two days later they travelled by train north to Bouranville where the men detrained and marched to Embry, a pretty little village which lay in a small wooded valley. It had white-washed cottages, a small church and a stream that ran through the middle of the village. The whole battalion, including a draft of twenty-seven men from the Royal Engineers, was housed in a large barn and friendly locals helped the soldiers find their way about.

As soon as the battalion was settled in there was a process of sorting out to accomplish. Officers and men busied themselves replacing lost equipment. Nearly every man had items missing, from gas helmets to socks. The only Lewis gun left – the one that Sergeant Major Bulson had used in the battle – now had no ammunition drums. New company rolls had to be made, which was a hard job as nearly all of the battalion's paperwork had been lost in the attack. Lists of the missing and known injured had to be filed, and the post for these men had to be sorted. Parcels which arrived for the missing or injured were divided up amongst the men's old sections so far as they existed.

No rations arrived the following day, which ironically meant that the men had a better breakfast of fresh meat, bread and butter, as well as potatoes bought from the two village shops. There were four estaminets in the village which also proved popular during the stay.

Slowly attempts were made to return former 7th Somerset officers to the re-forming battalion. Lieutenant Mitchell came back to the battalion after working on the 20th Division staff, as did Lieutenant Jones, who had been the brigade intelligence officer. Officers like Lieutenants Joyner and Butler returned from leave. Drafts of new men started to dribble in to increase the numbers as the weeks went by, including men from the depot battalion, the 3rd SomLI. These included officers new to the battalion, such as 2nd Lieutenant Powell who arrived with twenty-one men on 8 December.

Major Chappell's foot continued to cause trouble and for a while the battalion was commanded by Major Brocklehurst who had been with the divisional depot battalion. The recently promoted Captain McMurtrie described the new commanding officer:

> Major Brocklehurst was a typical dug-out major. He was old, always did everything to the letter of the law and was always pleased with any company commander who had his latrines clean, candles in fireproof tins, fire buckets outside the billet and a stock pot by the cooker. If you got all these things done, and it only took a little care to do it, then in his opinion you were a good company commander. He was a dear old man and a typical old grandfather but he never put the wind up the men as our old CO did and we company commanders did more or less what we pleased.

Over the forthcoming weeks the whole process that had begun in 1915 when the battalion arrived in France, began all over again. The men were formed into platoons on arrival, and training started to identify the specialists bombers and Lewis gunners. Training took place in the mornings and the men played football in the afternoons. One problem encountered was a difficulty in maintaining high standards in training because of a shortage of experienced NCOs.

On 12 December the battalion moved to La Belle Hôtesse as part of a general concentration of the 20th Division in an area about twenty-five miles south-west of Ypres. The men's thoughts started to turn to Christmas which was rapidly approaching. On Christmas Day the men dined on four porkers, killed by a butcher in C Company, and they also had plenty of vegetables as well as plum pudding doused in rum and set alight. Three barrels of beer were bought, and gifts of cigarettes as well as comfort parcels from children from Somerset were distributed. As the afternoon wore on most of the men moved into nearby estaminets. In the evening it started to snow.

For the battalion 1917 had been an eventful year. It had risen from the mud of the Somme and taken part in some of the most successful attacks, only to be destroyed in the last days of the year. By the end of 1917 the battalion had lost 539 men since formation, including seven more who had died of wounds in December following the German counter-attack.[1] Most of those who died of wounds had been captured by the Germans. One was 31-year-old Private John Penhorwood from Appledore in Devon. His wife Pollie would have been told soon after the battle that her husband was missing, but she would then have had a long wait before being informed through the Red Cross of his capture and death. Others would die of wounds into the New Year.[2]

Return to the Ypres salient

On New Year's Eve all of the battalion's officers were assembled for a meeting by Major Brocklehurst who had in his possession a map of the new sector into which the 7th Somersets were to go. It showed all of the tracks from the support area to the front line which the company commanders would be visiting the next day.

Captain McMurtrie was unimpressed: 'He fussed about and talked about how important and secret it was, should he trust anyone etc . . . The CO also brought up the question of whether all the battalion trench maps (every officer had about ten just to make his kit weigh a little more) should be locked up, silly old fool.' On New Year's Day the Somerset company officers met up with some from the DCLI and all were driven for a reconnaissance of the line to be held in the Ypres salient.

On 3 January 1918 the battalion moved to a camp closer to the front line where training continued. The battalion was now returning to fighting strength with companies mustering about 100 men each, although it was short of officers.

Three American officers were attached to the battalion for training during this period, and Foley and McMurtrie took them up to the front line to reconnoitre the positions into which the Somersets would soon move. The DCLI headquarters had been moved as their commanding officer, adjutant and the rest of their headquarters staff had been killed in a fire in a tunnel in which they were stationed. Captain McMurtrie:

> The duck board track curved just beyond the ridge and as we were going round the bend, Foley and I in front, two Americans fifty yards behind us and Berry and the third American fifty yards behind them, there was a sudden swish – bang and a shell exploded a yard off the duck board track, between Foley, I and the two Americans. A minute afterwards, Foley and I couldn't see the Americans for smoke, they had bolted off with the 'wind up' as the expression goes! We went on a little quicker and got to Iliad Trench, saw all the pill boxes and then returned.

On 13 January the Somersets returned to the front, replacing the 7th DCLI and occupying support trenches in the Mount Sorrel area which was to the south-east of Ypres along the Menin road. The following day they moved into the front line. This was a series of water-logged outpost positions in front, with low parapet trenches infested with rats immediately behind.

The area had been fought over as late as the middle of December, as the front-line positions which were on the forward slope of the ridge gave, or denied, observation over the salient.

Until the middle of January the winter was severe. Snow and heavy frosts were common, freezing the swampy ground solid and icing over the little streams that ran through the front line. Soldiers living in the front line often suffered from frost bite due to the extreme conditions and inadequate shelter. Because of the weather the battalions of the 20th Division were rotated through the front line on a forty-eight hourly basis.

The period at the front remained very quiet until 4 February 1918 when the battalion was withdrawn. During this time only one man had been killed.[3] Few incidents of note occurred. Once the battalion raided enemy trenches, throwing a few hand grenades at the Germans before scuttling back to British lines. One man accidentally shot himself in the hand while working on a wiring party in no man's land which required a full investigation with witness statements from all of the other members of the working party. Finally, an alarming incident occurred on 3 February when British artillery started to fire short on the Somersets' forward positions. A quick call stopped the fire and prevented casualties.

Reorganisation

While the Somersets were in the trenches on this last tour of duty, the 20th Division, along with all of the others in the British Army on the continent, was reorganised. The reorganisation was required because of the falling strength of battalions in the field. There had been a reduction in the number of replacements coming across the Channel as part of a deliberate government policy. Lloyd George, the Prime Minister, believed that if Haig were given sufficient men to maintain the strength of the BEF he would continue the costly offensives of 1917. An army starved of men could not sustain lengthy offensive operations and Lloyd George's idea was to await the build up of the American Army, until it was of sufficient strength to alter the balance on the Western Front.

The reorganisation was also to take into account the need to have extra men involved in defensive preparations for the expected German offensive. The Germans had effectively defeated the Russians and were rapidly transferring as many men as possible across to the Western Front to deliver a knock-out blow to the British and French before the Americans could arrive in sufficient numbers. A race had begun.

It had been decided to reduce all infantry brigades from four to three battalions each. Each division would retain a pioneer battalion, meaning an overall reduction from thirteen to ten battalions within each division. The 20th Division lost the 6th Ox & BucksLI, 10th KRRC and the 10th RB. The effect of the sudden implementation of the reorganisation on the morale of the men in these battalions was marked. The officers were given a choice of which battalion they would go to. The men were, as far as possible, sent to other battalions of their regiments. One commanding officer, Lieutenant Colonel Morgan-Owen, returned from a course to find his battalion, the 10th RB, had been disbanded.

Also as part of the reorganisation the 7th KOYLI were to leave the division on 15 February to become an 'entrenching' battalion. The 2nd Scottish Rifles, a regular battalion from the 8th Division joined the 20th Division as part of the 59th Brigade. The division's artillery and trench mortar contingents were adjusted, and about one week later an additional Vickers machine-gun company joined the division. The idea was to maintain a high level of firepower with fewer infantrymen through forming a divisional machine-gun brigade with four companies of machine guns.

On 7 February the 7th Somersets went back to the front line, occupying new positions. Company headquarters were in water-logged former German pill boxes. The men had to live in shell hole 'posts', modified shell holes that were themselves filling up with water. The whole area was littered with rotting British and German corpses from the earlier fighting.

Because of the conditions the men adopted a daily regime of massaging their feet for fifteen minutes in the evening, and each day clean socks were sent up the line in an effort to reduce trench foot. The efforts were largely successful.

This time in the front line the enemy became more active, regularly firing trench mortars at the British posts. On Sunday 10 February Private Arthur Hann was blown to pieces by a trench mortar bomb and Private Albert Lock was fatally wounded. Lock was only 19 when he died at a casualty clearing station in Poperinghe.

Monday the 11th was quieter and the men spent greater amounts of time improving the trenches. During the day Private Gosney, who was on gas sentry duty, rushed into company headquarters shortly after a shot had been fired outside. He was shrieking and fell down on the floor of the dugout having shot himself in the leg. The circumstances were highly suspicious as Gosney was already under arrest for failing to return to the battalion after his leave and an enquiry was immediately opened with statements being required of all nearby. Gosney was taken away on a stretcher.

After two days in support, on Wednesday 13 February the battalion went back to the front line, where it was shelled by trench mortars using high explosive and gas. Many men were injured on this and the next day and Lieutenant Date and a number of others were badly gassed. On Thursday 14 February William Way was killed by a trench mortar bomb. His body was never recovered.

On the night of 15 February 1918 the battalion was relieved by the 8th

SomLI and many men met former friends and comrades they had known from their training or service. One of the officers now in the 8th SomLI was Captain Peard, who had been badly injured while serving with the 7th Battalion in a trench raid in 1916. The men were nevertheless pleased to be out of the front line.

Over the next few days they made their way by light rail and marching to Campagne where they remained until 22 February. Colonel Troyte-Bullock resumed command of the battalion and the days were spent in training and cleaning. The battalion continued to suffer from the inexperience of the new officers and NCOs, and the longer serving officers had difficulty in getting the new men into proper order. Some of the things that were overlooked were of a fairly trivial nature to men who could be living or fighting in slimy mud in the very near future. The fact that buttons were not polished was perhaps not of the greatest significance, but it was symptomatic of general sloppiness. At a pre-parade inspection of one of the platoons, some men were found to have rusty ammunition and items of kit were often missing.[4]

On 22 February the battalion started their move south, into the sector held by General Hubert Gough's Fifth Army. The move started scrappily as the laxness of some in the battalion meant that not all of the equipment had been properly packed when it was time to go. Some of the cooker staff had got drunk the night before and were unable to pack all of the equipment and some had to be left behind. The two men responsible were later given field punishment and replaced. The men were at that time unaware that a relatively short distance away from their new location the Germans were preparing to launch a massive attack that would open the biggest battle of the war on the Western Front.

NOTES

1 Those who died of wounds were Private Frederick Alden (died 2/12/17), Private Albert Chandler (died 3/12/17), Sergeant Frederick Howse (died 4/12/17), Private John Penhorwood (died 7/12/17), Private Joseph Richardson (died 9/12/17), Corporal Arthur Woodman (died 13/12/17), and Private Thomas Heath (died 13/12/17).

2 These were Private William Stobart (died 4/1/18) and Lance Corporal Colin Wedlake (died 5/1/18).

3 He was Private James Chalmers who was killed while the battalion was in brigade support.

4 During this time Private William Trott died (on 18 February) at the Notre Dame Hospital at Hainout in Belgium, an area occupied by the Germans. The cause of death is unknown.

CHAPTER XVII
The Kaiser's Battle

Background

Throughout January 1918 the British Fifth Army gradually took over sections of the front line that had previously been held by the French, in the area facing and south of St Quentin. The extension meant that the British Army, which was about to undergo a reorganisation to reduce the number of battalions in each division, also had to assume responsibility for another twenty-five miles of front line.

That the Germans were planning a significant spring offensive was well known. They had been steadily moving reinforcements from their Eastern to the Western Front since the collapse of Russia. Some of the early arrivals had been committed in the counter-attack at Cambrai in November, but many more divisions had arrived since then. What was unknown was where the Germans would attack. Another fact known to the British High Command was that the British were in an extremely weakened state as the number of replacement soldiers coming out to British units had dwindled as part of Lloyd George's policy of restricting replacements. Also, following the Passchendaele offensive, many more officers and men were given leave through the winter and spring to maintain morale. This effectively further weakened the fighting strength of the formations.

The forward positions held by the British were not always adequate from a defensive standpoint. The British Army had been engaged in offensive operations from 1915 through to November 1917 and most front-line positions were the foremost points of a previous attack, or trenches and posts dug in preparation for a future attack. The dugouts were not deep, and support trenches were very often simply means of getting to or from the front line, rather than defensible lines on their own.

Tactically too the British were unused to defence in set-piece battles, although the principles of defensive schemes were well established by 1918. The British had invariably been counter-attacked by the Germans whenever ground had been captured, and local level tactical skills, like the deployment of Lewis guns ahead of the main defensive line to avoid them being precisely located and destroyed, were tried methods since 1916. The employment of forward posts ahead of the main defensive line was also a known and tried method of defence along the front line.

Through the winter of 1917–18 the British decided to concentrate defensive preparations in the area to the middle and north of their defensive line. This line ran from just north of Ypres in Belgium to La Fère which was approximately six miles south of St Quentin. The north and centre were where the vital communication and supply routes linked the army to Britain. In the south, Haig had received an undertaking of support from the French in the event of a German attack, and a German success here would have less strategic consequences for the British.

The Fifth Army in the south was accordingly more thinly spread than the other British armies. It also inherited many miles of French front line that needed considerable strengthening and reorganisation to suit British defensive plans.

The British scheme was to establish a 'forward zone' of posts along the entire front from a few hundred yards to a few miles deep in some places. The aim of these posts was to delay and disrupt any attack. Behind these posts was the 'battle zone'. This was formed by a series of mutually supporting redoubts and smaller posts which were sited for their fields of fire and to make use of the lie of the land. The battle zone was to be between one half mile to a mile deep, and these positions were expected to halt the German attack. Behind the 'battle zone' was a final line of resistance, called the 'brown line' in the Fifth Army area. These were final defensive positions to prevent a breakout should the Germans penetrate the battle zone

Against the Fifth Army, and the Third Army to its north, the Germans were preparing seventy-six divisions to assault the British line. These units were withdrawn from the front line, or kept back from the line as they came from the Eastern Front for training in offensive techniques. Specialist storm troop formations were trained to assault key defensive positions, and officers and soldiers were given training in infiltration tactics. The general principle was to advance through any gaps in enemy positions and either continue on through the enemy lines, or in some cases attack the positions passed from the rear or flanks. Specialist equipment like flamethrowers was to be used against some points of resistance and for the first time the Germans would deploy light machine guns in large numbers to support attacking infantry. The infantry assault would also be supplemented by light artillery and trench mortars which were assigned to follow up the advancing infantry and deal with pockets of resistance. The infantry assault would follow a short (five-hour) but fierce artillery barrage of key positions using a large number of gas shells.

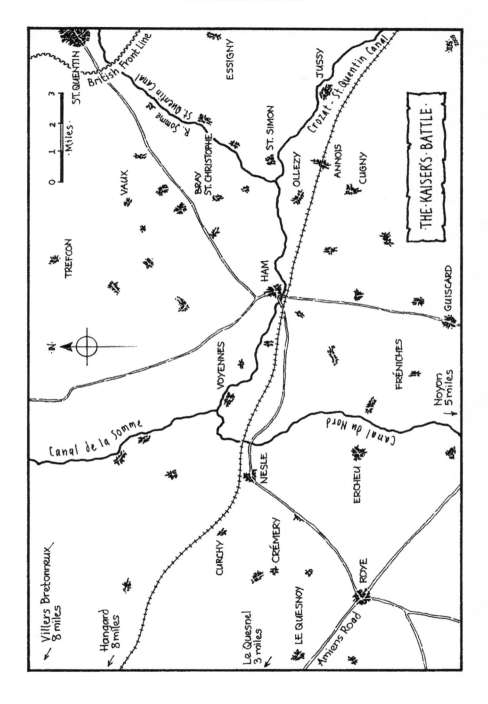

The 7th Somersets

On 22 February the 7th Somersets with the rest of the 20th Division found itself moved into the area of Nesle. This was at the time the Fifth Army headquarters. The GHQ held eight divisions as a general reserve, although two divisions were positioned behind each of the four army groups in the front line. The 20th and 50th Divisions were the two GHQ reserve divisions held behind the Fifth Army front. The 20th Division was approximately nine miles behind the front line, the 50th Division another twenty miles behind.

The Somersets themselves marched to the village of Fréniches, where the battalion set about training in earnest. That the Germans would attack was well known, even amongst the men at battalion level. The fact that the 20th Division was one of the eight GHQ reserve divisions also meant that whenever and wherever the attack came it was likely that the men would quickly be moved to the area of fiercest fighting.

Captain McMurtrie said:

> We would probably be taken by bus or train to a certain place and then have a long march to where the enemy had broken through and of course we should be fighting in open country and not in trenches. During this 'rest' therefore we were hard at work training the men in open warfare and its tactics, getting the men used to long route marches and in every way getting the men fit.

The men also provided working parties which quickly raised a discipline problem when some from C Company refused to join in. On Sunday 24 February Brigadier General Banbury assembled the battalion and addressed the men on the seriousness of the work involved which resolved the issue. In their spare time the men played football, went to Verey Lights concerts and also took part in the 20th Division race meeting.

In the event of an attack, the defensive scheme envisaged the 20th Division holding a nine-mile line from St Simon in the south to Trefcon to the north; positions along the 'brown line'. The 20th Division was to form the reserve division for Lieutenant General Ivor Maxse's XVIIIth Corps which comprised the 36th (Ulster), 30th and 61st (South Midland) Divisions. On 10 March 1918 officers were taken forward to reconnoitre the area the battalion would go into. While visiting this area the Somerset officers noted the extended line the battalion would hold, and also the incomplete defences. They also came across fenced-off areas containing Italian soldiers who had fled in the German Caporetto offensive. These were being used as a labour supply to improve local defences.

Despite all of the preparations for the battle that would soon take place, other battalion functions continued. Private Gosney, whose rifle had discharged while he was gas sentry shooting himself in the leg, was produced on a stretcher to be court martialled for causing a self-inflicted wound. In the meantime he had had his leg amputated and he appeared very ill when he arrived. The trial took place and Gosney was eventually acquitted.

Throughout this time the battalion, with the rest of the Division, was put on increasingly shortened notice to move. When the battalion arrived it had been on twenty-four hours' notice to move off. On 10 March 1918 this was reduced to twelve hours' notice. On the 20th March it was reduced to one hour.[1] With this reduction of notice the men packed their equipment and then turned in to sleep on a very cold night.

Battle stations

While stationed here the battalion had been split up. D Company was at Voyennes; the other companies at Curchy. Captain Foley with D Company: 'Voyennes was many miles behind the front line, but all that night and in the early morning of Thursday our billets shook with the sustained thunder of a heavy bombardment.'

Captain McMurtrie, who was even farther away with the rest of the battalion at Curchy: 'In the middle of the night, the enemy started a tremendous bombardment which could be heard distinctly at Curchy even though we were about fifteen miles from the front line.'

The men spent an anxious night, half sleeping, half awake with excitement and anticipation of news from the front. Packs and officers' valises were given a final sort to be ready to move as soon as orders were received. The men waited through the night and next morning against the back drop of the enemy artillery 'drum fire'. Finally, mid-morning, news came from a dispatch rider from corps headquarters at Nesle; the enemy had attacked and been held all along the front. That afternoon another dispatch rider brought orders for the battalion to go to its battle stations in buses. Captain McMurtrie recalled:

> On the way we had passed frightened peasants clearing out their homes and going back with as much of their household goods as they could carry. They had been through one German occupation and were not going to chance another. It was a pitiable sight seeing old men and women and young children hurrying along as best they could with terror in their eyes.

Several heavy shells burst near the buses as the battalion was driven towards the front and the men drove past piles of clothes left by the Italian prisoners. Captain McMurtrie:

Just outside Ham we passed a cooker overturned in the road and a stream of men came past us many wounded, amongst whom were a great many gunners, some carrying their gun sights. They told of an awful barrage, of swarms of Germans attacking, and of our men being shot down or surrounded. This was not very cheerful, evidently things were not going at all well so far.

Soon the men got within range of some enemy guns that were firing shrapnel which burst with black puffs of smoke. They de-bussed and moved forward by company crossed the Crozat–St Quentin canal and into their positions. Because of the delay in getting the orders through, A, B and C Companies arrived before D Company who were still on the road and the first three companies were ordered across the canal and told to dig in.

The battalion position was to the left of those the officers had previously reconnoitred. This area had no barbed wire in front and the men needed to deepen the trenches. Once the battalion had dug in and the men had had a very short rest, the orders were changed. The battalion was to retire to the west bank of the Crozat canal and dig new positions immediately along the canal bank. The bridges were to be prepared for demolition by Royal Engineers. This time D and C Companies were to dig in on the front, and A and B Companies were sent back about a mile through some wooded swampy ground on the western bank of the canal to be in support. The move behind the canal meant that the men were now digging into positions which were overlooked by St Simon on the far side of the canal, although the digging in this part was easier as some of the work had already been completed, and in some parts there was even barbed wire in front. The main problem with the dispositions remained the huge area to be covered by the battalion.

Captain Foley: 'We [D Company] had, I should think, some eight or nine hundred yards of the canal to hold, and this comprised two road bridges, two wooden pontoons, and half a dozen small foot bridges.' Three platoons held the forward posts which were mainly deployed to cover the approaches to the bridges. The fourth platoon was kept in reserve.

Most of the officers and men were exhausted after being awake for most of the previous night and having spent the day siting and digging two sets of defensive positions. Many of the sections would continue to deepen their posts throughout the next night. The Germans opened and then kept steady fire on the main road to the west of the main bridge throughout the time the battalion was digging in. During the day Private Wallace Creed from Stroud in Gloucestershire was killed by enemy shellfire.

That evening Colonel Troyte-Bullock summoned the company

commanders to battalion headquarters in order to outline the situation; he made things plain. The Germans were to be expected at any time the next day. When they did arrive the 7th Battalion was to fight to the last.

As dawn arrived on Friday 22 March the men peering over the entrenchments found themselves looking into a thick mist which permitted visibility only just across the canal. The night had been cold, and soon the battalion's cooks who were with the transport supplied tea, bacon and rum to warm the men up. Occasionally across a bridge on the front, figures would loom out of the mist; wounded British soldiers, gunners who had lost their batteries, and along the main road some heavy guns, all heading away from the fighting.

For the men of A and B Companies who were in support approximately one mile from the canal, Friday 22nd was relatively inactive. C and D Companies who were holding the canal bank had a much more lively day. D Company was on the left, C Company to their right.

Captain Foley with D Company:

> Exactly what the position was in front we could not at that time ascertain, and among the first things I had to do on that Friday morning was to send forward patrols to try and get in touch with some of our troops to the front. This they failed to do in the time allotted. It was fairly obvious, however, that things were not going altogether well with us; every now and then we could hear a sudden burst of rifle fire, and the bursts always seemed to be getting nearer.

The mist cleared at 10am and at 11.30am there was a sudden and fierce burst of rifle fire close to the British front line, immediately followed by a burst of machine-gun fire along a road in D Company's area.

Captain Foley was on this road: 'We hurried on as fast as we could up the road, meeting on the way Jones, the Brigade Intelligence Officer, who shouted to us that the Germans had reached the canal bank (thereby living up to his title), various excited R.E. personnel making good their escape, and a runaway mess cart.'

The Somersets in the front line quickly returned fire and large explosions followed as the Engineers detonated the explosive charges on the bridges. Captain Henry Foley set about ascertaining the extent of damage caused to the bridges and was extremely concerned to find an engineer-built wooden bridge, capable of carrying heavy traffic, complete. Lieutenant Mitchell, one of the platoon commanders, also reported that a foot bridge farther along also remained undamaged as the charges had failed to fire.

It was found that the Engineers, upon firing the charges, had disappeared leaving an empty dugout. Mitchell volunteered to try to destroy the foot bridge with a box of bombs. Captain Foley:

Having armed himself with a couple of Mills, he stood up on the bank in full view of the opposite side, and proceeded to hurl them in the prescribed manner at the centre of the bridge. This I consider required no little courage, because, although the firing had ceased, yet we had no reason to suppose that the enemy had withdrawn.

Despite his courage, the Mills bombs were unable to damage the structure.

Captain Foley decided to call upon Corporal Peppard, a man with knowledge of explosives, to help in the demolition of the remaining bridges, and the corporal spent the rest of the day destroying any remaining bridges with zeal.

By the evening of the 22nd the battalion was firmly established on the western bank of the canal. C and D Companies now held the canal bank, B Company was in support and A Company in reserve near battalion headquarters. To the north of the 7th SomLI were three companies of the 7th DCLI who carried on the line until it joined up with a brigade of the 36th (Ulster) Division who had retired from their original front line. To the south of the 7th Somersets was the single company of the 7th DCLI who carried the line towards positions of the 14th (Light) Division. The battalion on the extreme left of this division was the 6th SomLI who held the village of Jussy. Another cold and dreary night awaited the men sheltering in their entrenchments, the Germans sending over the occasional shell.

23 March

The early morning of 23 March 1918 was shrouded in a heavy fog, which cleared much more quickly than it had the previous day. During the night the Germans had deployed in force on the opposite side of the canal, and were now dug in on the commanding high ground opposite. The effect on those in the front line was dramatic, as the men came under fire as soon as they showed themselves. No one was able to move about without attracting fire.

Captain Foley: 'From an early hour – another fact which caused us some uneasiness – we could hear heavy rifle fire to our rear, as though an attack in some force were being made there.'

Behind the foremost positions movement and communication was better. At 8am battalion headquarters were ordered back to Annois to maintain better contact with brigade. When they got to Annois they were met by some men from the 14th Division, when the reason for the sounds of fighting to the rear of the Somersets became clear – the Germans had launched an attack on the 14th Division at Jussy. The 6th SomLI, who had been heavily mauled in the first day of the offensive, together with the 9th Scottish Rifles, had borne the brunt of the attack. The charges on their bridges had failed and the Germans crossed the canal in strength. The 14th

Division had been pushed back about one and a half miles exposing the right flank of the 7th Somersets and the company of the 7th DCLI to their right.

Quickly a message was sent to Captain McMurtrie's A Company, the only company which at this time was in direct contact with headquarters, to form a defensive flank on the right of the Somersets' line from Annois to the canal. The impossibility of this order is apparent when one sees that the distance to be defended by A Company was over one mile in swampy and wooded country. The three other companies remained along or immediately behind the canal bank and were unable to move because of the dominant German positions on the far side of the canal.

Captain McMurtrie with A Company:

> About an hour afterwards [10am], [Lieutenant] Berry came up and showed me a place on the map, on the canal on which I had to take my company. I got the company out of the trench and we started to go across country in artillery formation. Soon however, Berry came rushing up to tell me he had made a mistake and that we were to get back ready for a counter attack or to form a right defensive flank. We got back just as the enemy began to fire with heavy machine guns and soon I got a message from the CO to form a defensive flank against the enemy who were expected to attack by an encircling movement at any moment. I got my men out and soon found three posts already dug very deep and were partly facing the wrong way but I ordered the men to dig a fire step and then we were ready for as many Germans as wished to come.

Headquarters had also deployed themselves in the Annois area along a sunken cart track that ran across the railway line through the village. The men could now only await their fate.

Captain McMurtrie: 'We soon saw some men on the horizon but it was impossible to make out whether they were Germans or our own men. The machine gun fire was pretty hot and these men began running and at last reached us. They were men of the KRRC who had been fighting on the canal bank and had had no rations or water sent up. They had been forced out of their positions and were withdrawing.' At that point Captain McMurtrie went back to headquarters to report the position as the signallers were unable to communicate with battalion headquarters.

While McMurtrie was away the Germans closed with A Company. Heavy machine guns were brought up and the German artillery found its mark dropping fairly heavy fire on the defensive posts. A Company initially fought back with rifle and Lewis gun fire being directed at the attackers, but soon gave way, falling back towards the headquarters positions.

Captain McMurtrie recalled:

> The CO was glad to see me and also pleased to get my information. He wanted me to wait while he wrote a message to all company commanders ordering them to withdraw back to the St Simon–Annois road. He showed me the message, sent it off and then I started back with my runner. I had gone half way and was just crossing a very marshy piece of ground when the enemy started shelling heavily. Machine gun and rifle fire increased and then I saw the remainder of my company, headed by an officer running back as fast as they could in terror, men dropping in all directions. It was impossible to form up the remainder in the swamp so I led them over to battalion headquarters. Here I found that the enemy had advanced and was pushing forward his machine guns to try and encircle us. I think one of the most bitter moments I have had was to see my company, being killed and wounded, broken up and nothing to remain of four months hard work, except dead, wounded and maimed.

At the canal bank posts C and D Companies held their positions through the morning. Their posts were fired upon regularly by rifles and machine guns. Despite this fire the odd effective burst was fired by the Lewis gunners against Germans who were showing themselves fairly freely within the village of St Simon.

Captain Foley:

> One German walked out as bold as brass apparently with the object of examining the iron bridge more closely. He was picked off neatly by one of my snipers. Shortly after one, when Mitchell and I were debating on the situation, I got a message from Whitworth, commanding C Company on my right, saying that he was withdrawing, under orders from the CO to the railway cutting at Annois, in other words to battalion headquarters. From the runner I learnt that a similar message was on its way to me. It had not yet arrived, however, so that I was still my own master. I gave Mitchell orders to withdraw to the line held by A and B Companies, and to report himself to battalion headquarters. Meanwhile with company headquarters and the other three platoons I decided to hang on and await developments on the left of the main road.
>
> But Mitchell had hardly disappeared down the road towards Annois, when we saw a man in a great state of excitement running towards us waving and shouting for us to come back. This put a fresh complexion on things. There could be no doubt that matters were more serious on the right than I had estimated, and I no longer felt

justified in keeping the company in a position which, entirely in the air as it had become through the withdrawal of C Company, would merely have been a trap had we been subject to an attack from the rear. I therefore sent two runners along to Sergeants Wood, Hayward and Squibb, telling them to withdraw to the railway cutting at Annois. I was about to move off down the road when it occurred to me that Sergeant Wood, being without a map, would have great difficulty in finding Annois; so I sent off company headquarters under Sergeant Francis, who was then acting company sergeant major, and myself set off to follow the two runners.

While the orders from battalion headquarters were getting through to the three front-line companies, the retreat of the remnants of A Company continued, until they joined up with the headquarters detachment in the sunken road across the railway line. The pursuing Germans were quick to attack these men and a fierce fight began. Among these defenders Colonel Troyte-Bullock was shot through the neck by a rifle bullet and many others were similarly injured or killed. Many of the injured, including the colonel, made their way to the rear as the fighting progressed. Colonel Troyte-Bullock arrived some time later at the 7th DCLI headquarters, exhausted through shock and blood loss, where he was able to apprise their commanding officer, Lieutenant Colonel Burgess-Short DSO, of the situation unfolding to his right before retiring to seek medical attention for his wounds.

Captain McMurtrie who was now with battalion headquarters:

Huns attacked us and for about an hour we kept shooting at them and kept them at bay. I saw one Bosch, who pretended to be dead, suddenly open fire on us. He got more than he bargained for.

[Lieutenant] Berry who was next to me firing away, got up to look over the bank, over which we were shooting. He got a bullet right through the head and was killed instantly, falling on top of me with a groan. Berry was one of the best and kindest men I have ever come across. I was very upset to see him killed. I now had to take command of the battalion headquarters. Ammunition was giving out and the Germans were gradually working around us and threatening to surround us any minute. I considered it would be a waste of life to hold on any longer, having done all we could to delay the enemy for as long as possible. A great many men had already been killed or wounded and I decided that it was time to withdraw.

The remnants from headquarters and A Company made their way along the railway line towards Ollezy, where they eventually came across Lieutenant Colonel Burgess-Short. He had been organising groups of men from a number of regiments to face the attacking Germans. The defenders arranged themselves into three groups, two on small hills on either flank and a main group in a small valley in between. Here the battle ended for these men on 23 March.

Meanwhile the forward companies, following their orders, retired towards battalion headquarters. Some of the men made their way back across small streams and ditches, through small woods until they came close to Annois.

Captain Foley said:

> I left [Sergeant] Hayward with the two platoons in a little wood, and went myself with an orderly to report to battalion headquarters. We had not gone many yards up the line, when straight ahead of us we saw some men crossing it in single file. I immediately took it to mark the spot where battalion headquarters were established, and was hurrying on when my orderly, whose sight was considerably better than mine, suddenly stopped short. He took a good look at the figures ahead of us, and then announced in no uncertain voice that they were Germans. He was a bit of a booby, this man, and at first I thought he was mad, but only a few steps were enough to convince me that what he had said was perfectly true.

Captain Foley immediately lined the small wood with his two platoons facing Annois; he was now at a loss to know what to do. He had no idea where any friendly soldiers could be found, the other two platoons from his company had not arrived, nor was there any sign of C Company. The dilemma was resolved by the arrival of an officer from the Durham Light Infantry who said that there were men from the King's in nearby Cugny. Foley led his two platoons back to this force where Colonel Vince of the King's was assembling a composite force that comprised two companies of King's, two platoons of Shropshires and the newly arrived Somersets who were grouped with the Shropshires to make a third company. The men were lined up in a field as the evening drew in, listening to the sounds of fighting going on ahead.

Some of the men retiring towards the headquarters position from the front-line companies got completely lost. Sergeant Francis, who had been sent to guide Sergeant Wood's platoon from D Company from the canal bank to Annois, got himself and his platoon lost. Sergeant Francis later recounted what happened:

> On getting my platoon together we marched back, as I thought, by the right road, but unfortunately it was the wrong one, as it was a fork road. Anyhow, on marching along I saw what I thought was a party of British soldiers, beckoning us to come on, but imagine my

surprise on coming closer to discover it was a party of Germans. I immediately gave the order to about turn and make for the wood which was on my left. On getting through the wood we were further hampered by a river which was several feet deep, so I asked Lance Corporal Haines who was a stretcher bearer with my platoon to find out how deep it was with the aid of his stretcher, and found it was about five feet deep. In we went and got across, of course like drowned rats; nevertheless we got over and started for a building which I thought was an old barn, and you should have seen us when we discovered it to be nothing else but an old quartermasters stores, with a liberal supply of tunics, trousers and puttees. Of course, we soon divested our wet clothes and put on the new and made our way towards our retreating soldiers. I might say that we were under fire all the time this was happening, and of course were disorganised; anyhow, I came in touch with a Scottish Regiment and we were attached to them for three days until they found out where the 7th SomLI were, and then they sent us back to be made up to strength again.

Given their location, the Scottish soldiers were doubtless from the 9th Scottish Rifles who had been fighting alongside the 6th Somersets in Jussy.

As evening closed Captain Foley and his men lay in a field near Cugny together with the groups of Shropshires and King's that had been gathered together by Colonel Vince. The Germans advanced towards Cugny, evidently intending to capture it before the end of the day, and they clearly located the composite force and started shooting at the men in the field. The King's commanding officer decided to withdraw his men after nightfall and orders were issued for the Somersets and Shropshires to line a sunken road and provide cover for the retreating King's, which they duly did. Groups of men in twos and threes came back from Cugny as the Germans advanced towards it. They joined the men already in the sunken road.

Captain Foley said:

It was extraordinary at times like that how any formed body of men, under proper control, however small it might be, seemed to attract to it the stragglers from miles around. In an incredibly short time the banks of our sunken road were thick with men, belonging, I suppose, to a dozen different brigades. A major of the 14th Division, who had arrived at this time, took over command of the whole force.

As soon as the main body of the [King's] Liverpools started moving back, we got the order to open rapid fire on the village, immediately to our front. Seldom I suppose has such a hail of shot swept across no man's land at an unsuspecting enemy. The men were literally shoulder to shoulder, and for five minutes at least the vicinity of Cugny must have been extremely unhealthy.

After the King's had retired, the composite force sped back to a position about eight hundred yards on the main road from Cugny where the officers sorted the men into their respective units. The Germans seemed to have no intention of following that night, and Foley and the Major from the 14th Division went back to try to make contact with a brigade headquarters rumoured to be in the next village down the road. They ran into the 7th Somersets' transport on this road, meeting Lieutenant Scott who accompanied the men back to the village. The ill-tempered brigadier they found here simply told them all to return to the transport lines which Foley found 'ludicrous'.

Foley returned to where he had left his men and met up with Colonel Vince of the King's who had started to deploy his men across the road. Food was distributed to this group of men from the Somersets' transport and they started to dig in to await the Germans the next day. The Somersets and King's formed an outer perimeter, with the Shropshires in the middle in a 'keep' position. Some smaller posts were created ahead of this main line of resistance along the road to Cugny. The men spent a very cold night digging in.

24 March

All around this area stragglers from a variety of battalions moved about the battlefield through the afternoon of the 23rd and overnight into 24 March. Many who were unable to find friendly formations spent anxious hours listening to noises in the darkness. The Germans were advancing in strength up to the new front line and through any gaps they could find, often running into British soldiers who frequently surrendered, sometimes put up a fight or fled.

Captain McMurtrie at Ollezy:

All that night which was bitterly cold, there was fitful shooting, we heard transport on the road and shouted only to be answered in German voices. Two German cavalrymen came down the road across which my men were lined, we shot both of their horses dead but the men got away. That night we had orders from brigade to hold in our position, instead of withdrawing and making a good strong line a little further back. We all thought it likely that by night fall we would either be killed, wounded or prisoners for there was no chance to get back being almost completely surrounded.

Dawn on 24 March was again shrouded in a thick and cold mist which protected the British soldiers from being detected in their positions. Everything would soon change.

In Captain McMurtrie's area, in front of the village of Ollezy, as soon as the mist cleared the Germans discovered the British positions. Almost immediately they opened fire with machine guns and artillery that had been brought up over night and placed in a commanding position over the British entrenchments. The men here were without food or water and were by now extremely tired.

Captain McMurtrie said:

> About this time I received a verbal message by a runner from the Colonel [Vince] to the effect that my party was to cover the withdrawal of the rest and then was also to withdraw. Almost immediately the rest started withdrawing and after they got clear, I gave the order to withdraw too. I had learnt a lesson from Cambrai and I was determined not to let the men start running for once they did in such a situation it was impossible to hold them. I had my revolver out and anyone who tried to run I immediately threatened to shoot. This stopped all the running but it was the worst hour I have ever been through, with only the Cambrai counter-attack on the 30th November.
>
> The enemy were lining the right ridge and pouring a deadly fire into us, shells and shrapnel were bursting everywhere. German aeroplanes started flying over us and firing into our midst. Men were dropping everywhere, some were wounded and calling out for help, others were dying and groaning in their pain. It was a ghastly situation. 2nd Lieutenant Butler was killed. The Colonel had given me no place where we were to withdraw and so I steered a course straight to our rear. The end was very near and soon we ran bang into a huge number of German artillery and transport and were captured.
>
> A German on a horse came up and led me to believe that he wanted my revolver and kit and so I gave him my revolver. He took it and fired it into the ground. I had heard as everyone else had of the awful treatment by Germans of their prisoners and so thought this German was trying my revolver in order to shoot me. I waited but nothing happened. I was told to take the rest of my kit off and then being very thirsty got my water bottle out, filled it from a stream and at last got a drink, the first one for twenty four hours.

Captain McMurtrie and the nine remaining men from his party were taken into Ham, the town near to where they were captured. Here they witnessed Germans looting the town; men were everywhere with boxes of biscuits, bottles of wine and cigarettes taken from ransacked buildings. Wounded Germans were seen making their way back for help, and the party led by McMurtrie were given an injured man to carry. On their way back they passed a seemingly endless stream of German artillery, tractors, infantry and transport heading in the opposite direction. Eventually they stopped for a rest.

Captain McMurtrie continued:

> We waited outside the village [St Christophe] for about ten minutes and during the wait an officer and some men came up to us. The officer spoke English and was quite friendly and amongst other things asked me my rank and my age. The Germans could not believe that an officer of nineteen could be a captain, but I believe a captain in the German army has a larger body of men to command.

Captain McMurtrie would spend the remainder of the war in captivity.

The other large group of 7th Somersets were those with Captain Foley deployed in defensive positions along the road to Cugny. Dawn for these men also brought the mist which cleared after a few hours. The positions which had been made overnight were hardly complete, and contact had been lost with all soldiers behind.

The morning passed with a long-range British gun firing shrapnel rounds over the road, and the Germans started firing rifle grenades from Cugny at the forward posts which resulted in these posts being withdrawn.

Captain Foley was still with the Shropshire men in the 'keep' position:

> At noon the enemy machine gun fire showed a marked increase, and this we knew to be the harbinger of a fresh attack. The advance was made at first on our extreme right, and we had a perfectly clear view of the whole thing. We let the enemy get well out from the village, which they did by short rushes in excellent order, and then with our sights at only 300 yards, started a steady fire on them as they lay in the open fully exposed to our view. I took the rifle from the man next to me, who had nearly blown my head off with his first shot, and getting him to act as loader, settled down to killing Germans with a lust which, when considered in cooler moments afterwards, rather amazed me. We could hardly miss at so short a range, and their casualties were very heavy, especially amongst the machine gunners, who made a conspicuous target by reason of their heavy weapon which they carried on a kind of stretcher.

The stocks of ammunition quickly started to dwindle and parties of men were sent back to find more.

Captain Foley continued:

Proportionally as our fire slackened, the Germans had pushed on. Finding themselves quite unopposed on their immediate front, they were able to start an encircling movement on our right. Meanwhile on the left a similar movement was going on, hidden from our view by a slight rise in the ground. Our position had now been spotted by the enemy, who swept it with heavy machine gun fire. A man near me was shot through the head. Their advance at this point became very rapid, so that soon large numbers of them actually came between us and the main line.

In a kind of fascination we watched them push on covered by the fire of a 4.2 inch battery, until suddenly our main line broke, and we saw its garrison [including the men of the 7th Somersets] running in a confused mob down the road. It was a depressing sight, but I suppose only the natural result of an attack in force on such a weak and isolated position. Almost immediately we could see batches of our men who had failed to get away coming back towards us as prisoners. I observed that the garrison of my position had been reduced, through departure to the rear and casualties, to only a couple of men besides myself. We three were thus an island, entirely surrounded by a sea of victorious enemies. The gravity of the situation came home to me with sparkling clearness.

Groups of enemy soldiers now started to advance on this last position. Captain Foley:

We were now in one of those plights when a soldier has to consult whatever conscience he may possess and, choose between a death of doubtful glory, but obvious futility, or surrender.

At twenty yards distance the leading Hun raised his rifle and aimed it with dispassionate care at my head. It seemed to me that to be shot like a pig in a poke was in no way furthering the cause of the Allies. Consequently, and in rather less time than it takes to tell (the man had large fingers playing about his trigger), I indicated that we were willing to capitulate. Somewhat to our surprise, the Hun, evidently a gentleman, lowered his weapon, at the same time pointing out that our best course was eastward. We complied. I discovered then that my eyeglass, which had so assisted me in my scrutiny of these goings on, was still firmly stuck in my right eye. Perhaps this had acted on the man with hypnotic effect, and contributed towards saving us from a summary execution.

The capture of Ham by the Germans on 24 March prompted a further general retreat as units continued to retire or be driven back by the victorious Germans. The 7th Somerset Light Infantry ceased to exist as an organised force on 24 March, although many soldiers fought on with other units in the general retirement and efforts were made to try to regroup any small remnants that came forward.

On 24 March the remnants of the 61st Brigade fell back towards a stream to the south-east of Guiscard, with the idea of covering the town of Noyon for the night. They were grouped with two French battalions that had been rushed into the battle to try to stem the enemy advance.

The last days of March

Overnight the 61st Brigade was withdrawn to Ecuvilly which the men reached by 10am on the 25th. Here the brigade was reorganised into a 'composite battalion' of three companies – one from each of the three original battalions, and a headquarters company from the original 61st Brigade headquarters. The complete strength of this composite 'battalion' was nine lieutenants and 440 men.

The 61st Brigade was placed at the disposal of the French 22nd Division and was sent by lorry to the Gruny area with the 7th Somersets 'company' holding Crémery. The French were retiring here too, and the role of the 61st Brigade was to cover the left flank of the retirement that night. The 61st Brigade remained in the rearguard role until ordered to withdraw at 7am on 25 March. The 'battalion' retired to positions near Le Quesnoy en Santerre, a village on high ground with an old trench system including barbed wire. The Germans followed up the 61st Brigade quickly and attacked the village throughout the day. This village was held mainly by the 7th DCLI 'company'. At dusk the remaining eleven men out of the original 100 Cornwalls retired on orders, having stopped the German advance all day.

On the night of 26 March a further roll call was taken and the 7th Somersets now had only twenty-one men under 61st Brigade command. The brigade now numbered 151 men.

Officially the 20th Division was withdrawn from the front line on 27 March. Its headquarters was established at Le Quesnel which was to act as a centre to regroup the survivors. These remnants formed a reserve behind the 30th Division which at that time was across the road that ran from Roye to Amiens – the immediate goal for the Germans.[2]

The 20th Division was unable to take any significant part in the rest of the battle, remaining mostly in reserve positions immediately behind the front line. The one exception was when men of the 59th Brigade were called on to launch a local counter-attack on 29 March and another when the 61st Brigade were to form a small bridgehead in front of the village of Hangard on 31 March.

By this time the defending soldiers started to get dependable artillery support which was invaluable on 31 March and 1 April when German attacks were held along the front. Successful local counter-attacks were made by men from the 60th Brigade after the Germans penetrated the front line. None of this fighting directly involved the few 7th SomLI who remained.

On the night of 1 April the shattered remnants of the 20th Division infantry formations were finally relieved and were driven away to Quevauvillers which was ten miles south-west of Amiens. The 20th Division had suffered such heavy casualties and was now so disorganised as to be unfit to take the field.

Analysis

The 7th Somerset Light Infantry casualties for this period are difficult to calculate with precision as the dates given for the deaths of many of the men are plainly wrong, and were probably only guesses given the confusion of the front at this time. A day-by-day description is given in the notes.[3]

The battalion diary prepared by Major Chappell at the end of the month showed that only one officer and ten men were known to have been killed and three officers and fifty-seven men were known to be injured. Fifteen officers and 390 men were still missing. The battalion had lost 476 men, which included nearly the whole of its fighting complement. In fact sixty-one men were killed in this battle or as a immediate result of it; scores were injured and hundreds captured.

A proper analysis of British infantry tactics in this battle is almost impossible. It was fought as a series of rearguard actions from hastily formed defensive works. Because of the sparseness of defenders and the lack of artillery support by the time the Somersets became involved, no cohesive defence was possible. From the casualty figures, higher than in most other battles, it is clear that the 7th SomLI fought their ground in many places.

The German infiltration tactics were very effective against the defences put up by the British. Wherever a breakthrough was achieved, the Germans reinforced the success by pressing on through any gaps. The effect of this tactic is amply demonstrated by the collapse of the 7th SomLI on 23 March when their right wing gave way, after the Germans attacked from an unexpected direction. The three forward companies were quickly cut off, as the whole German attack fell on A Company first and then headquarters. Command and control of the battalion was quickly lost and the three remaining companies lost all cohesion with each other.

German low-level tactics were an improvement on those used at Cambrai. The infantry used short rushes towards British defences after they had deployed machine guns to suppress the defenders. This no doubt considerably reduced their casualties, while the use of forward machine guns effectively supported the attacks using the infantry's own integral firepower.

There has long been a debate about the effect of the morning mists during this battle. Evidently it both assisted and hindered both sides throughout the battle depending upon what was happening. Initially the defenders had their field of fire reduced, which, given the large distances they had to hold, was no doubt a big disadvantage to them. Later the mist protected the British positions from being detected. On a number of occasions the Germans used mounted scouts to locate the Somersets' positions, which were then attacked in strength whenever visibility improved sufficiently. The delay and confusion among the Germans trying to locate the defenders accurately was no doubt a considerable problem for German commanders who were striving to maintain offensive momentum in the critical days following the breakthrough.

NOTES

1 During this time three men from the battalion died. Private John Nurton who died on 13 March, was buried in the Ham cemetery; Lance Corporal Arnold Duley, on 14 March; on 20 March 42-year-old Private Henry Kew is listed as being killed in action – this is probably an error. He is buried at the Cabaret Rouge cemetery in the Pas de Calais and it is likely he died of wounds.

2 Because of the role played by the 20th Division, the three brigades fought almost completely independently from each other. Both the 59th and 60th Brigades were initially deployed behind the 36th (Ulster), 30th and 61st (South Midland) Divisions. This part of Gough's Fifth Army was the only part which held its battle zone positions on the first day of the offensive, retiring later as both flanks were exposed. This may in part be because the Corps Commander of these divisions, Ivor Maxse, was regarded as an excellent infantry commander who devoted a lot of attention to training his men. It may also be because this part of the Fifth Army line had reserve soldiers who were immediately available to be used to stabilise the front where the enemy threatened to break through.

3 The twenty-four men listed as killed on 22 March 1918 were Lieutenant Samuel Berry, Private Frederick Carpenter, Private James Doyle, Private Thomas D'Oyly, Private Harry Every, Private Charles Greenslade, Private Frank Harvey, Private Francis Huxham, Private Edwin Liddicoat, Private Oliver Martin, Private John Newton, Private Henry Osman, L/Corporal William Page, Private Albert Pageter, Private Robert Paramour, Private Richard Park, Private Alexander Powell, Private Charles Spearing, Private Albert Watson, Private Arthur Westwood, A/CSM George Wheadon, Private Albert Wilcocks, Private David Williams and Private Ellis Williams.

The sixteen men listed as having been killed on 23 March were Private Leonard Broom, Private John Carpenter, L/Corporal Reginald Carter, Private Sidney Chesterman, Private Albert Foot, L/Corporal James Heal, Private Frank Hembrow, L/Corporal David Jennings, Private John McQuilliams, Private Edward Peach, Private Arthur Reading, Private Cyril

Sheasby, Private Harold Smith, Private Jack Smith, Private William Tucker and Lieutenant Herbert Whitworth.

No men were listed as killed on 24 March 1918 – the day of the German attacks toward Ollezy and from Cugny.

Two men reported to have died on 25 March 1918 were Sergeant Herbert Soloman (died of wounds) and Sergeant Lyndell Tizzard.

Four men were said to have died on 26 March 1918. These were L/Corporal William Brine (died of wounds), 2nd Lieutenant Wilfred Powell (attached to 61st Brigade trench mortars), Private William Roberts and Private Theodore Tudgay.

Listed as killed on 27 March is 2nd Lieutenant Stanley Butler MM. He died on the 24th.

Listed as killed on 29 March were Privates William Middleton (died of wounds) and John Wilcock. The battalion was not officially in action on this date, but, because the men were so scattered, it is conceivable that either of these could be correct.

Said to have died of wounds on 30 March is Private Charles Harris.

Said to have died on 1 April were Privates Herbert Small and Robert Brotherton. Private Edward Marimer died of wounds.

Listed as killed in action on 2 April is Private Walter North. While the 7th Battalion was not in the line on 2 April, men from the battalion were still involved in combat roles after becoming mixed up in one of the many composite forces.

On 8 April Private Percy Hancock died. He was a German prisoner – details of the cause of death were unknown.

On 10 April Private Howard Stanley was killed in action.

On 11 April Private Howard Stanton died of wounds.

On 23 April Private Eric Noble died a prisoner. The cause of death is unknown.

On 26 April 23-year-old Private Thomas Powell died of injuries in hospital in Rouen.

On 4 May Private Frank Mitchell died in German hands. The cause of his death is not known.

On 5 May 23-year-old Private David Willmott died in German hands. The cause of death is unknown.

CHAPTER XVIII
Would It Stop?

Aftermath

The strength and effectiveness of the German March offensive shocked the allied command structure. It would result in bitter recriminations, in particular between Haig and Lloyd George, who each sought to blame the other for the collapse of the Fifth Army front and for the subsequent treatment of Hubert Gough, the Army commander, who was effectively dismissed with accusations made about his fitness to command.

One immediate result of the German offensive was that a unified command structure was created with General Foch, the French commander, being appointed overall Commander in Chief of the British, French, American, Belgian, Portuguese and Russian soldiers on the Western Front. From then on this would enhance co-ordination of allied efforts until the end of the war.

One of the aspects which came to be bitterly disputed was the number of trained men who had been available in the UK prior to the German offensive. This acrimony was particularly heightened because of the reduction and reorganisation within the British divisions immediately prior to the offensive and the consequences during it.

Lloyd George countered the accusations stating that: 'We were astonished to ascertain that there were 88,000 men on the establishment in France who were on leave in this country.' There were a further 170,000 men on Lloyd George's figures who were immediately available to be sent abroad, including some 50,000 18- and 19-years-olds who were trained, but whom the government had undertaken not to use unless there was a national emergency. It was conceded by all that this had now occurred.

Whatever the motives of all parties in apportioning blame, it is evident that there were significant numbers of men available, as ships started carrying thousands per day at first, and then tens of thousands per day across the Channel to France and Flanders over the next few weeks.

With the likelihood of the German offensives continuing with vigour, every effort was made to quickly rebuild the 20th Division. On paper the 20th (Light) Division was listed in GHQ as a reserve division. On 3 April 1918 Major General Douglas-Smith was relieved of divisional command

and sent to a home command in England. He was replaced by Major General Carey who had publicly acquitted himself well in the German offensive.

7th Battalion

The 7th Somersets arrived at Quevauvillers on 2 April and remained there until the 30th. During this time twelve officers and 510 men joined the battalion in replacement drafts. Major Chappell said:

> By this time the Battalion was practically at full strength with other ranks, although there was a lamentable shortage of officers, and most platoons were commanded by NCOs. The reinforcements were mainly composed of youths of eighteen or nineteen years of age, keen as mustard and anxious to get into action. They had reacted splendidly to the intensive training undergone during the month the Battalion had been out of the line, and when orders were received to proceed to the trenches the Battalion was in a highly efficient state.

The move, when it came on 1 May, was to a camp to the west of a hill called the Notre Dame de Lorette. Men from the battalion visited the hilltop which was littered with French dead from the attacks of the year before. Major Chappell: 'A magnificent view of the line was obtained, with Vimy Ridge standing prominently to its immediate front; shells could be seen bursting over the line from Ypres in the north right down to Peronne in the south.'

The battalion relieved a Canadian battalion in the Lens area on 3 May. For veterans and new soldiers alike, the trenches the battalion occupied were strange. The front line ran through the battered streets of Ablain St Nazaire, the support and reserve trenches situated in the western end of the town. In the rear area the houses were still standing although badly damaged. All had lost their roof slates leaving the skeletal rafters which had an eerie effect at night. The whole position overlooked Lens which was held by the Germans. Major Chappell:

> The battalion quickly shook down to trench warfare again and for the first tour in the front line the new troops were carefully instructed in trench discipline and routine. They showed a splendid spirit, quickly absorbed all that was taught them and began to look around for trenches to capture and an enemy to conquer.

Despite the aggressive tendencies of the new soldiers, the first tour was quiet and after nine days the battalion was relieved. During this time four men from the battalion died of wounds.[1]

The battalion returned to a more combative front on 20 May 1918. The division's artillery had been 'hotting up' the front. The retaliatory fire included a high percentage of mustard gas, and because of the inexperience of the men, the battalion suffered ninety-eight casualties from the fire; most were treated in the battalion aid post. Twenty-five suffered more serious effects and one man, Private Ernest Thompson, died from gas effects on 25 May.

While the battalion remained in this sector of the line for two months until 13 July, trench warfare routine returned. Regular occurrences during this time were small amounts of shelling and German air raids every three or four nights. Also a British railway gun would be pushed up behind the front line, fire off a few rounds and then depart before the German barrage could sever the railway line. Morale was maintained by keeping the men busy patrolling when in the front line and working on trench improvements or training when behind the front line. Forty-eight men were killed in action, died of wounds or sickness during these two months.[2]

One particularly tragic event occurred when a train carrying a working party was hit by shellfire. The men scattered under the shelling but not before two men, Private Frederick Webber and Sidney Robinson, were killed. Another twenty-one were injured, five of whom would die of their injuries the following day. Another man died later.[3]

On 16 June a raid was carried out to capture a German for identification purposes. The plan was to slip quietly over a railway embankment that ran across part of the front, enter a German dugout, a number of which were known to be on the far side of the embankment, capture a prisoner and return. An artillery barrage would be fired twenty minutes after the start of the raid to cover the retirement.

At the appointed hour the two platoons set out. All went well at first, but as the men started to cross the embankment and were shown up against the sky, heavy machine-gun fire was opened up on the raiders. Men were shot down and chaos followed. The two platoons retreated quickly to their starting positions, with two men dead – Privates White and Manning – and nine men injured. Private Parsons was found to be missing – it was discovered later that he had been killed. Another man was found to be suffering from shell shock.

During this time of rebuilding and development of the new soldiers, efforts were made to train all men to a high standard. Gas protection, for example, became well practised and although the Germans continued to fire gas shells, there were no gas casualties during the latter part of this period. The tactical emphasis changed to platoon tactics, with occasional company level training.

While the 20th Division was rebuilding its fighting abilities in a quiet part of the front, great events were taking place elsewhere.

An overview

Following their March offensive, the Germans had continued to launch strong offensives against the British and French lines.

While continuing the attacks towards Amiens in the south, the Germans launched the 'Georgette' offensive on 9 April against the northern part of the British line between Armentières and Ypres. The aim was to capture the Channel ports. Although some ground was given up after a Portuguese division was broken through, the line held and the Germans suffered heavily. Against the French they launched a surprise attack on 27 May which drove a wedge into the French defences nearly as large as that in the March offensive against the British. The battlefield this time was mainly along the Chemin des Dames, the scene of the French attacks of 1917 that had nearly led to the mutinous collapse of the French Army. The aim of this offensive was the capture of Paris and the assault was stopped at Château Thierry, fifty miles north-east of Paris. A subsidiary attack was launched on 8 June between Noyon and Montdidier which, although pushing the French defenders back six miles, also failed to break through.

While the Germans pressed home their attacks, the significant numbers of additional British soldiers had their combat skills raised. Also, the American forces were increasing in numbers so that they now had nearly 600,000 battle-ready men in France. The Americans were deployed into battle in increasing numbers and became actively involved in the defensive actions.

Gradually the pendulum was swinging in favour of the Allies who were able to contain the German attacks while growing in strength. By 14 July German attacks had largely been fought to a standstill, although the French and British had suffered heavily in the process.

The German High Command put their faith in one last great attack, which was launched against the fifty-mile front of the French and Americans between Château Thierry and Main de Massignes on 15 July. The attack had been anticipated. Not only was it held, but it was defeated and the limited extent of the German advance in the next three days was the farthest they would reach into France in the war. Three days later – on 18 July 1918 – the French and Americans started the counter-offensive that commenced the final stage of the war. A succession of hammer blows by the French, Americans and British would drive the Germans out of the war.

The Somersets

The great battles and momentous events on the Western Front that followed the March offensive by-passed the 7th Battalion, other than in rumour and through the newspapers. Lens was still a relatively quiet part of the line with the offensives happening to the north or south.

On 14 July, the day before the last German offensive of the war, the battalion returned to the front line near Lens. The relief came under fire and Corporal Barron was killed and eight others were injured. One of those injured, Private Reginald Newing, would die the next day at a casualty clearing station at Ligny St Flochel.

The battalion found the front line changed with the enemy having lost all initiative in no man's land. Strong fighting patrols were sent out every night with orders to attack any enemy they found. The Germans now rarely entered no man's land, and relied on sporadic shelling of the British lines, usually with a mixture of high explosive and gas.

Raiding of enemy trenches was also stepped up. These were organised with one officer leading three sections of the 'raiding party' while another would control a 'covering party' with the Lewis gun. Raiding and fighting patrols would be the primary offensive activity of the battalion up until the end of the war.

One of the raids took place on 30 July, after the artillery had spent the last eight days incrementally damaging the German wire. One platoon from B Company was led out by 2nd Lieutenants Shillson and Moorhouse,[4] the events being described in a poem written by one of the raiders:

In the dead of night over the top we went,
Creeping stealthily through No Man's Land,
Flitting like ghostly shadows from hole to hole,
Silent on our murderous business bent.
Then the silence was torn and shattered and rent in twain,
As swift with a shriek and a roar the barrage began,
And night was as day in the flash of the shells,
While death was unleashed and there rained a terrible rain,
On, ever on, we went to the enemy's wire,
Crossed it and passed right over an enemy post,
Down a steep bank where the train used to rumble and roar,
Until to our backs the enemy opened fire.
We had passed their post in the darkness and would never have known,
Except that our sergeant engaged them and drove one out,
He ran back towards his line in the face of us,
The nest of the hawk was raided and the bird had flown.
'Halt there' we yelled, and revolver shots rang out,
He yelled and seemed to be dead, but he rose again,
Holding aloft his hands, turning this way and that,
Caught fast in a trap, a prey to terror and doubt.
Oh! The mad race to our lines over No Man's Land,
Over the bank and down through aprons of wire,

Leaping from crest to crest of those terrible holes,
Back to the trench where sentries eagerly stand.
Back to the dugout at last, coming in one by one,
Our officer cries 'Is anyone missing or lost?'
'No, thank God, all are safe,' we shout
And after the action, weary, but happy withal,
Our cellars we reach ere daylight has begun,
To sleep the sleep of victors whose duty is done.

Anon.

Two men were slightly wounded in the raid. The sergeant in the poem, Sergeant Smith, who was part of the covering party, received a bar to his Military Medal for rushing the enemy post and killing or injuring three of the occupants with a revolver. 2nd Lieutenant Shillson was awarded the Military Cross for his capture of the fleeing fourth man.

In the following two weeks rumours began to circulate that the enemy were likely to retire soon. The foundation was no doubt the hugely successful British offensive at Amiens which had commenced on 8 August. Massed formations of tanks had again been used to crush a huge gap in the German defences and in five days pushed the Germans back to their old Somme defences.

Lieutenant Colonel Chappell: 'The rumour most favoured by Higher Command was that the enemy were retiring, so on the 19th August strong patrols were sent out to penetrate the enemy front line. This proved to be still strongly held and 2nd Lieutenant Larter was wounded on one of those patrols.' There was no retirement in this sector, and the battalion left for the front line at Acheville where it arrived on 27 August 1918.

The Germans in the new sector initially showed fight. Lieutenant Colonel Chappell:

> The relief of the 2nd Rifle Brigade [on 27 August] was not completed without loss: halfway through the relief the front line was severely shelled, and Privates [Charles] Darby, [Matthew] Manchip and [James] Williams were killed, several others being wounded. Lieutenant Stewart had a narrow escape, a 5.9 shell bursting practically at his feet, leaving him quite unharmed.

Seven others were injured.

The following bright and clear night a patrol of 2nd Lieutenant Smith MM and his orderly set out never to return. They were last seen by a sentry moving towards the enemy wire. It was presumed that they had been killed, but in fact they were captured by German raiding parties. That night two separate raids were made by the Germans, both fought off, leaving one Somerset soldier injured. Although the British held a dominance in no man's land, the Germans unsuccessfully tried to raid the Somerset's trenches again on 6 and 9 September.

During this time active patrolling continued with nightly attempts to force a passage through the German barbed wire. The Germans would open up strong rifle and machine-gun fire on the patrols and so the tactics were modified. A grappling hook would be thrown across the wire and, when the patrol were in sufficient cover, often a shell hole, the rope on the grappling hook would be tugged to simulate a man moving through the wire. The Germans would usually open a heavy fire on the grappling hook. When everything went quiet the patrol would throw a few grenades at the German positions and then move along the line to cause problems elsewhere. The hooks were frequently left in place for future use. During this time camouflaged posts were established approximately 200 yards into no man's land which would be covered by day and used as patrol bases at night.

Despite the three German raids in September, casualties during the period from 27 August to 25 October, when the character of the fighting again changed, were far lighter than before. There was a considerable drop in enemy aggression as time passed and only seven men were killed during this time.[5] This was despite the Somerset men taking greater risks because of the lack of enemy activity. Frustration at the lack of enemy fight began to show towards the end of this period. Lieutenant Colonel Chappell recalled:

B Company took over the whole of the front line on the 25th [October] and continued the offensive policy. Five months of trench warfare in quiet sectors had not affected the fighting spirit of the battalion; to use a term much in vogue at that time, it 'had its tail well up'. This can best be judged by the following incident. A fighting patrol of B Company was inspecting the enemy wire when one of the men, evidently incensed by the lack of initiative shown by the enemy, addressed the unseen ones as follows in broad Somerset dialect, 'Eh, you ruddy shisters, bisn't comin' out t'ave a scra-a-ap?'

A significant number of deaths of men formerly of the battalion during this time was among prisoners of war. Between 24 June and 4 November 1918, twelve prisoners of war from the 7th SomLI died in German captivity more than three months after their capture. Three are shown in records to have died of wounds, the other eight have 'unknown' causes of death which may be attributable to disease as conditions and food allowances for prisoners was poor, and what became known as 'Spanish Influenza' began to sweep through Europe in the autumn. The prisoner-of-war camp in East Prussia where Captain McMurtrie was detained was plagued by flu in November 1918. The Germans also used their prisoners of war as a labour supply.[6]

When out of the line the men started training in open warfare techniques and also practised offensive manoeuvres with tanks.

The Central Powers collapse

The German occupants of trenches in front of the 20th Division had shown no sign of voluntarily giving up their positions and it was decided that stronger attacks would be mounted to dislodge them.

On the night of 26 October 7th DCLI on the right of the Somersets attacked and captured the enemy front line positions taking twelve prisoners. At the same time Somerset patrols chased the few Germans holding their front line into their support trenches. The raid could not be followed up as the enemy effectively blocked the communication trenches with barbed wire.

Morale, already high, continued to rise as the next day news came through that the Bulgarians had asked the Allied powers for an armistice. Bulgaria surrendered unconditionally on 28 October 1918.

On the night of 29 October at 2am two platoons of A Company pushed forward and occupied the German front-line trench with little opposition. The two platoons had to withdraw later as they had no support on their flanks. Remarkably this raid, like that carried out three days earlier, resulted in no casualties amongst the raiders.

Lieutenant Colonel Chappell said:

> An experiment was tried on 1st October to see how far the enemy would allow patrols to advance in daylight – if they were allowed to advance at all – and a patrol of D Company under 2nd Lieutenant Tarbit was selected to reconnoitre the Acheville line [the enemy front line raided by A Company], crossing no man's land, a distance of about 600 yards, in broad daylight. A good deal of nervousness could be observed among the onlookers as they watched the steady progress of the patrol, but the enemy front line was entered without a shot being fired. Each of the three communication trenches examined by the patrol was held by the enemy and 2nd Lieutenant Tarbit engaged one to test its strength, which was found to be considerable, but beyond defending their positions the enemy made no attempt to drive the patrol from their front line. An hour later 2nd Lieutenant Tarbit withdrew his patrol to his own lines, once again without drawing hostile fire.

Over the following rainy days, patrols from the 7th DCLI initially, and then the 7th Somersets, engaged the Germans, progressively pushing them farther back through their trench systems. Good communication was effected between each battalion in the 61st Brigade through dedicated liaison officers from each battalion being attached to the other two in the brigade. If significant resistance was encountered, artillery fire was brought to bear on the enemy – demonstrating both the good communication with, and flexibility of, the artillery at this stage of the war.

By 5 October the Germans had effectively withdrawn to what the British called the 'Village Line'. This was a series of trenches behind the village of Fresnoy. On the night of 5 October Somerset patrols from B and D Companies were pushed through the village testing the strength of the defences. The Germans retired quickly in the face of their advance with only the occasional sniper to hold up the patrols. The men explored the cellars and houses and found many signs of the recent habitation by the enemy. In one cellar they discovered a lit candle.

D Company continued to advance through Fresnoy and started digging themselves in within 100 yards of the Village Line. Because the enemy started heavy machine-gun and rifle fire on the entrenching soldiers, a request was put in for artillery support. Very quickly an accurate barrage fell on the enemy positions, both stopping the fire and apparently causing many casualties.

Just before dawn on 6 October a battle patrol from B Company in conjunction with men from the division to the right of the Somersets tried to force the Germans back fully to the Village Line which meant an attack on any posts ahead of this line. 2nd Lieutenant Dean led the Somerset platoon along the trenches until they encountered a strongly held trench block which they attacked. Private Frank Gay was able to rush along the trench and tried to climb over the block when he was shot and killed. A number of other casualties were caused and the attack was called off with the men establishing a post nearby.

As the night passed into daylight, the rain continued to fall keeping the trenches very muddy. The German defences were now easily identifiable and accurate artillery fire was brought all along the German front line through the morning. B Company was ordered into Fresnoy with orders to prepare to attack the German line in conjunction with a battalion of the Sherwood Foresters to their north. Lieutenant Colonel Chappell described the action:

> At midday the climatic conditions were bad, rain pouring down, trenches waterlogged and full of mud, while a number of gas shells added to the general unpleasantness. At about 4pm, Sherwood Foresters, holding the southern end of Fresnoy Trench, requested that a battle patrol be sent up Chapel Trench to work in conjunction with their patrol moving up Coke Trench, the two patrols forming a post at the junction of these two trenches. Lieutenant McCracken ordered 2nd Lieutenant Greedy with his platoon to carry out the patrol which,

on reaching the block just west of Coke Trench found it unoccupied. They also found the body of Private Gay.

The patrol continued past the block but were unable to make contact with the Sherwood Foresters. With the battalion relief imminent the patrol returned. The day's activities resulted in another three men dying. These were Privates Frederick Smith and Ernest Marler who were killed outright, and Private Sidney Saunders who died of wounds.

On 6 October the battalion retired from the front line for the last time of the war, having advanced the line some 400 yards in one day. They moved to the small village of Monchy-Breton that was out of enemy range. Battalion headquarters was set up in an estaminet, and the men spent their time resting, training and playing sports. Lieutenant Colonel Chappell said:

> It was during the 13th October that, during mess, a message was received from Brigade that an armistice had been signed. After the news had thoroughly sunk into the minds of be-dazed headquarters officers, the CO ordered a battalion celebration and made gifts of a barrel of beer to each company to assist in it. Battalion headquarters indulged in an orgy of toasts from Commander in Chief down to the last joined platoon commander, after which the CO and adjutant made a tour of companies to ensure that the great event was being kept up to the spirit it deserved. It is recorded that both survived the ordeal, although retiring somewhat tired and worn, but the climax arrived at 4am the following morn, when, the adjutant was wakened to receive another message which read 'Cancel message re armistice stop. Previous message referred to Greeks stop. Carry on training as usual. Message ends'.

On 30 October 1918 the battalion was moved at very short notice by lorry to the outskirts of Cambrai which was now in British hands. After a three-day wait the battalion marched by stages in pursuit of the now rapidly retiring German army. A series of villages, at which the battalion would stop for two or three days and then set off again, – Avenes, Vendegies, Wargnies-le-Petit and Bavai – were visited by the soldiers who marched cross country to ease congestion on the roads which were used by the artillery and transport.

The battalion remained in fighting spirit and was once again passing scenes of vandalism of French property. The liberated civilians had mixed emotions; they had their freedom, but often at a heavy price – their crops destroyed and homes frequently damaged by artillery fire. Food shortages now posed a real problem as winter approached. Lieutenant Jenne recalled one encounter at this time:

I was introduced to an old peasant well over seventy at Wargnies-le-Grand whose brother had died during the occupation at Wargnies-le-Petit only a few kilometres away. The German regulations were so stringent with regard to any communication between one village and another that he was not allowed to attend his brother's funeral. As he told me this the depths of his nature were stirred to real emotion – and yet he said it without bitterness – resignation had become such a habit with him.

At daybreak on the morning of Monday 11 November 1918, the battalion marched into Feignies, situated to the south of Mons, where 61st Brigade headquarters passed on details of the cessation of hostilities to the 7th Somersets. The war would end at 11am.

Lieutenant Colonel Chappell recalled the occasion:

As the hour approached there could be easily discerned from the conversation of those around the varying feelings which predominated within them. In the far distance, perhaps ten miles away, a large gun could be heard booming with great regularity, once every three minutes; much nearer a battery of field guns were intermittently barking their last defiance at the enemy. A group of young officers who had not yet seen an engagement or even trench warfare were enthusiastically chatting of a broken armistice and the chances it would give them of taking part in some big action and perhaps distinguishing themselves. Nearby three veterans were seated on the ground and it was clearly evident that vastly different emotions filled their hearts; silent, their eyes were fixed on the not far distant front from whence, for long years, Death had come unceasing day and night. It seemed as if their memories ranged over the many encounters they had won from the Old Man with the Scythe and as if, although they yearned for a cessation of hostilities they would not allow themselves to contemplate its joys until it became an actual fact.

Eleven am was now very near and the synchronised watches were frequently inspected; the field battery was silent, but the booming of the heavy gun continued at regular intervals. An anxious look appeared in the eyes of the veterans; would it stop on the stroke of eleven or would it continue and bring disaster in its path? At last the hour arrived and a dead silence reigned everywhere. Twenty-five seconds later the silence was horribly shattered by the boom of the heavy gun: and then dead silence again. The one question that beat into the brains of the veterans was 'Would it stop? Would it stop? Would it stop?' One minute passed, a minute and a half, two minutes, and still silence reigned. Then groups of watchers and listeners seemed to waken; they heard the sound of a soft wind passing overhead, of birds whistling; they heard conversation commence, and reverently they glanced upwards and whispered 'Thank God. At last'. The war was over.

NOTES

1   The four men who died of wounds were Private Frederick Stidder (10 May) Privates Ernest Briggs (14 May), Frederick Sharp (16 May) and Thomas Duff (24 May).
2   Soldiers not specifically referred to in the text or other notes were L/Corporal George Porter (died at home 24 May). Private Charles Chaplin (25 May), Private George Shore (29 May), Private William Reed (29 May), Private William Tarr (30 May),Private Thomas Chivers (31 May), Private William Guy (3 June), Private Robert Hill (6 June), Private William Mayne (7 June) Private James Maddick (7 June), Private Oliver Parsons (died of gas effects in Britain on 10 June), Private Sidney Yeomans (13 June), Private William Perry (died in hospital in London on 21 June), Private Ernest Hemmens (died 22 June a prisoner of war), Private Ewart Read (died 24 June), L/Corporal James Roberts (died 25 June a prisoner of war), Private Hubert Barnard (died 29 June a prisoner of war), Private George Keeves (died 4 July in a German hospital), and Privates Maurice Kerly (died 6 July), Frederick Priscott (died 6 July), George Trigger (died 11 July) and Sidney Carver (died 13 July).
3   Privates John Hunt, Bertram Cottle, Archibald Wyatt, Alfred Davies and Samuel Wooton died of wounds on 11 June.
4   No relation to the author.
5   They were Private Robert Evans (killed 30 August), Private William Male (died of wounds 11 September), L/Corporal William Brambley (died of wounds 20 September); Privates Joseph Smart, Harry Sewell and William South (killed by shellfire on 21 September), Private Frederick Smith (shellfire on 24 September)
6   The three men were Privates Frederick Rodway (died 26 July), Walter Clatworthy (died 4 August) and Edwin Thorne (died 24 August). On 28 August Private William Darville died a POW and on 3 November 1918 Private William Gillett died in Cologne. See also note 2 above.

CHAPTER XIX
A Land Fit For Heroes

The peace

The war was over but the peace had yet to be secured. Each division was required to choose one battalion which was to be maintained at full strength to be ready to enforce the armistice if necessary. From the 20th Division the 7th SomLI was chosen for this role – a great disappointment to many.

The battalion moved back to the Cambrai area almost immediately and then to Vauchelle les Artois on 8 December where it took possession of a nissen hut camp for the next five months. The men built a small parade ground, painted the buildings, planted gardens, shored up the pathways and built a guard house from which a guard was mounted. At dawn and dusk the Union flag was raised and lowered with due ceremony.

The only men for early release from the battalion were those who were required back immediately for economic reasons. Thirty-one miners were released from the battalion to return to their pits, although this shortfall was made up by the arrival of replacements from the division.

The battalion continued the training of the men in tactics and rifle skills, and fatigue parties were supplied to build or improve other camps or to fill in old trenches. Many new activities were introduced like the lectures on flying or 'life and adventure in South Africa' as well as educational training.

Slowly, in dribs and drabs, men began to be demobilised from 13 January 1919, with the largest group – 300 NCOs and men – demobilised on 11 March. By 27 May 1919 the 7th Somersets were down to a volunteer cadre strength of thirty-three men and a few officers. These were driven in lorries to Calais where, after completing the inventory for battalion equipment, they travelled by ferry to Folkestone. On 11 June the last of the battalion returned to Taunton to hand over the battalion colours to the care of the Depot, which was officially done after a civic reception and speech by the Mayor of Taunton.

The next day the small group of men met up at Taunton railway station at 2.30 in the afternoon. The last of the 7th Somerset Light Infantry bade each other farewell and parted company to return to their former lives.

On 17 April 1920 another small group of men gathered again at Taunton to form a guard of honour to escort the battalion colours to its final home at Bath Abbey where it can still be seen hanging today. The group of familiar names included Captain McMurtrie, Company Sergeant Major Steele, Sergeant Sorrell, Sergeant Smith MM, Lieutenant Colonel Troyte-Bullock DSO, Major Galsworthy, Captains Spark MC, Holt, Foley MC, Andrews, and Lieutenants Colsey, Phelps, Lewin, White, Cox, Chambers and 2nd Lieutenants Gurnett and Snook.

Aftermath

The war had seen remarkable changes in military terms, with a dramatic change in tactical thinking on all sides of the conflict. The 7th Somersets had started the war with tactical schemes that worked at battalion or company level at the lowest. The war ended with platoons as the primary combat unit. The army had learnt to co-ordinate artillery, aeroplanes, tanks and infantry with varying degrees of success, but to a remarkable extent considering the huge technological advances during the war. Support weapons such as the Lewis gun and Stokes mortar had been fully integrated into battle tactics, and artillery had become far more flexible and accurate.

Although the war ended on 11 November 1918, in many ways it never ended for the men involved and their families. Some men died from the injuries they had sustained in the terrible struggle. On the day that the war ended two men from the 7th Somersets died in hospital from their injuries. Private Wilfred Carver was only 21 years old when he died. Private Edward Mitchell from Plymouth was the other man who died. Another ten would die as a direct result of the war within a short time after the end of fighting.[1]

The battalion had 663 men killed during the war. This amounted to nearly the full fighting strength of the battalion. It had nevertheless fared better than the three Somerset Light Infantry battalions that fought solely on the Western Front for over three years. The 1st Battalion lost 1,315 men; the 6th Battalion 849 and the 8th Battalion 821.

Many hundreds more were injured, some repeatedly. The last commanding officer of the 7th Battalion, Lieutenant Colonel Preston-Whyte DSO, was injured four times. Many of these injuries would leave permanent disfigurements like severe facial scarring or loss of body parts. Lieutenant Addis had his foot blown off in a raid in 1916 and Private Beale's hand was shattered by a grenade in Havrincourt Wood. Others would suffer from their injuries in years to follow, like the many injured from poison gas who would later get chest problems caused by damage to the lung lining. Most of these men returned to their communities and homes to try to get on with their lives as best they could.

The effect of the war on British society was equally socially disfiguring. There were hundreds of thousands of bereavements leaving widows and orphans. The 7-year-old daughter of furniture packer George Price, who died in the attack on Langemarck, would no doubt forever associate her birthday with the news of her father's death. Many children would grow up only knowing that their father was killed in the Great War.

The realities and consequences of the Great War were so terrible that a divide between the survivors and those who remained at home was perhaps inevitable. The people at home could not, and perhaps understandably did not want to know the true details of the war. They could see the evidence of the 'lost generation'.

Lloyd George had promised the returning soldiers 'A Land fit for heroes to live in'. The realities of the economic situation in the 1920s was very different, and battalion papers at the Light Infantry Office contain a number of letters from former soldiers seeking references from Colonel Troyte-Bullock for the sometimes menial jobs they were applying for.

For many of the soldiers who returned, the bonds that had formed in the course of the war were too strong to be left behind. In the case of the 7th Somersets officers' reunions were initially organised by 'Ack Ack' Andrews and attended by many in the battalion.

Many former officers could not attend, like Lieutenant Colonel Preston-Whyte who returned to his home in Bloemfontein in South Africa. He later found, when requested to recall his experiences, that he was unable to convey in words the things that had happened: 'If I try to write things down it looks so small.'

Henry Foley, whose brother had been killed, emigrated to South Africa at the end of the war. He would write to friends complaining about the price of beer; eventually returning to the United Kingdom, he married and had a son called Michael. He died at Stoke Mandeville hospital on 17 May 1991 aged 95 after working as a solicitor in Buckinghamshire. Lieutenant Grigg also emigrated, in his case to Canada to make his home in Vancouver.

Others did not travel so far. Captain Jones who had served as battalion and brigade intelligence officer, became a lecturer at Bangor College and died after a short illness in February 1942. He had just fathered a young child. Lieutenant Jenne MC, who was awarded the Military Cross for his actions at Lesboeufs, obtained a first class honours degree in 1923, became a teacher and fathered a baby boy. 'SOS' Smith gave up a legal career and went into farming which he 'infinitely prefer[ed]'. Lieutenant Berry took an honours degree at Oxford, and became a twice published barrister of the Inner Temple by 1922. 2nd Lieutenant Brown MC, whose Military Cross was awarded for his actions on 27 February 1917 when a post had been blown in by a 5.9 shell, became a politician and Secretary of State for Mines in the National Government in 1932. Sergeant Ellis returned to work in his sweet shop.

A small number remained in the Armed Forces. Colonel Troyte-Bullock joined the Machine Gun Corps after recovering from his injuries, and Lieutenant Atkinson joined the 2nd Somersets and was sent to Egypt. Major Percy Chappell, one of very few lucky survivors from the 1st Somersets 'Old Contemptibles' who had passed through the the war uninjured, apart from treading on a nail just before the German counter-attack at Cambrai, remained in the Somersets after the war and served in intelligence in Ireland. He retired from the army in 1925 and was later involved in Civil Defence committee work in the 1950s. He was made an MBE.[2] Captain George McMurtrie, upon release from captivity, joined the 1st Somersets and served with them in Ireland. He later spent time with the Royal West African Frontier Force and remained in the Army until after the Second World War attaining the rank of Lieutenant Colonel. In September 1944 he took command of a Light Infantry holding (transit) battalion at Clacton-on-Sea and then Plymouth, and after the war was appointed Permanent President of Courts Martial in Palestine. His last brush with enemy action came when Jewish terrorists blew up a train he was travelling in killing all those in the next compartment. He died peacefully in 1994. His son David became a Lieutenant Colonel in the Light Infantry, his grandson achieving the same distinction in 2002.

When the Second World War came, Colonel Troyte-Bullock DSO, Captain Foley and Lieutenants Jenks, Phelps and Liddon all served again with the Home Guard. Andrews became a fire warden. Many of the soldiers' children were of the generation that would see action too. Both of Captain Mitchell's sons were to fight against Germany. Mitchell himself died on 15 March 1942, a direct result of the machine-gun bullet injury to his thigh he received in the Somme fighting.

NOTES

1   Those who died were Private Frank Smith (15 November 1918), Private George Wall (19 November 1918), Private Arthur Hussey (26 November 1918), Private Sidney White (28 November 1918), Private Maurice Reugg (30 November 1918), Private William Richards (11 December 1918), Private George Seaward (11 December 1918), Lance Sergeant Arthur Jones (27 January 1919), Private Bertram Cox (21 February 1919) and Private Edward Pearce (28 February 1919).
2   Rather curiously I found a newspaper cutting referring to Major Chappell, dated 24 January 1951, underneath a floorboard of my house in Bath in 1999.

Appendix I

20th (Light) Division
Organisation in early 1915

59th Brigade (four battalions)
    10th King's Royal Rifle Corps (10th KRRC)
    11th King's Royal Rifle Corps (11th KRRC)
    10th Rifle Brigade (10th RB)
    11th Rifle Brigade (11th RB)

60th Brigade (four battalions)
    6th Oxfordshire and Buckinghamshire Light Infantry (6th Ox &
       BucksLI)
    6th King's Shropshire Light Infantry (6th KSLI)
    12th King's Royal Rifle Corps (12th KRRC)
    12th Rifle Brigade (12th RB)

61st Brigade (four battalions)
    7th Somerset Light Infantry (7th SomLI)
    7th Duke of Cornwall's Light Infantry (7th DCLI)
    7th King's Own Yorkshire Light Infantry (7th KOYLI)
    12th King's Liverpool Regiment (12th King's)

Pioneers 11th Durham Light Infantry (11th DLI)

Artillery (four brigades – sixty-four guns)
    90th Field Artillery Brigade (four batteries of four 18pdr guns each)
    91st Field Artillery Brigade (as 90th Bde)
    92nd Field Artillery (Howitzer) Brigade (four batteries of four 4.5 inch
       howitzers each)
    93rd Field Artillery Brigade (as 90th Bde)

Engineers
83rd, 84th and 96th Field Companies
   Royal Engineers

Signal Services
20th Division Signal
Company Royal Engineers

Medical
60th, 61st and 62nd Field Ambulances

Divisional Supply Train

Appendix II

20th (Light) Division
Organisation from February 1918

59th Brigade (three battalions)
2nd Scottish Rifles
11th King's Royal Rifle Corps (11th KRRC)
11th Rifle Brigade (11th RB)

60th Brigade (three battalions)
6th King's Shropshire Light Infantry (6th KSLI)
12th King's Royal Rifle Corps (12th KRRC)
12th Rifle Brigade (12th RB)

61st Brigade (three battalions)
7th Somerset Light Infantry (7th SomLI)
7th Duke of Cornwall's Light Infantry (7th DCLI)
12th King's Liverpool Regiment (12th King's)

Pioneers 11th Durham Light Infantry (11th DLI)

Artillery (three brigades – seventy-two guns)
91st Field Artillery Brigade (three batteries of six 18pdr guns each and
one battery of six 4.5 inch howitzers)
92nd Field Artillery Brigade (as 91st Bde)
93rd Field Artillery Brigade (as 91st Bde)

Trench Mortar Batteries
Two Heavy TMBs (each ten Newtons) and 59th, 60th, 61st Trench
Mortar Batteries (Stokes)

Engineers
83rd, 84th and 96th Field Companies
Royal Engineers

Signal Services
20th Division Signal
Company Royal Engineers

Medical
60th, 61st and 62nd Field Ambulances and stretcher company

Machine-Gun Companies
59th, 60th, 61st and 217th Companies
(as A, B, C and D Companies 20th Division Machine-Gun Battalion)

Divisional Supply Train

Appendix III

Gallantry Awards

1st level	2nd level	3rd level
Victoria Cross	Distinguished Service Order (DSO)	Military Cross (MC)
All ranks (from 1850s)	Officers (from 1880s)	Officers (from 1915)
	Distinguished Conduct Medal (DCM)	Military Medal (MM)
	Soldiers (from 1850s)	Soldiers (from 1916)

Both officers and soldiers could also be 'mentioned in dispatches' – a 4th level of gallantry recognition.

Select Bibliography

Imperial War Museum

Sir Gerald Clauson,	Private papers
Major P P Curtis,	Private papers
H M Dillon,	Letters
Capt G D J McMurtrie,	WWI Diary
J B Nevitt,	Private papers
Major H D Paviere,	Private papers
Lt Col P F Storey,	Private Papers

Light Infantry Office, 14 Mount Street, Taunton

7th Battalion War Diary 1914–1919
Light Bob Gazette 1919–1925
War Time Notes, 7th Battalion Officers Club, Issues Dec 1939, March
    1940, April 1942, April 1943
7th Battalion Scribbling Diary
Colonel Troyt-Bullock manuscript
61st Brigade Operational Orders G/1574/6
Notes on Tank and Infantry Training (20th Division) JFC Fuller
20th Division Operational Orders No 1 23/7/17 and No 15 G732 12/8/17
20th Division Notes on 38th Divisional Orders for the Attack G484
Notes on Patrolling (20th Division)
2nd Lieutenant Spark – Report on Battle of Langemarck
20th Division Defensive Scheme Plan G/1874/6
7th Battalion Roll

Royal Engineers Library, Chatham

181st Tunnelling Company RE War Diary   Royal Engineers Library,
                                                       Brompton Barracks,
                                                       Chatham

Liddle Collection, Leeds University

2nd Lieutenant H Langdon,	Diary
Arthur Hendon,	Private papers

HMSO

Soldiers died in the Great War 1914–19 Part 18, Prince Albert's (Somerset
    Light Infantry)

Books

Boyle, R C, *A Record of the West Somerset Yeomanry 1914–1919*, London: St Catherine Press

Blunden, Edmund, *Undertones of War*, London: Penguin, 1982

Cana, Frank, *The Great War in Europe (8 vols)*, London: Virtue

Carver, Field Marshal Lord, *Britain's Army in the 20th Century*, London: Macmillan, 1998

Connors Nesbitt, Roy, *Eyes of the RAF – A History of Photo Reconnaissance*, Stroud: Alan Sutton Publishing, 1996

Coombs, Rose, *Before Endeavours Fade*, London: After the Battle,1983

Dungan Myles, *Irish Voices from the Great War*, Dublin: Irish Academic Press, 1995

Lloyd George, David, *War Memoirs (2 vols)*, London: Odhams Press, 1936

Fisher, W G, *History of the Somerset Territorial Units*, Taunton: The Phoenix Press, 1924

Foley, H A, *Three Years on Active Service and Eight Months as a Prisoner of War*, London: 1920

Foley, H A (ed), *The Scrap Book of the 7th Somerset Light Infantry*, Taunton

Gliddon, Gerald, *The Battle of the Somme – A Topographical History*, Stroud: Sutton Publishing Ltd, 1998

Gliddon, Gerald, *The Somme – VCs of the First World War*, Stroud: Sutton Publishing Ltd, 1995

Griffith, Paddy, *Battle Tactics of the Western Front*, New Haven and London: Yale University Press, 1994

Hesketh-Prichard, *Sniping in France*, London: Leo Cooper, 1994

Horsfall and Cave, *Cambrai the Right Hook*, London: Leo Cooper, 1999

Inglefield, V E, *The History of the Twentieth (Light) Division*, London: Nisbett & Co Ltd, 1921

Ireland, Maj Gen, *Medical Aspects of Gas Warfare*, USA Govn't Printing Office, 1926

Ivelaw-Chapman, J, *The Riddles of Wipers*, London: Leo Cooper, 1997

Laver, James, *Between the Wars*, London: Vista Books, 1961

Macmillan, Harold, *Winds of Change 1914–1939*, London: Macmillan, 1966

MacDonald, Lyn, *They Called It Passchendaele*, London: Papermac, 1983

MacDonald, Lyn, *The Roses of No Man's Land*, London: Penguin, 1993

MacDonald, Lyn, *To the Last Man*, London: Viking, 1998

Middlebrook, Martin, *The First Day on the Somme*, London: Penguin Books, 1984

Neillands, Robin, *The Great War Generals on the Western Front 1914–18*, London: Robinson, 1999

Popham, Hugh, *The Somerset Light Infantry*, London: Hamish Hamilton, 1968

Richter, Donald, *Chemical Soldiers*, London: Leo Cooper, 1994

Samuels, Martin, *Command or Control*, London: Frank Cass, 1995

Sassoon, Siegfried, *Complete Memoirs of George Sherston*, London: Reprint Society, 1940

Stedman, Michael, *Guillemont*, London: Leo Cooper, 1998

Steel and Hart, *Passchendaele – the sacrificial ground*, London: Cassell & Co, 2000

Stephen, Martin, *Poems of the First World War*, London: Orion Publishing Group, 1993

White, B T, *British Tanks 1915-1945*, London: Ian Allan Ltd

Prior and Wilson, *Command on the Western Front*, Oxford: Blackwell, 1992

Winter, Denis, *Death's men – Soldiers of the Great War*, London: Penguin, 1978

Wyrall, Everard, *The History of the Somerset Light Infantry 1914–19*, London: Methuen, 1927

Newspapers

Bath Chronicle, Bridgwater Mercury, Bristol Times and Mirror, Burnham Gazette and Somerset Advertiser, Central Somerset Gazette, Chard and Illminster News, The Cork Advertiser, Langport and Somerton Herald, Keene's Bath Journal, The Kerryman, The Killarney Echo, The Rhondda Leader, Somerset County Gazette, Somerset Guardian, Somerset and Wilts Journal, Taunton Courier, Wells Journal, Western Gazette.

General Index

277

Names Index

Note: Ranks are shown at highest attained, even on temporary basis. The names index does not include footnote names.